A Letter from Dr. Charles Hull Wolfe
President, Plymouth Rock Foundation

Dear Christian Friend,

Recently President Barak Obama, while on a trip abroad and without giving the matter sufficient thought, casually declared that the United States is not a Christian nation. If the President had been a little more analytical, and especially if he'd read the remarkable new book you now hold in your hands, in all probability he would never have made such a statement. For page after page, from the beginning to the end, *The Book that Made America* by the gifted and scholarly Dr. Jerry Newcombe tells us America was born a Christian nation and has been one ever since.

This book begins by exploring America's Christian roots with the Bible as the country's basic textbook, the Bible's law and covenant illustrated in the lives of the Pilgrims and the Mayflower Compact, becoming our guide to individual self-government, structured constitutionalism, and a free market.

If you turn all the way back to this book's Appendix, what do you discover? The United States Supreme Court made it official: *America Is a Christian Nation!*

No matter what books you now own about our Christian history, *I encourage you to get this one!* – for an adult Sunday School or Teen Sunday School, for your pastor, or simply for your own edification. Become a more knowledgeable Christian citizen! After you learn about the significance of the Pilgrims, come visit their home in Plymouth.

– CHW

DECLARATION OF INDEPENDENCE   PAINTED BY JOHN TRUMBULL
OIL ON CANVAS, 12′ X 18′ . COMMISSIONED 1817; PURCHASED 1819, PLACED IN THE U.S. CAPITOL ROTUNDA IN 1826.

The signing of the Declaration of Independence in 1776. Our nation's birth certificate, the Declaration proclaims that our rights come from God. Period. What God has given, the state cannot take away.

Praise for The Book that Made America . . .

*S*AY that America is a Christian nation and you'll be brought up on hate crime charges—or at least thought an ignoramus. But what are the *facts* of history? *The Book That Made America* demonstrates that there once was a Book even more integral to this nation than Al Gore's *Earth in the Balance*. I recommend Dr. Newcombe's book highly!

Ann Coulter
New York Times #1 Author

*T*he *Book That Made America* is a most welcome addition to the growing literature that documents the foundational and pivotal role that the Bible played in the founding of our nation and the forming of our government. Dr. Jerry Newcombe combines accurate scholarship and careful analysis with engaging writing. This arsenal of historic wisdom from our Judeo-Christian heritage should be in your library. If you have funds to buy only one book on this topic, this is the one!

Peter A. Lillback, PH.D.
Prof. of Historical Theology, Pres., Westminster Theological Seminary
Pres., The Providence Forum, Sr. Pastor, Proclamation Presbyterian Church, Bryn Mywr, PA

*H*ISTORICAL revisionism is alive and well in our nation's classrooms and in the media. So what has been the Bible's role in American history? It certainly had a profound impact on the founding of this country as well as in the framing of the government. And where did we go astray as a nation? How can we return to our Biblical roots? Jerry Newcombe answers these and many other questions in *The Book That Made America*. Read this book to learn the history our nation has forgotten.

Kerby Anderson
National Director, Probe Ministries International
Host of "Point of View," USA Radio Network, and author of many books and articles

*J*ERRY NEWCOMBE has created a masterpiece of apologetics that skillfully portrays the power of Scripture in the transformation of the American wilderness into the world's first Christian constitutional republic. His writing is profound and well documented, yet easy to read. This great book will become a timeless educational resource that catapults the centrality of Christ and His Word back to the heart of our civilization where it belongs.

Marshall Foster, D.D.
Founder and Pres., The Mayflower Institute and World History Institute, Speaker, and Coauthor
of *The American Covenant: The Untold Story*, Thousand Oaks, CA

In The Book That Made America, Jerry Newcombe quickly cuts through the fog of agenda driven rhetoric to give a brilliant and unbiased examination of what made America unique among the nations of the world. Jerry's commanding knowledge of history provides clear and undeniable evidence that the Bible was a key formative influence in America's culture, economy, and form of government.

William J. Federer
Best-selling author and speaker, nationally known radio host on *AmericanMinute.com*
Pres., Amerisearch, Inc., St. Louis, Missouri

Jerry Newcombe has furnished Christian believers with a major weapon for the moral and spiritual civil war we are waging for the soul of America. He carefully provides us in a readable and engaging way with quotable evidence of the Christian roots of our nation. This book should be in the home of every American patriot.

Peter J. Marshall
Evangelist, speaker, and co-author of best-selling books, including
The Light and the Glory, Cape Cod, MA

Jerry Newcombe does an excellent job in documenting and telling the story that almost all Americans used to know: that is, without the Bible there would be no America as we know it. The Bible was the central most important influence in the birth, growth, and development of this nation. The principles in that book produced the most free, prosperous, just, and virtuous nation in history. As we have forgotten this truth, we have gradually lost our liberties. To preserve this great nation, Americans must know the ideas in *The Book That Made America.*

Stephen McDowell
President, Providence Foundation and
Biblical Worldview University, Charlottesville, VA

With the skill of a journalist experienced at interviewing others, Jerry Newcombe reveals the one book that built America. He digs deep into the documents, individuals, and spirit of America and lets the evidence speak for itself. Understanding the development of ideas from the Reformation through the planting of America, as well as admitting the faults that had to be repaired, Jerry has done a service for Americans by bringing the Bible back into historical focus at a time when it is most needed.

Paul Jehle, M.Div., Ed.D.
Executive Director, The Plymouth Rock Foundation
Senior Pastor, The New Testament Church and School, Plymouth, MA

The Book that Made America

HOW THE BIBLE FORMED OUR NATION

Jerry Newcombe, D.Min.

Nordskog Publishing inc.

Ventura, California

2009

The Book that Made America:
How the Bible Formed Our Nation
by Jerry Newcombe, D.MIN.

Copyright © 2009 by Jerry Newcombe

International Standard Book Number: 978-0-9824929-0-1

Library of Congress Control Number: 2009929285

Manuscript and Theology Editor: Ronald W. Kirk
Copy Editors: Kimberley Winters Woods and Mary-Elaine Swanson
Typography and Design and Editing: Desta Garrett
Cover Design: Timothy R. Moore, Donald E. Van Curler
Flying Dutchman Management, Inc.
Photographs (except where otherwise noted) are the author's.

Copyright notice: Unless otherwise indicated, all Scripture quotations are from The Holy Bible, English Standard Version®, copyright © 2001 by Crossway Bibles, a publishing ministry of Good News Publishers. Used by permission. All rights reserved.

Scripture quotations marked "NIV" are taken from the HOLY BIBLE, NEW INTERNATIONAL VERSION®. NIV®. Copyright © 1973, 1978, 1984 by International Bible Society. Used by permission of Zondervan. All rights reserved.

Scripture quotations marked "NKJV" are taken from the New King James Version. Copyright © 1982 by Thomas Nelson, Inc. Used by permission. All rights reserved.

Scripture quotation from The Geneva Bible (TGB), by permission, Tolle Lege Press (www.tollelegepress.com).

No part of this publication may be reproduced, stored in a retrieval system, or transmitted, in any form or by any means—electronic, mechanical, photocopy, recording, or otherwise—without prior written permission.

Printed in the United States of America.
Evangel Press, Nappanee, Indiana

Published by

Nordskog Publishing, Inc.
2716 Sailor Avenue
Ventura, California 93001, USA
1-805-642-2070 • 1-805-276-5129
www.NordskogPublishing.com

Member

Christian Small Publishers Association

PHOTO BY DAVID EXTERKAMP

DEDICATION

To the Memory of

D. James Kennedy, PH.D.

(1930–2007)

The author and the late Dr. D. James Kennedy on location at Independence Hall in Philadelphia for a Coral Ridge Ministries-TV special, "What if America Were a Christian Nation Again?" based on the book by the two of them.

PHOTO BY DOUG ROHM

Foreword

Jennifer Kennedy Cassidy

$\mathcal{A}$s the daughter of the late Dr. D. James Kennedy, I had the privilege of hearing my dad preach for years and years. One of his favorite topics he would return to from time to time was the Christian roots of America. He knew that modern Americans enjoy the fruit of America's Christian foundation—but many want nothing to do with the root of that foundation because it is Christian. My dad was able to cut through what he himself called "the miasmic fog of secularism" and document America's true history, which was very Christian.

Here is what my dad said on the subject of our nation's Christian roots:

> The Scripture states, "Blessed is the nation whose God is the LORD: and the people whom He hath chosen for His own inheritance." The Bible asks, "If the foundations be destroyed, what can the righteous do?" (Psalm 11:3). There is no doubt this is, indeed, a nation built upon the foundation of God—that the Lord was the God of this nation; that it was founded upon the principles of God's Word, upon the teachings of Christianity, and for the advancement of the Kingdom of Christ. All of that has been under enormous attack for the last few decades. In fact, so effective has been that attack that the historical revisionists have all but removed every vestige of our Christian heritage from our schools' textbooks. Even the very monuments in the nation's capital that point to the Christian origins of this country are being changed or removed.
>
> My subject: "America: A Christian Nation." That is a concept that has been so systematically blotted from the collective memory of this country as to sound in the ears of most people in America

to be an alien philosophy, an intrusion of religion into the tranquility of a secular nation.

All nations that have ever existed have been founded upon either some theistic or anti-theistic principle, whether we think of the Hinduism of India, the Confucianism of China, the Mohammedanism of Saudi Arabia, or the atheism of the former Soviet Union. If we know our history, we know that America was a nation founded upon Christ and His Word. Those foundations, indeed, are crumbling in our time.

There are those in our country today who are busily tearing apart that foundation, who would gnash their teeth at the idea that this is a Christian nation. They will not be satisfied until they have removed every vestige of our Christian heritage from not only the minds of the people, but also from the monuments of this country.

As my dad knew so well, and proclaimed so often, anybody with an open mind who studies our true history cannot help but conclude that we began as a Christian nation. Because we began as a Christian nation, people of all faiths or no faith are welcome here.

Several of the last books my dad wrote he co-labored with one of the key producers in his television ministry, Dr. Jerry Newcombe—who, by the way, earned his doctorate at Knox Theological Seminary, which was founded by my dad and for which he served as the chancellor until his recent illness and death. This book is adapted from Jerry's doctoral thesis at Knox. He shares my dad's grasp of America's rich Christian heritage. Jerry loves America, but he loves Jesus first.

That's why I am pleased to recommend this book. Oliver Wendell Holmes, Jr. was a man whose judicial philosophy I do not agree with. Nonetheless, he once said that a page of history is worth a volume of logic. Well, Dr. Jerry Newcombe has presented here page after page, documenting our nation's true Christian roots. Jerry cuts through all the political correctness that has infected this great country.

There is a lot at stake including, ultimately, our freedom. America was founded upon the notion of religious freedom for all. That liberty is in jeopardy if the present trends of secularism continue. I pray that God may use this book to help awaken a new generation of Americans to learn our true history and rediscover what it is that made America great in the first place.

About the Author

PHOTO BY GEORGE ROLLER

*J*ERRY NEWCOMBE, D.MIN., of Coral Ridge Ministries is a professional communicator whose research and media productions have been seen by millions. He has helped shape the media output of one of the most influential U.S. Protestant churches in the twentieth century.

Dr. D. James Kennedy, the late founder and head pastor of Coral Ridge Presbyterian Church and Coral Ridge Ministries, became a national leader as one of the first pastors in our time to apply the Biblical faith to the realm of civil policy in light of Christian America's historical civil stewardship and participation. In this work of national influence, Dr. Kennedy made Jerry Newcombe a trusted friend and collaborator.

As senior producer for Coral Ridge Ministries television Dr. Newcombe has produced or co-produced more than fifty documentaries. He is the host of two weekly radio shows. He has been a witty, humorous, and engaging guest on numerous television and radio talk shows, including Fox News and *Politically Incorrect* with Bill Maher. He is the author or coauthor of twenty-one books. *What If Jesus Had Never Been Born?*, *How Would Jesus Vote?*, *Christ's Passion: The Power and the Promise*, and *The Presence of a Hidden God* are among the fourteen books co-authored with Dr. Kennedy.

With a Bachelor of Arts degree in history from Tulane University (1978), Dr. Newcombe is an accomplished historian. His research in the realm of early American history inspired numerous books regarding the faith of the founding fathers, notably *George Washington's Sacred Fire* (co-written with Dr. Peter Lillback) and *One Nation under God: Ten Things Every Christian Should Know about the Founding of America* (co-written with Dr. David C. Gibbs, Jr.).

Dr. Newcombe also holds a Master's degree in communications from Wheaton College (1983) and a Doctor of Ministry from Knox Theological Seminary (2008). Dr. Newcombe wrote his thesis on the importance of "Preserving Our Christian Heritage" and how pastors and their congregations can pass on that heritage.

Dr. Newcombe met his wife Kirsti at Wheaton Graduate School. They were married two years later in her home church (the Lutheran Free Church of Kristiansand, Norway). The service was bilingual; they said, "Ja, I do" on 28 June 1980. They have two children, Annie and Eric. The Newcombes, residing in South Florida, have co-authored two books together: *I'll Do It Tomorrow* and *A Way of Escape*.

Contents

Acknowledgments

*T*HERE are many people that I could thank for this book — perhaps too many to list. But let me try. First of all, I must thank my wife, Kirsti Newcombe, who helped me at every step, carefully reading and rereading (and rereading and rereading) every sentence. Her advice has proved invaluable.

In addition, I thank those who have taught me along the way about the true facts of American history. These include (in alphabetical order):

* David Barton
* John Eidsmoe
* William J. Federer
* Marshall Foster
* Paul Jehle
* D. James Kennedy
* Peter Lillback
* Peter Marshall
* Charles Hull Wolfe

I am also most appreciative of my book agent, Bill Jensen, and publisher, Gerald Nordskog.

Also, I am grateful to the professors at Knox Theological Seminary who read through my thesis, which was the basis for this book: Dr. James Garretson and Michael Morales.

Above all, I am grateful to Jesus Christ for His redemption of my undeserving soul.

PHOTO BY BRENT NIMS

Publisher's Word

Gerald Christian Nordskog

$\mathcal{G}$EORGE WASHINGTON, my personal hero, and the beloved Father of our Country, was indeed "first in the hearts of his countrymen." After the ratification of the Constitution was assured, on June 29, 1788, he penned:

> No one can rejoice more than I do at every step the people of this great Country take to preserve the Union, establish good order and government, and to render the Nation happy at home and respectable abroad. No Country upon Earth ever had it more in its power to attain these blessings than United America. Wondrously strange then, and much to be regretted indeed would it be, were we to neglect the means, and depart from the road which Providence has pointed us to, so plainly; I cannot believe it will ever come to pass. The Great Governor of the Universe has led us too long and too far on the road to happiness and glory, to forsake us in the midst of it. By folly and improper conduct, proceeding from a variety of causes, we may now and then get bewildered; but I hope and trust that there is good sense and virtue enough left to recover the right path before we shall be entirely lost.[1]

Today, exactly 221 years later, America has long gone down that rocky road of folly and improper conduct, that our general of the colonial army, and first president of our nation hoped and trusted would never happen, and we are leaning toward becoming entirely lost nearing the end of this first decade of the twenty-first century. Do we, as Americans, have the good sense and virtue enough left today to recover the right path? Or are we too divided and secular a nation to recover? We have indeed greatly and sorely departed from the road to which Providence had pointed us so plainly during our colonial and founding era; regrettably it has come to pass. We appeal to the Great Governor of the Universe not to forsake us in our grievous national sins in this land. Americans all, we must repent and return to our first love, the love of Christ and His Law-Word, and love for one another.

This book will excite and cause us to remember and resurrect our roots, and give us the way back to George Washington's vision for a United America. This was the dream and goals of all of our founding fathers, who based our nation, one nation under God, on the life-giving words and laws of the Holy Bible, that *Book that Made America*. We must recapture our heritage of the Christian character and government of our, the world's first, Christian constitutional republic.

James Madison's famous phrase in *The Federalist Papers*, has echoed down over two centuries of American history:

> It is evident that no other form would be reconcilable with the genius of the people of America; with the fundamental principles of the Revolution; or with that honorable determination which animates every votary of freedom: To rest all our political experiments on the capacity of mankind for self-government.[2]

Verna Hall and Rosalie Slater's 1983 Year of the Bible work affirmed, "History shows that mankind's ability to govern itself is in direct proportion to the relationship of the individual to God, to Christ.... The history of the Bible and the history of American liberty are inseparable. The Bible is the source of individual liberty—salvation from sin through Jesus Christ. It is also the basis for external or civil government."[3] As Noah Webster wrote:

> It is extremely important to our nation, in a political as well as religious view, that all possible authority and influence should be given to the Scriptures; for these furnish the best principles of civil liberty, and the most effectual support of republican government.[4]

Chief Justice Joseph Story in expounding upon the uniqueness of our Constitution and the founding of our nation, concluded his *Commentaries* with this warning—which we need to heed immediately in America today:

> The structure has been erected by architects of consummate skill and fidelity; its foundations are solid; its compartments are beautiful, as well as useful; its arrangements are full of wisdom and order; and its defences are impregnable from without. It has been

reared for immortality, if the work of man may justly aspire to such a title. It may, nevertheless, perish in an hour by the folly, or corruption, or negligence of its only keepers, THE PEOPLE. Republics are created by the virtue, public spirit, and intelligence of the citizens. They fall, when the wise are banished from the public councils, because they dare to be honest, and the profligate are rewarded, because they flatter the people, in order to betray them.[5]

Robert C. Winthrop, descendant of the first governor of Massachusetts Bay Colony, one and a half centuries ago, warned the audience of the Massachusetts Bible Society:

All societies of men must be governed in some way or other. The less they may have of stringent State Government, the more they must have of individual self-government. The less they rely on public law or physical force, the more they must rely on private moral restraint. Men, in a word, must necessarily be controlled either by a power within them, or by a power without them; either by the Word of God, or by the strong arm of man; either by the Bible or by the bayonet.[6]

Our nation's second president, John Adams, wrote this in a letter to our third president, Thomas Jefferson, on Christmas day, 1813:

I have examined all [religions], as well as my narrow sphere, my straightened means, and my busy life would allow me; and the result is, that the Bible is the best Book in the world. It contains more of my little philosophy than all the libraries I have seen.[7]

Dr. Jerry Newcombe, whom I thank exceedingly for allowing Nordskog Publishing the opportunity of publishing his twenty-first book (as author or co-author), has brought us in *The Book That Made America* a definitive work on the stupendous influence of Holy Scripture in the founding and development of our great nation, the United States of America. We must learn and recapture the godly principles that our founding fathers knew from a deep and abiding knowledge of God's roadmap and His commandments contained in the Bible—now, more than ever. Read the author's book, study it, and then turn to the Bible for study and application in our lives, homes, institutions, and civil government. Will we be ruled, as today, by the strong arm of man, or by the Word of God—by the Bible or by the bayonet? That decision is yours.

I end this Word with a proclamation and a prayer from George Washington's April 30, 1789, First Inaugural Address:

> It would be peculiarly improper to omit, in this first official act, my fervent supplications to that Almighty Being who rules over the universe, who presides in the councils of nations and whose providential aids can supply every human defect.... In tendering this homage to the Great Author of every public and private good, I assure myself that it express your sentiments not less than my own.... [W]e ought to be no less persuaded that the propitious smiles of Heaven can never be expected on a nation that disregards the eternal rules of order and right which Heaven itself has ordained.[8]

Notes

SPECIAL PUBLISHER'S NOTE: Numerous citations listed were taken from the monumental book, *The Bible and the Constitution of the United States of America*, Commemorating the Year of the Bible, 1983, Verna M. Hall and Rosalie J. Slater (San Francisco: Foundation for American Christian Education, First Edition, December 11, 1983). This book was greatly influential to me and distributed widely in my roles as Los Angeles County Chairman, Year of the Bible Committee, and as Chairman of the Southern California Constitution Education Committee, during our events: The Bible and the Constitution conferences during the bicentennial era. The Year of the Bible was declared in 1983 by Public Law 97-280 on October 4, 1982 by Joint Congressional Resolutions, signed by President Ronald Reagan.* (GCN)

1 George Washington, letter to Benjamin Lincoln, in *Writings of George Washington*, John C. Fitzpatrick, Ed. (1930), 29:525. As quoted in *The Bible and the Constitution* (see above), 36.

2 Alexander Hamilton, James Madison, John Jay, *The Federalist, A Commentary on the Constitution of the United States, Being a Collection of Essays in Support of the Constitution Agreed Upon September 17, 1787, by the Federal Convention*, Number 39. (Washington & London, M. Walter Dunne, Publisher, 1901), 256. As quoted in *The Bible and the Constitution* (1983), 3.

3 Hall and Slater, *The Bible and the Constitution*, (1983), 3, 4.

4 Noah Webster, 1832, as quoted in Verna M. Hall, "Principles of Liberty Drawn from the Bible," *The Christian History of the American Revolution: Consider and Ponder* (San Francisco: Foundation for American Education, 1975), 21.

5 Joseph Story. *Commentaries on the Constitution of the United States*, Abridged by the Author, Boston, 1833, 111, sec. 141. As quoted in *The Bible and the Constitution*, 37.

6 Robert C. Winthrop, *Addresses and Speeches on Various Occasions*, Boston, 1852. As quoted in Hall, *Christian History of the American Revolution*, 20.

7 John Adams, a Letter to Thomas Jefferson, in William J. Federer, *Treasury of Presidential Quotations* (St. Louis: Amerisearch, 2004), 31; and Norman Cousins, ed., *In God We Trust: The Religious Beliefs and Ideas of the American Founding Fathers* (NY: Harper & Brothers, 1958), 255-56.

8 George Washington, First Inaugural Address, in *America's God and Country Encyclopedia of Quotations*, William J. Federer, (Coppell, TX: FAME Publishing, Inc. 1994), 651-52.

*See adjoining page for President Ronald Reagan's *Year of the Bible Proclamation* of February 3, 1983.

Year of the Bible, 1983
By the President of the United States of America
A Proclamation

Of the many influences that have shaped the United States of America into a distinctive Nation and people, none may be said to be more fundamental and enduring than the Bible.

Deep religious beliefs stemming form the Old and New Testaments of the Bible inspired many of the early settlers of our country, providing them with the strength, character, convictions, and faith necessary to withstand great hardship and danger in this new and rugged land. These shared beliefs helped forge a sense of common purpose among the widely dispersed colonies—a sense of community which laid the foundation for the spirit of nationhood that was to develop in later decades.

The Bible and its teachings helped form the basis for the Founding Fathers' abiding belief in the inalienable rights of the individual, rights which they found implicit in the Bible's teachings of the inherent worth and dignity of each individual. This same sense of man patterned the convictions of those who framed the English system of law inherited by our own Nation, as well as the ideals set forth in the Declaration of Independence and the Constitution.

For centuries the Bible's emphasis on compassion and love for our neighbor has inspired the institutional and governmental expressions of benevolent outreach such as private charity, the establishment of schools and hospitals, and the abolition of slavery.

Many of our greatest national leaders—among them Presidents Washington, Jackson, Lincoln, and Wilson—have recognized the influence of the Bible on our country's development. The plainspoken Andrew Jackson referred to the Bible as no less than "the rock on which our Republic rests."

Today our beloved America and, indeed, the world, is facing a decade of enormous challenge. As a people we may well be tested as we have seldom, if ever, been tested before. We will need resources of spirit even more than resources of technology, education, and armaments. There could be no more fitting moment than now to reflect with gratitude, humility, and urgency upon the wisdom revealed to us in the writing that Abraham Lincoln called "the best gift God has ever given to man.... But for it we could not know right from wrong."

The Congress of the United States, in recognition of the unique contribution of the Bible in shaping the history and character of this Nation, and so many of its citizens, has by Senate Joint Resolution 165 authorized and requested the President to designate the year 1983 as the "Year of the Bible."

NOW, THEREFORE, I, RONALD REAGAN, President of the United States of America, in recognition of the contribution of the Bible on our Republic and our people, do hereby proclaim 1983 the Year of the Bible in the United States. I encourage all citizens, each in his or her own way, to re-examine and rediscover its priceless and timeless message.

In Witness whereof, I have hereunto set my hand this third day of February, in the year of our Lord nineteen hundred and eighty-three, and of the Independence of the United States of America the two hundred and seventh.

Ronald Reagan

PHOTO: J. NEWCOMBE

Statue honoring Rev. John Harvard on the Harvard campus square. Notice the gigantic Bible on his lap. Like so many institutions in the beginning of America, Harvard got its cues from the Scriptures.

The Book
that
Made America

How the Bible
Formed Our Nation

PHOTO: J. NEWCOMBE

George Washington, the father of our country, was a committed Christian in the Anglican tradition. He warned Americans in his 1796 Farewell Address not to undermine religion and morality, which are indispensable supports for our political prosperity. This statue of Washington is in front of Independence Hall, where he presided over the constitutional convention in 1787.

Introduction

Bless the Lord, O my soul,
and forget not all His benefits.
(Psalm 103:2)

ONE time I came across an unbelievable sight at the beach. This was in August 1994 during the crisis when many desperate refugees were trying to flee from Cuba on makeshift rafts. I stumbled across one of these ramshackle contraptions off the shores of Deerfield Beach, north of Ft. Lauderdale. It is about 300 miles or so from Cuba. This raft reflected the anguish that its makers must have felt. It was composed primarily of three wooden doors. There was some sort of Styrofoam or flotsam at the bottom to keep it afloat. One of the doors was at the bottom of the structure and the other two made up the raft's sides, with pieces of wood nailed across to serve as crossbeams. Some of the wood used included wooden shutters. It was literally as if someone had torn apart his own home, under cover of darkness, in order to put this thing together. Then they would have had to float or row over in the treacherous waters, in the grueling sun, with the potential threat of sharks along the way, to try and get into America. Why? So that maybe—just maybe—they could get a chance to enjoy what you and I enjoy every day: freedom, and the chance for a better life.

I saved a small remnant of pieces from that raft. I understood that the next day the Coast Guard would come and haul it away to destroy it, while putting out the alert that approximately ten new Cubans had made it secretly to our shores. I guess that the number was ten, based on discarded clothing items in the raft. There were two makeshift lanterns in the vessel.

One was a large Ball jar, and the other was a small round jar, the latter of which I saved and still have. Both had wicks in them and some sort of kerosene-like liquid to keep them lit. What must that voyage have been like? How many hours or days through shark-infested waters did it last? How did they get here without any kind of motor or sail? What did they eat or drink along the way? Meanwhile, these two lanterns would surely have helped them during the nighttime—long after they got away from Cuba. (It was virtually certain that they launched their departure from the communist island under cover of darkness.)

And everyday, millions of Americans born here think little or nothing of the freedom we have. Again, this freedom is so great that some people would risk *everything* to come here.

What makes America so different? How is it that the vast majority of nations on the earth have patterned their constitution after ours? How is it we ever came up with a constitution in the first place? What role does Christianity play in this? What does it matter, anyway, about what happened in the past? Some people, even Christians, would say all that matters is the present and the future—not the past.

But our heritage does matter. Our twenty-eighth president, Woodrow Wilson, was once the president of Princeton University. He made the following remark, which gets at the very heart of this book:

> A nation which does not remember what it was yesterday, does not know what it is today, nor what it is trying to do. We are trying to do a futile thing if we do not know where we came from or what we have been about....
>
> The Bible...is the one supreme source of revelation of the meaning of life, the nature of God, and the spiritual nature and needs of men. It is the only guide of life which really leads the spirit in the way of peace and salvation.
>
> America was born a Christian nation. America was born to exemplify that devotion to the elements of righteousness which are derived from the revelations of Holy Scripture.[1]

I agree with President Wilson. Our present and future depends in large part on our understanding of the past. We have forgotten God's many benefits in helping to found this nation. Furthermore, for the sake of the liberty to proclaim the gospel, it matters that we pass on this freedom.

What President Wilson wrote reminds me of the statement George

Orwell wrote in his classic novel, *1984*: "Who controls the past, controls the future: who controls the present controls the past."[2] In our time, the history books have been rewritten and God has been erased.

Nonetheless, the unparalleled religious freedom we have enjoyed in America is an outgrowth of Christianity and not any other worldview. As Rabbi Daniel Lapin once observed, secular humanism is a jealous faith. Militant secularism and radical Islam stand ready in the gap should Christianity fail in America. Much is at stake—if nothing else, precious souls.

This book is dedicated to the memory of the late Dr. D. James Kennedy, with whom I had the privilege to coauthor many books, some of which touched on our godly heritage and why it matters. He once said, "You and I were born in a Christian nation. That may not be said for your children or grandchildren, unless we who have received this marvelous patrimony do something other than let it sift through our fingers like sand because we are engaged simply in personal peace and prosperity, as Dr. Francis Schaeffer used to say."[3]

One of our key founding fathers and our fourth president, James Madison, noted that nations are more likely to fall from within than from without. Specifically, he warned, "Since the general civilization of mankind, I believe there are more instances of the abridgement of the freedom of the people by gradual and silent encroachments of those in power than by violent and sudden usurpations."[4] Radio commentator Mark Levin constantly cites nineteenth-century French philosopher Alexis de Tocqueville's phrase "a soft tyranny." He is concerned that we are constantly giving away our rights in exchange for protection and supposed economic security. We should remember what Benjamin Franklin said on this point: "Those who would give up essential liberty to purchase a little temporary safety deserve neither liberty nor safety."[5]

Thus, our nation's heritage is too great to squander.

Here is a quick overview of this book. Part I gives us a clear picture of the role the Bible played in making America. We will begin with a quick survey of our nation's Christian roots. Then we will explore Biblical considerations on government in general and on remembering what God has done in the past (individually and nationally). Then we will get an overview of our Christian roots by using a fifty-question quiz. First I will present the quiz and then provide detailed answers. It provides a memorable way to learn some important facts of our history.

In Part II, we will explore the Bible and the Settling of America. For our purposes, the settling era of the United States is essentially from 1607 (Jamestown) to 1774 (the first Continental Congress). We begin this section by considering the fact that many of the settlers of this country came for Christian reasons. Then we look at how education in America (even through the founding era) was thoroughly Christian. In one way or another, the Bible was the chief textbook for the first two hundred years or so of America. Next, we will look at the fact that many of the colonies, especially those with a Biblical basis, began with a covenant. This helped pave the way for the Constitution, which is still our guide today.

In Part III, we look at the Bible and the founding of America. We begin with a look at the fact that almost all of our nation's founders were committed Christians. We will also explore what the founders intended in the Constitution, particularly in the first amendment. Next, we will consider an important question: What about America's shortcomings? Do they permanently discredit the notion that America ever was a Christian nation?

In Part IV, we tie up some loose ends. We will consider where America went astray from our Biblical roots. Also, we will look at the Bible and regeneration, noting the point that all change begins in the human heart and proceeds outward from there. Finally, we have a concluding chapter on where we should go from here. In the Appendix, we will see an excellent summary of our Christian roots (much of which we will have covered in the book). This summary comes from a surprising source—a former Supreme Court Justice. Please note that throughout this book, you may find that certain facts keep coming up—but from different angles. That is because these key facts cannot be underscored enough, documenting for all time our nation's Christian roots.

America has great roots and a great foundation.

I hope America is not through with God. I certainly hope God is not through with America. That is especially ironic when you consider our nation's true history.

PART ONE

The Book that Made America

*T*HE purpose of these opening chapters is to provide an overview of how the Bible played a unique role in the creation of America. First, we will introduce and survey the subject. Next, we will consider the Bible and government. What principles can we cull from the Word of God that deal with a nation's remembrance of what God has done for them in the past? Finally, we will have a fifty-question quiz that tests one's knowledge of the unique role the Scriptures and the Christian faith played in the founding of America.

We are standing on a threshold. Unless we teach the next generation about our unique heritage, it will be lost in the revisionist mishmash of half-truths and political correctness. Understanding our foundation and our godly roots is the first step to preserving them.

PHOTO BY J. NEWCOMBE

St. Paul's Chapel in New York City.

At this Anglican church on April 30, 1789, just after being sworn in on the Bible, George Washington and other leaders of our new republic participated in a two-hour worship service, consecrating the new nation to God. President Washington worshiped here weekly for two years while the city served as our national capital.

This church miraculously survived the attack on September 11, 2001, and became a focal point for the 9/11 rescue operations. For eight months, hundreds of volunteers worked 12-hour shifts serving meals, making beds, counseling and praying with fire fighters, construction workers, police, and others. "Unwavering Spirit: Hope and Healing at Ground Zero," a new interactive exhibit at the church, honors that ministry and its legacy of love and compassion.

The open sky directly behind the church is where the World Trade Center towers stood.

CHAPTER 1

Our Christian Roots

Blessed is the nation whose God is the LORD.
(Psalm 33:12)

*E*ARLY in his presidency President Barack Obama, during an official overseas trip, declared that the United States is not a Christian nation. To my knowledge, this is the first time in our nation's history that a president has made such a statement. Meanwhile, numerous presidents throughout our history have said the opposite. Most importantly, our founders declared that our rights come from God. That is the essence of the American experience.

The same week President Obama made his declaration, *Newsweek* magazine had a cover story—just in time for Holy Week 2009—on the decline and fall of Christian America. In fact, on the first page of the article itself, they have a large sidebar with large words, "The End of Christian America." The article quoted one of my modern heroes, Dr. Albert Mohler, Jr., the president of Southern Baptist Theological Seminary, who said, "The so-called Judeo-Christian consensus of the last millennium has given way to a post-modern, post-Western cultural crisis which threatens the very heart of our culture." Jon Meachem of *Newsweek* adds this comment to Mohler's insight: "There it was, an old term with new urgency: *post-Christian*. That is not to say that the Christian God is dead, but that He is less of a force in American politics and culture than at any other time in recent memory."[6] The reason *Newsweek* sees the demise of "Christian America" is the growing numbers of non-religious

Americans, juxtaposed with a shrinking Christian population. About three-quarters of Americans yet claim to be Christians, though many apparently profess faith, while not possessing it.

There is an irony to the statistics this magazine cites. John Rabe, my colleague at Coral Ridge Ministries-TV, who serves as the host for the *Learn 2 Discern* commentaries, points out: "The *Newsweek* cover story, entitled 'The Decline and Fall of Christian America,' noted that the percentage of professing Christians in America had fallen to 76 percent. If we had a basketball game where the final score was 76-24, somehow I doubt that we'd describe the team with 76 as having 'declined' or 'fallen.'"[7]

Well, is Christian America dead? Sean Hannity had a roundtable discussion on this on his Fox News program, and guest Steven Mansfield observed, "We're living on a borrowed legacy."[8] I agree, but the legacy is still there. Just because President Obama or *Newsweek* declares we are no longer a Christian nation does not change our origins. We are still one nation under God because of our roots—despite what some liberal politicians, activist judges, or the secular media may say. Until the Declaration of Independence is no longer our nation's birth certificate, America will always be one nation under God.

Anybody familiar with the true facts of American history has no other reasonable conclusion than that we began as a Christian nation. But if you say that America is or was a Christian nation, you will have quite a controversy on your hands.

This conflict is not new. In late 2007, presidential candidate, John McCain, made such a reference and was hammered for it by the forces of political correctness. Senator McCain said, "But I just have to say in all candor that since this nation was founded primarily on Christian principles, personally, I prefer someone [as president] who I know has a solid grounding in my faith." He also said, "The Constitution established the United States of America as a Christian nation...in the broadest sense." While people from all faiths or no faiths are welcome here, they ought to "...know that they are in a nation founded on Christian principles." This angered Ira N. Forman, executive director of the National Jewish Democratic Council, who said of McCain, "Someone running for president ought to understand the Constitution a little better. Nowhere does it say the United States is a 'Christian' nation. How can we trust someone to uphold the Constitution who doesn't even know what's in it?"[9]

Quoting McCain and then Forman's response in his article, Jewish conservative columnist, Don Feder, rebuts this routine type of criticism:

> Nowhere does the Constitution say that there's a high and impregnable wall of separation between church and state. That hasn't kept liberals like Forman from repeatedly reading those words into the Constitution over the last sixty years. *The idea of America as a Christian nation is at the heart of the culture war. The concept of Christian America has profound implications for the political tug-of-war over abortion, euthanasia, embryonic stem-cell research, human cloning, gay marriage, hate crimes legislation, pornography, sex education and other issues whose outcome will determine our survival as a free people.* [emphasis mine]
>
> In politics, as in the physical world, nature abhors a vacuum. Everything must be something.
>
> If America isn't a Christian (or a Judeo-Christian) nation, what is it to be—a Muslim nation, a Marxist nation, a nation inspired by the French Revolution, the *Humanist Manifesto II* or...*Earth in [the] Balance* (prequel to *An Inconvenient Truth*)? A survey of the twentieth century—with particular attention to Europe, Asia, the Middle East and San Francisco—will show how successfully those belief systems have worked in terms of promoting human dignity.[10]

This reminds me of the observation of Rabbi Daniel Lapin, another Orthodox Jew who defends the notion of "Christian America." I have interviewed him repeatedly for Coral Ridge Ministries-TV.

Rabbi Lapin points out that the United States of America has protected well the Jewish people: "No country in the last two thousand years has provided the same haven of tranquility and prosperity for Jews as has the United States of America. And, this is not in spite of Americans being Christian; it is because of it. You might say that America's Bible belt is the Jewish community's safety belt."

Therefore, says the rabbi, the very safety of Jews (and others) is put at risk when the Christian faith is undermined in America: "Jews need to understand that our safety and security in the United States is dependent upon the health and vitality of American Christianity."[11] How great it would be if more Jews and other non-Christians in our country were as insightful as Don Feder and Rabbi Lapin.

THE ANNALS OF AMERICA

Many people today chafe at the notion that America began as a Christian nation. But look at the facts of history. For example, I have a set of encyclopedia-type volumes called *The Annals of America*.[12] It was published in the 1970s by *The Encyclopedia Britannica*. This series contains many of the original writings of American history. The first several volumes deal with the settling and founding era. These provide indisputable facts that America had a Christian beginning. But many modern people just ignore this information, as if the greatness of America just appeared out of thin air. It is when you read these writings from our founding fathers, in *their* own words, you realize just how much God and the Christian faith have to do with America. That is why this book is filled with quotes, some of which are lengthy, so you can see for yourself that the Bible is the book that has made America.

WHO CARES?

I care that the presupposition of American freedom is that our rights come from God, not the state. You should care too, if for no other reason than the sake of the unhindered proclamation of the gospel.

If you argue, like Cal Thomas does,[13] that persecution is good for the gospel, my comment is twofold: 1) That is not always the case, and 2) Why should a nation founded by Christians for religious freedom *for all* be so twisted as to deny Christians full religious freedom?

First, let's examine one example where persecution does not necessarily lead to the growth of the church. Consider how Islam in several centuries taxed Christians into becoming Muslims.

In the Middle East, North Africa, and Spain, Muslims conquered former Christian territory, causing mass conversions to Islam. A lot of the conversions had to do with laying heavy tax burdens on those that would not convert to Islam.

Dr. James White, a Christian scholar who has debated Muslims (and others) in more than fifty debates, says this about the effect of those taxes: "It became far more effective to wipe out those Christian communities by, in essence, taxing them, than it did by using the point of the sword. The point of the sword creates martyrs; taxation just creates poor people over time. And it is that long-term type of pressure that creates the most converts."[14]

Robert Spencer, author of *The Politically Incorrect Guide to Islam (and the Crusades)*, is the director of Jihad Watch. He has written several other books on Islam. He says about this taxing of the Christians by the Muslims: "This is what happened to the great Christian majorities that had been in Syria, in Egypt, in North Africa; this is what happened to those populations. They now either don't exist at all or they are very tiny minorities because of the wearing down of those communities by the [taxes] and by the regulations that accompanied it over the centuries."[15]

Church historian, Kenneth Scott Latourette, points out that by A.D. 950, 50 percent of what had been Christendom was lost to Islam. For example, all seven of the churches to whom the book of Revelation was written had come under the crescent. So, while it may be generally true that persecution causes the church of Jesus Christ to grow, the example of Islam shows that that is not always the case.

Second, I maintain that it is important that we pass on our Christian heritage to the next generation, so that we will not be swindled out of our religious liberty by those with a very different agenda for America. For example, why should churches and ministries have to spend precious resources and donations defending themselves against frivolous lawsuits related to domestic partnerships or against false accusations of "hate crimes"? Why should a pastor's sermon in his own church become the basis for lawsuits? In other words, the reason our Christian heritage matters, ultimately, is the freedom to preach the gospel and to live out the Christian faith. Religious freedom is the lynchpin of all other freedoms. Remove religious freedom, and other liberties will soon be taken away as well.

It is ironic that religious liberty is now in jeopardy in a nation founded primarily for religious liberty. Consider some basic facts of our founding.

"OUR FOUNDING DOCUMENT"

More than two decades ago, in December 1982, on the eve of the International Year of the Bible (1983), *Newsweek* magazine did a cover story discussing the Bible's impact on America. Many *Newsweek* readers were probably startled to hear this refreshingly honest assessment, from a surprising source:

> [F]or centuries [the Bible] has exerted an unrivaled influence on American culture, politics and social life. Now historians are discovering that the Bible, perhaps even more than the Constitution,

is our founding document: the source of the powerful myth of the United States as a special, sacred nation, a people called by God to establish a model society, a beacon to the world.[16]

I do not agree with the notion that America's special calling is a "myth." However, the great aspect of this quote is the idea—from a secular source—that the Bible is our founding document. Later, *TIME* magazine came out with this assessment in an article called, "Looking to Its Roots."

> Ours is the only country deliberately founded on a good idea. That good idea combines a commitment to man's inalienable rights with the Calvinist belief in an ultimate moral right and sinful man's obligation to do good. These articles of faith, embodied in the Declaration of Independence and in the Constitution, literally govern our lives today.[17]

So we see that even secularists will sometimes acknowledge the Christian origins of this nation, when they are honest. Recently, atheist author Sam Harris wrote his monograph, *Letter to a Christian Nation*, attempting to persuade Americans to shed any remaining shred of a Christian nation. He uses the phrase "Christian nation" in the sense that the majority of Americans identify themselves as Christian.

DEFINING OUR TERMS

At the outset of our study, let us clarify a few terms. When I use the term the settlers of America, I am generally referring to those people who came from Europe between 1607 and 1774. When I refer to the founders of America, I am generally talking about those American colonists from the first Continental Congress of 1774 roughly through 1800. What do we mean by a "Christian nation"? I believe that America began as a Christian nation and intended religion (Christianity) to play a robust role in our national life, but in a way that gave everyone freedom of conscience. I believe our founders intended the separation of the institution of the church from the institution of the state, so that no one Christian denomination would lord it over the others—again, respecting the consciences of individuals. I believe the founders intended that religion would play a role in public life—on a voluntary basis. If that were not the case, then they contradicted themselves repeatedly. For instance, George Washington said "religion and morality" are "indispensable supports to our political prosperity."[18]

When we talk about the notion of a "Christian nation," I have no illusions that America is a Christian nation today. It certainly does not retain the Christian character of the settling and founding eras of North America. I must point out early in this book that the settling of America was more directly Christian than the founding of America. Most of the settlers were clearly and explicitly Christian. It would not be accurate to say that the founders were as directly Christian in the same way the settlers were. Nonetheless, there is a strong case for the Christianity of the vast majority of the founders, as well. The Great Awakening touched many of our key founding fathers, such as Samuel Adams, who played a greater role to incite us toward independence than any other man.

I do not believe America should be a *theocracy*. What I mean is that America should not be an authoritarian regime, run by a particular sect and imposing its peculiar theology on the rest of us. I mean that I repudiate an Islamic-style civil order run by imams of whatever stripe. It is disingenuous of modern secularists to say that those of us trying to regain and to preserve our Christian heritage actually want to create such a theocracy. The late Dr. D. James Kennedy (my pastor for more than twenty years) spoke on this critical issue conclusively. I had the privilege of writing thirteen books with him while he was alive. For one of them, I sat down with a tape recorder in hand and asked him about the charge that he and his colleagues want a theocracy in America. Here is what he said, as we included in our book, *The Gates of Hell Shall Not Prevail* (Thomas Nelson, 1996):

> [M]any people who actively engage in the attack against Christianity in this country accuse the religious right of trying to establish a theocracy here. That's not true. Despite the claims of our critics, we are not advocating a theocracy in America.

We are advocating America's tradition of liberty and the protection of *everyone's* rights, based on America's Biblical heritage. Again, here's Dr. Kennedy:

> In the history of Biblical religion, there has only been one theocracy and that was...the state of Israel in the Old Testament. God alone ruled, for there was no legislature in Israel. The Sanhedrin

was not a legislature or parliament; it was simply a supreme court.
There was only one lawgiver in Zion, who was God. He was the
one who gave them all of their laws.

Many of those laws were special, given to discipline the people away
from gross paganism, to make them painfully aware of their sin and, most
importantly, to prepare them to birth the Christ. Again, Dr. Kennedy:

> Most Christians have always believed that that system of law
> ended with the destruction of Israel. Therefore, we as Christians
> do not by any means advocate the re-establishment of a theocracy.
> I would not agree with any push to reinstitute the Old Testament
> civil, legal system as replacing our whole governmental legislation.
> That is not what we favor. But those laws do give us guidance as
> to the kinds of laws that civil government should form. And I do
> believe that the laws of every nation should be in harmony—not
> with all the special laws of the Old Testament—but at least with
> the moral laws of the Ten Commandments. It is important to
> understand that America's historic common law derives from the
> English system, which in turn has its roots in *ancient rights of
> Englishmen*. These were a Biblically derived system of laws under
> Alfred the Great, King of England.
>
> [Jesus lived under a debased form of the Hebrew theocracy.] . . .
> But His death and the subsequent dispersal of Israel brought an
> end to it. By His Spirit working through the early Church, I think
> it is very clear that He did not mean to perpetuate that system
> into the whole world. Even at the first Council at Jerusalem,
> they said, we had a system of laws that we ourselves could not
> bear and now we should not try and impose this on the Gentile
> world (paraphrased from Acts 15:1-21). I believe the Church has
> been acting in accordance with Christ as He revealed His will
> through His Spirit to the early Church. So, therefore, I would
> say Jesus is not in favor of trying to restore the theocracy to the
> whole civilized world.
>
> Somebody asked me if I was out to Christianize America.
> And I said, "No, of course not. I'm out to Christianize the whole
> world!" And what else does the Great Commission mean but that?
> That we are to proclaim the gospel to every creature and pray that
> they will respond positively to the invitation to receive Christ and
> the gift of eternal life.

And if they do, they will become Christians, with its appropriate fruit, and that will result in a greater *Christianization* of any country where they live. By Christianization, we mean that as the people increasingly hearken to His Law-Word, living according to the Spirit of God with liberty, equal justice, and loving one's neighbor as oneself increasingly becomes the norm. America represents perhaps the highest expression of this understanding of Christianization ever known. Here's more from Dr. Kennedy:

> It's amazing that that is seen as somehow unAmerican or alien or foreign, whereas 99.8 percent of the people in this country as late as 1776, 150-plus years after the Pilgrims landed here, professed themselves to be Christians; 99.8 percent.[19] And so, the idea that we would Christianize this country is only an effort to return to where the country started—not to introduce something foreign, alien, or strange.

Indeed, the known alternatives are forms of statism, where the government imposes itself on the people and liberty is increasingly destroyed. Dr. Kennedy concludes:

> The founding fathers did not give us a government which they expected us to change with every shifting wind, but also it's true that 78 percent of people in America still profess themselves to be Christians.[20] We probably have a higher percentage of Christians today in this country than exist as a percentage of one religion than most of the nations on earth.[21]

This point that we do not advocate an authoritarian theocracy must be underscored because our position is often misrepresented. Those who say that we cannot legislate morality are only too willing to impose their own view of morality. In her acerbic style, Ann Coulter made this cutting observation, when I interviewed her for Coral Ridge Ministries: "Liberalism is the official state religion. People don't even notice it anymore, because liberalism denies it's a religion, so it proceeds, it advances and affects the entire culture, so that people don't even notice it anymore. And ordinary people are constantly on the defensive on the 'separation of church and state.' *Separation of church and state?* Well, that's a separation of *YOUR* church and state. Their church *IS* the state." [emphasis hers][22]

Someone's view of morality will be represented. The question is not, *if* morality will be legislated, but rather *whose* view will prevail?

UNIQUE NATION

The United States of America is unique. Survey the history of the world, and you will not find another nation like it. Other great nations have patterned their constitutions after ours and reaped similar benefits.

America is the lone superpower. We are the model nation that many try to emulate. More constitutions are based on ours than are based on any other. We are the envy of the world. Many potential immigrants risk their lives to make it to these shores. Some of them die in the process. Some illegal immigrants from Mexico, who suffocated in the airtight compartments in the back of a truck in the Southwestern desert of the U.S., come to mind.

What is the source of our greatness?

There are certainly many historical *threads* that have made us great, just as there are multiple threads that make up Western civilization. Just as Christianity is the single most important thread in Western civilization, so is the Christian faith the single most important contribution to America's uniqueness.

Sounds far-fetched? Consider the fact that we are governed by one document—the Constitution. As we will see, this is a direct outgrowth of the Puritan covenants, which bound one man to another under God and gave cohesiveness to their colonies, which, at their creation, were little more than outposts in a howling wilderness.

I believe the reason we are great is our rich Christian heritage. In a very real way, North America began, "In the name of God" as the Mayflower Compact, our first constitution, puts it.

In 1954, the threat of atheistic communism from halfway around the world was on the march in various satellite states. There was even the threat of communists within our own borders. In this context, when the contrast between God-based government and anti-God-based government could not have been greater, Congress decided to add the words "under God" in our Pledge of Allegiance. Here is what President Eisenhower said at the time he signed that law:

> FROM THIS DAY FORWARD, the millions of our school children will daily proclaim in every city and town, every village and rural school house, the dedication of our nation and our people to the Almighty. To anyone who truly loves America, nothing could be

more inspiring than to contemplate this rededication of our youth, on each school morning, to our country's true meaning.[23]

In 1955, President Eisenhower said this: "Without God, there could be no American form of Government, nor an American way of life. Recognition of the Supreme Being is the first—the most basic—expression of Americanism. Thus the founding fathers of America saw it, and thus with God's help, it will continue to be."[24] Without God, there would be no America.

Listen to what British scholar, historian, and author, Paul Johnson, has to say. In *A History of the American People* he writes, "America had been founded primarily for religious purposes, and the Great Awakening had been the original dynamic of the continental movement for independence. The Americans were overwhelmingly church-going, much more so than the English, whose rule they rejected. There is no question that the Declaration of Independence was, to those who signed it, a religious as well as a secular act...."[25] He also added, "And it is important to remember that America, as a whole, was a religious breakaway from Anglicanism...Anglican arrogance in the early seventeenth century came home to roost in the 1770s."[26] In the context of the Pilgrims and Puritans, Johnson writes, "religion was the biggest single motive in getting people to hazard all on the adventure...."[27]

I believe that ours is a peculiar country with a unique history. Again, I believe that what is best in the country is that which can be traced back to our Judeo-Christian heritage. What is lacking in our nation is our departure from that heritage.

CONSIDER JUST A FEW FACTS

Christopher Columbus changed history by discovering the New World. While he was not the first European to visit our continent—that honor belongs to Norway's Viking, Leif Eriksson—nonetheless, Columbus was the one who paved the way for others to follow in his train. Despite his significance in history, his *Christian* motivation is little known today. Why did he persevere for at least seven years requesting funding of his voyage? Why did he suffer repeated rejections of his proposal and even ridicule? Why did he defy death and risk mutiny to sail west into unknown waters? He tells us in his own words: "It was the Lord who put into my mind

(I could feel His hand upon me) to sail to the Indies. All who heard of my project rejected it with laughter, ridiculing me. There is no question that the inspiration was from the Holy Spirit, because He comforted me with rays of marvelous illumination from the Holy Scriptures."[28]

Jumping ahead to 1607 to the first permanent British settlement in North America, Jamestown, we find that the colony began with a ceremony of planting the cross at the beach and claiming the new land for Jesus Christ.

In the late 1500s, Great Britain made an abortive attempt to settle in Virginia—a land named after the Virgin Queen, Elizabeth the First, who reigned at that time. But not until Jamestown in 1607 was England able to create a permanent colony. They named it after the current monarch, King James the First. The first charter of Virginia, written in 1606, before they set sail, listed as one of the colony's goals being the "propagating of Christian religion to such people as yet live in darkness and miserable ignorance of the true knowledge and worship of God."[29]

When they arrived in 1607, they opened sealed instructions that had been written for them back in England the year before. One of those statements reminded them that unless they did things God's way and unless He helped them, the colony would be in vain. "Every plantation which our heavenly Father hath not planted shall be rooted out."[30]

The permanency of Jamestown paved the way for the Pilgrims, a small group of Separatists who could not agree with the premise that the Church of England at the time was in conformity with what they read in the Geneva version of the New Testament. The Pilgrims who settled Plymouth in 1620 explicitly began their colony "In the name of God. Amen."[31] Furthermore, they stated why they came: "for the glory of God and the advancement of the Christian faith."[32]

The Pilgrims intended to settle in the "northern parts of Virginia." Indeed, Jamestown made Plymouth possible. However, they were providentially blown off course. They created the first permanent European colony in New England. After the Pilgrims had come, so did the Puritans. The rest of the New England colonies were explicitly Christian and Puritan in tone.

Let me clarify the differences between the Pilgrims and the Puritans. Members of both groups were committed, Bible-centered Christians. The difference lay in their relationship with the Church of England. The

Pilgrims who settled Plymouth in 1620 differed from the Puritans in the sense that the former believed that the Church of England was so hopelessly corrupt that it could never be redeemed. The Pilgrims were Separatists and were persecuted for it. The Puritans worked for the purity of the Church of England, hence their name. In one sense, the Pilgrims were a subset of Puritans, with perhaps a more refined theology with regard to relational government. They both were committed to a strict interpretation of the Bible. The Pilgrims came to New England first, and, as it turns out, they blazed a trail for the Puritans, who wanted to stay and change the Church from within. Instead, monarchs like King James I and Charles I made it so difficult for religious nonconformists that eventually thousands of Puritans emigrated to the New World. Meanwhile, historian John Eidsmoe points out that by the end of the seventeenth century, any distinctions between the Pilgrims and the Puritans were virtually erased.

After the Pilgrims gained a tiny toehold in the New World, thousands of other Christian nonconformists—that is—the Puritans, came in, wave upon wave, after them. Plymouth had made Boston, Connecticut, and Rhode Island possible. During the tumultuous seventeenth century when England was rocked by civil war (which was driven by religious reasons in great part), thousands of Puritans saw the futility of trying to purify the Church of England by staying in England and joined their spiritual cousins, the Pilgrims (who were Separatists), in the New World.

The Puritans sometimes disagreed with each other. Branching out from Massachusetts, Puritan pioneers settled Connecticut and created the first complete constitution in America, the Fundamental Orders of Connecticut in 1639, which states that they established their colony "to maintain and preserve the liberty and purity of the gospel of our Lord Jesus which we now profess."[33]

In 1636, Puritan Roger Williams established Providence (named after God), Rhode Island. It was created to provide a safe haven for people to worship however they saw fit. Furthermore, the Rhode Island Charter of 1663 showed a desire to reach the Indians for Jesus Christ:

> …whereby our said people and inhabitants, in the said Plantations, may be so religiously, peaceably and civilly governed, as that, by their good life and orderly conversations, they may win and invite the native Indians of the country to the knowledge and obedience of the only true God, and Savior of mankind….[34]

In the 1630s and 1640s, Queen Christina of Sweden permitted a colony to be established in Delaware. One of the stipulations of the colony was that "all persons, but especially the young, shall be duly instructed in the articles of their Christian faith; and all good church discipline shall in like manner be duly exercised and received." Furthermore, there was provision for the Indians, which she called "the wild nations," to be gradually "instructed in the truths and worship of the Christian religion."[35]

Meanwhile, Catholics from England, intent on religious liberty, founded Maryland. Eventually, the colony would lose its Catholic flavor because it was overrun by so many Protestants.

In the 1670s and 1680s, Quakers founded a haven for Christians of all kinds. The Quaker William Penn laid this foundation, and to this day, Pennsylvania, named in honor of his father, enshrines the family name. Penn created what he called a "Holy Experiment," allowing for Christians of all denominations to worship freely as they saw fit. He too desired that the Indians be reached with the gospel. They desired to bring, as he put it, "the savage natives by gentle and just manners to the Love of Civil Societ[y] and Christian religion."[36]

In 1669, John Locke, author of *The Reasonableness of Christianity*, was chief author of the Charter of Carolina, which later split into two colonies. The charter stipulates that "God is publicly and solemnly to be worshipped."[37] The charter also instructs the colonists to act kindly toward the Indians for Christianity's sake and it entreats the colonists to live in such a way "that civil peace may be maintained amidst diversity of opinions." Why? In order "that Jews, heathens, and other dissenters from the purity of Christian religion may not be scared and kept at a distance from it, but, by having an opportunity of acquainting themselves with the truth and reasonableness of its doctrines, and the peaceableness and inoffensiveness of its professors, may, by good usage and persuasion, and all those convincing methods of gentleness and meekness, suitable to the rules and design of the gospel, be won ever to embrace and unfeignedly receive the truth."[38]

Jumping ahead to 1733, when Georgia was founded by James Oglethorpe, that colony also was to provide for the conversion of the Indians through the colony's good discipline and example of just, moral, and religious behavior. Oglethorpe's first official act as a Trustee in Savannah was to kneel with his company to offer thanksgiving and prayer to God.

BUT TODAY...

Despite Christianity's unique role in the shaping of America, there are daily assaults on our religious liberty from various sectors and on various fronts. Groups like Americans United for the Separation of Church and State and the American Civil Liberties Union (the ACLU) are doing everything possible to remove any influence of Christianity from the public square. Unfortunately, they have been very effective.

The newspapers are filled with accounts of the assault on religious liberty. Even now, legislation is in the works, such as Hate Crimes Laws or ENDA (the Employment Non-Discrimination Act), which some have quipped would be "the ENDA religious liberty," if it passed.

Alleged hate-crimes laws ("thought control") have gone into effect in other countries, resulting in a loss of religious freedom. For example, Ake Green, pastor of a small church in Sweden, preached a sermon in which he labeled homosexuality a sin. A tape of his message was sent to the local police, who determined that a "hate crime" had been committed. He went on trial and was sentenced to a month in jail, but the homosexual activists wanted him to spend a longer time. Thankfully, with the help of legal missionaries from America, Pastor Green won his case on appeal. The legal missionaries came from the Alliance Defense Fund (ADF), which D. James Kennedy helped create in the mid-1990s. Why should a pastor be threatened with jail time for preaching what the Bible says? Peter Sprigg of the Family Research Council says, "I cannot imagine anything more chilling to the freedom of religion than the prospect of a pastor being arrested and put in jail for preaching Biblical truth from his own pulpit in his own church in his own Sunday-morning worship service. But that's exactly what happened in Sweden."[39] Pastor Green notes, "We must be aware of the fact that faith is under fire."[40] And there are those who are trying to make hate-crime laws the law of the land in America.

We have reached the point where sexual libertinism of a homosexual and heterosexual nature trumps everything else. Religious liberty is subservient to abortion rights (which is an outgrowth of sexual politics). In the minds of many in our culture, the rights of homosexuals trump the rights of Christian people to practice their faith. In the last generation or so, conservative Christians are becoming second-class citizens. Jesus told us we can expect persecution, and so it comes.

Take the example in Australia of Danny Nahlia, a traveling preacher originally from Sri Lanka. He was a victim of hate-crime laws after the state of Victoria, where he lives, passed such a law in January 2002. Two months later, in March, someone asked him to give a seminar in a church on the subject of Islam (because of 9/11). He and a colleague put on a seminar and, unbeknownst to them, there were some Muslims in the audience (Australians of European-origin who had converted to Islam). At the seminar, Danny and his associate critiqued some verses from the Koran—verses along the lines of "kill the infidel." The Muslims then filed a complaint with the government under hate-crime laws. This then mushroomed into a big case. Danny Nahlia points out, "In total, the case has run now for almost five years. We have spent more than 650,000 Australian dollars [approximately U.S. $540,000] for the case. And the tribunal judge found myself and my [colleague], Daniel Scottwood, guilty, and said that we needed to apologize, pay $67,500 for newspaper advertisements, and not to be engaged in conduct such as that in future. I said, 'I will take the jail [time]. I will not apologize and compromise speaking about Jesus.' So, we were very close to going to prison, but we appealed our case. And the three judges in the Supreme Court, in the month of December [2006], cleared us from all wrongdoing and relinquished all orders made against us. This [hate-crime law] is a dangerous piece of legislation, because it's a subjective law, not an objective law."[41]

Some of the modern charges against Christians go to ridiculous lengths. I think one of the most odious I have ever heard about was the five-year-old American girl in kindergarten who wrote, "I love God" on her palm and was censured for it. How ironic that we go from a nation founded for religious liberty to a situation where such liberty is now at risk.

Because most Americans have attended the public schools, there is a great deal of ignorance on our Judeo-Christian heritage. This comes from virtually all quarters of society. Most pastors went to public school and were exposed to the revisionist view of history. Those of us wanting to restore a knowledge of our Christian heritage have our work cut out for us.

As secularism continues its stranglehold on American education, we move further and further away from retaining our Christian roots.

CONCLUSION

America was founded for liberty, in particular, religious liberty. But we have forgotten our heritage. I believe we will help increase the spread of the gospel by regaining our true history. Why should pastors and ministries be embroiled in costly lawsuits that are essentially forms of harassment when the goal of the founders was that we be free to live according to our consciences? Why should Christians be singled out for persecution, when George Washington said we would never be a happy nation unless we lived like good Christians, living in imitation of Jesus Christ? [42]

People of other views are welcome here. However, we find that in modern times, tolerance of viewpoint (which was a gift of American Christians) is being abused against those with the very worldview from whence it came. Note what author and speaker, Bill Federer, said in one of our programs on the Christian roots of America:

> Tolerance was an American Christian contribution to the world. Just as you drop a pebble in the pond, the ripples go out, there was tolerance first for Puritans and then Protestants, then Catholics, then liberal Christians, and then it went out completely to Jews. Then in the early 1900s, tolerance went out to anybody of any faith, monotheist or polytheist. Finally, within the last generation, tolerance went out to the atheist, the secular humanist and the anti-religious. And the last ones in the boat decided it was too crowded and decided to push the first ones out. So now we have a unique situation in America, where everybody's tolerated except the ones that came up with the idea. And so when people say Christians are intolerant, we really need to correct them and say, "No, we're the ones that came up with the idea of tolerance." [43]

In short, our Christian heritage counts because it defines what the nation is at our very core. Our future liberty depends on our present actions. Our amnesia of the past jeopardizes our future.

Next, we consider Biblical principles related to our heritage and our responsibility.

Pohick Church in Lorton, Virginia. Sketch by Benson J. Lossing

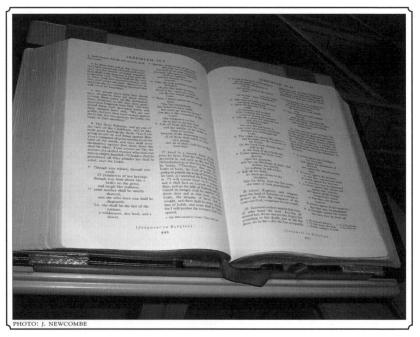

PHOTO: J. NEWCOMBE

The Bible at Pohick Church. This Anglican church is where George Washington, as a young man, attended and served as a vestryman. Dr. Donald Lutz, scholar on American history, notes that virtually all the founding fathers knew the Bible "down to their fingertips." Two social scientists, Hyneman and Lutz, studied thousands of writings from the founding era to see which sources were quoted or cited. They found that the Bible was quoted four times more than any human author.

CHAPTER 2

Biblical Considerations

Righteousness exalts a nation,
but sin is a reproach to any people.
(Proverbs 14:34)

THE most important consideration of any matter is God's opinion. What, if anything, does God's Word say on the subject?

While the Bible is not a political textbook, it certainly has political implications. It is God's political sourcebook for men—our guide for living with one another. The Word is the "Good Seed" of our understanding (Matthew 13:24). In this chapter, we want to look at Biblical implications for government and Biblical teaching on remembering what God has done in the past.

WARNINGS AGAINST OPPRESSIVE GOVERNMENT

We have already made the point that God only recognized one theocracy in the history of the world, that of ancient Israel. Even that did not work out too well. The ancient Israelites rebelled against God and His prophet, Samuel. They demanded a king. God granted their request, but He warned them in a lengthy admonition about how oppressive a king could be. What He said to mankind three thousand years ago still has implications for today. Today we are completely overtaxed. This is even more true in other countries. Because of the sinful heart of man, rulers often lord it over their subjects. This is a condition that the Bible warned humanity against all those centuries ago.

Here is the backdrop of God's warning regarding oppressive government:

> When Samuel became old, he made his sons judges over Israel. The name of his firstborn son was Joel, and the name of his second, Abijah; they were judges in Beersheba. Yet his sons did not walk in his ways but turned aside after gain. They took bribes and perverted justice.
>
> Then all the elders of Israel gathered together and came to Samuel at Ramah and said to him, "Behold, you are old and your sons do not walk in your ways. Now appoint for us a king to judge us like all the nations." But the thing displeased Samuel when they said, "Give us a king to judge us." And Samuel prayed to the LORD. And the LORD said to Samuel, "Obey the voice of the people in all that they say to you, for they have not rejected you, but they have rejected Me from being king over them. According to all the deeds that they have done, from the day I brought them up out of Egypt even to this day, forsaking Me and serving other gods, so they are also doing to you. Now then, obey their voice; only you shall solemnly warn them and show them the ways of the king who shall reign over them" (1 Samuel 8:1-9).

In His mercy, God grants their request. Then He spells out the details and implications of what they are asking for—the people will be oppressed by their rulers:

> So Samuel told all the words of the LORD to the people who were asking for a king from him. He said, "These will be the ways of the king who will reign over you: he will take your sons and appoint them to his chariots and to be his horsemen and to run before his chariots. And he will appoint for himself commanders of thousands and commanders of fifties, and some to plow his ground and to reap his harvest, and to make his implements of war and the equipment of his chariots. He will take your daughters to be perfumers and cooks and bakers. He will take the best of your fields and vineyards and olive orchards and give them to his servants. He will take the tenth of your grain and of your vineyards and give it to his officers and to his servants. He will take your male servants and female servants and the best of your young men and your donkeys, and put them to his work. He will take the tenth of your flocks, and you shall be his slaves. And in that day

you will cry out because of your king, whom you have chosen for yourselves, but the LORD will not answer you in that day" (10-18).

Modern Americans can relate to this. We work so hard that we may pay off our ever-increasing tax bills. Some politicians want to keep increasing these taxes. It can be argued that they do this so that their own power base may increase. Despite the warnings from the Lord, the Israelites were adamant on getting a king. This is what they had set their hearts on. The Bible continues:

> But the people refused to obey the voice of Samuel. And they said, "No! But there shall be a king over us, that we also may be like all the nations, and that our king may judge us and go out before us and fight our battles." And when Samuel had heard all the words of the people, he repeated them in the ears of the LORD. And the LORD said to Samuel, "Obey their voice and make them a king." Samuel then said to the men of Israel, "Go every man to his city" (19-22).

The Bible is clear that man's heart is wicked and is inclined toward sin. That is why those who have power are so inclined to abuse that power.

Part of the genius of the founding fathers of America was their recognition of the fact of man's sinfulness. They set things up in such a way so that no one individual or group could grab too much power. Knowing what the Bible teaches about man's sinful nature, they acted very carefully to avoid the kind of abuse that Samuel warned against.

For example, John Adams said any man holding political power was "a ravenous beast of prey."[44] His power must be contained and balanced by other governmental powers.

"BLESSED IS THE NATION"

Another teaching of Scripture related to government can be found in Psalm 33: "Blessed is the nation whose God is the LORD, the people whom He has chosen as His heritage!" (v. 12). Of course, this applied to ancient Israel. It is interesting to note that Abraham Lincoln quoted this on March 30, 1863, when he made this "Proclamation for a National Day of Fasting."

> [I]t is the duty of nations as well as of men to own their dependence upon the overruling power of God; to confess their sins

and transgressions in humble sorrow, yet with assured hope that genuine repentance will lead to mercy and pardon; and to recognize the sublime truth, announced in the Holy Scriptures and proven by all history, that those nations only are blessed whose God is the Lord.[45]

So, although this is viewed as being true first and foremost to ancient Israel, it can also be viewed as applying as a generality to any nation in which a multitude strive for godliness. Similarly, we find this statement in the poetic literature: "Righteousness exalts a nation, but sin is a reproach to any people" (Proverbs 14:34). Again, this general principle still holds.

CIVIL DISOBEDIENCE

Sometimes, the government tries to force believers to disobey God. It is usually not a case where the state sets out to force disobedience. In most cases, the state does not care what people think, believe, and worship. They just demand some type of nominal, outward obedience. In ancient Rome, for instance, you could worship any god you wanted to (including Jesus), but you also had to worship Caesar. Those who refused to engage in this act were punished. Sometimes they paid with their lives.

For example, the Roman Emperor Decius (201-251) demanded that citizens sacrifice to the empire. Many Christians could not do this in good conscience. Here is what historian Dr. Paul Maier says about that persecution:

> [T]here was no systematic empire-wide persecution of the Christians until the Emperor Decius. He was in charge from A.D. 249 to 251. He issued a general proclamation that Christians were to be eliminated on the basis of province by province, city by city, ward by ward, block by block, house by house. He sent his inspectors along; they would knock on the door and they would say, "Could I see your certificate?" If you had a certificate that you would sacrifice to the Emperor, fine, they would bless you and go to the next door. If you didn't have a certificate, no problem, they would bring in a bust of the emperor; they would light a little votive candle in front of it and give you some incense and say "Throw it on the candle." And if you did, they'd write you out a certificate. If you refused to do that, they then would immediately execute the men and sell the women and children into slavery.

That could have been a horrendous persecution of the church, but fortunately, Decius was only able to implement it for a short time and he was killed in the northern frontier, thank God.[46]

Consider another case where believers in the one true God were persecuted for not worshiping a false god. This was at the time of the Jewish exile in Babylon. The authorities established an example of forced idolatry. Daniel writes:

> King Nebuchadnezzar made an image of gold, whose height was sixty cubits and its breadth six cubits. He set it up on the plain of Dura, in the province of Babylon. Then King Nebuchadnezzar sent to gather the satraps, the prefects, and the governors, the counselors, the treasurers, the justices, the magistrates, and all the officials of the provinces to come to the dedication of the image that King Nebuchadnezzar had set up. Then the satraps, the prefects, and the governors, the counselors, the treasurers, the justices, the magistrates, and all the officials of the provinces gathered for the dedication of the image that King Nebuchadnezzar had set up. And they stood before the image that Nebuchadnezzar had set up. And the herald proclaimed aloud, "You are commanded, O peoples, nations, and languages, that when you hear the sound of the horn, pipe, lyre, trigon, harp, bagpipe, and every kind of music, you are to fall down and worship the golden image that King Nebuchadnezzar has set up. And whoever does not fall down and worship shall immediately be cast into a burning fiery furnace." Therefore, as soon as all the peoples heard the sound of the horn, pipe, lyre, trigon, harp, bagpipe, and every kind of music, all the peoples, nations, and languages fell down and worshiped the golden image that King Nebuchadnezzar had set up (Daniel 3:1-7).

Daniel's three Jewish friends fell afoul of the law because of their refusal to engage in idolatry. They engaged in civil disobedience.

> Therefore at that time certain Chaldeans came forward and maliciously accused the Jews. They declared to King Nebuchadnezzar, "O king, live forever! You, O king, have made a decree, that every man who hears the sound of the horn, pipe, lyre, trigon, harp, bagpipe, and every kind of music, shall fall down and worship the golden image. And whoever does not fall down and worship shall

be cast into a burning fiery furnace. There are certain Jews whom you have appointed over the affairs of the province of Babylon: Shadrach, Meshach, and Abednego. These men, O king, pay no attention to you; they do not serve your gods or worship the golden image that you have set up" (8-12).

Upon hearing this, the king was furious. However, the Jews were adamant in obeying God (to worship Him alone), despite the personal cost. By obeying God in this context, they were engaging in civil disobedience.

Then Nebuchadnezzar in furious rage commanded that Shadrach, Meshach, and Abednego be brought. So they brought these men before the king. Nebuchadnezzar answered and said to them, "Is it true, O Shadrach, Meshach, and Abednego, that you do not serve my gods or worship the golden image that I have set up? Now if you are ready when you hear the sound of the horn, pipe, lyre, trigon, harp, bagpipe, and every kind of music, to fall down and worship the image that I have made, well and good. But if you do not worship, you shall immediately be cast into a burning fiery furnace. And who is the god who will deliver you out of my hands?"

Shadrach, Meshach, and Abednego answered and said to the king, "O Nebuchadnezzar, we have no need to answer you in this matter. If this be so, our God whom we serve is able to deliver us from the burning fiery furnace, and He will deliver us out of your hand, O king. But if not, be it known to you, O king, that we will not serve your gods or worship the golden image that you have set up."

Then Nebuchadnezzar was filled with fury, and the expression of his face was changed against Shadrach, Meshach, and Abednego. He ordered the furnace heated seven times more than it was usually heated. And he ordered some of the mighty men of his army to bind Shadrach, Meshach, and Abednego, and to cast them into the burning fiery furnace. Then these men were bound in their cloaks, their tunics, their hats, and their other garments, and they were thrown into the burning fiery furnace. Because the king's order was urgent and the furnace overheated, the flame of the fire killed those men who took up Shadrach, Meshach, and Abednego. And these three men, Shadrach, Meshach, and Abednego, fell bound into the burning fiery furnace.

Then King Nebuchadnezzar was astonished and rose up in

haste. He declared to his counselors, "Did we not cast three men bound into the fire?" They answered and said to the king, "True, O king." He answered and said, "But I see four men unbound, walking in the midst of the fire, and they are not hurt; and the appearance of the fourth is like a son of the gods" (13-25).

God chose to miraculously deliver them (through the pre-incarnate Christ). But even without the happy ending, these three heroes chose to obey God rather than man.

> Then Nebuchadnezzar came near to the door of the burning fiery furnace; he declared, "Shadrach, Meshach, and Abednego, servants of the Most High God, come out, and come here!" Then Shadrach, Meshach, and Abednego came out from the fire. And the satraps, the prefects, the governors, and the king's counselors gathered together and saw that the fire had not had any power over the bodies of those men. The hair of their heads was not singed, their cloaks were not harmed, and no smell of fire had come upon them. Nebuchadnezzar answered and said, "Blessed be the God of Shadrach, Meshach, and Abednego, who has sent His angel and delivered his servants, who trusted in Him, and set aside the king's command, and yielded up their bodies rather than serve and worship any god except their own God. Therefore I make a decree: Any people, nation, or language that speaks anything against the God of Shadrach, Meshach, and Abednego shall be torn limb from limb, and their houses laid in ruins, for there is no other god who is able to rescue in this way." Then the king promoted Shadrach, Meshach, and Abednego in the province of Babylon (26-30).

What an amazing passage with an amazing outcome. The only ones who died that day were the soldiers bringing the three to the fire. If a government tries to force its citizens to directly sin, then the conscientious believer has no option but to disobey, even if it costs him his life. As we will see in a moment, this theme of civil disobedience on occasion carries over into the New Testament as well. Christians today might not always agree on where or when to draw the line between obedience and disobedience, but we all should see the principle established in Scripture.

This idea of civil disobedience is reinforced a few chapters later when Daniel is cast into the lions' den because he chose to pray to God, as was his custom. The passage is so familiar that we will not recount it. It, too, had a happy ending. Here are the two most critical verses for our purposes (6:7 and 10). Motivated by jealousy against Daniel, his enemies convinced the king to create a law by which they were sure to catch Daniel: "All the presidents of the kingdom, the prefects and the satraps, the counselors and the governors are agreed that the king should establish an ordinance and enforce an injunction, that whoever makes petition to any god or man for thirty days, except to you, O king, shall be cast into the den of lions" (Daniel 6:7). Despite the decree set up to trap him—a decree sentencing anyone to death who dared to pray—Daniel obeyed God, not man: "When Daniel knew that the document had been signed, he went to his house where he had windows in his upper chamber open toward Jerusalem. He got down on his knees three times a day and prayed and gave thanks before his God, as he had done previously" (6:10). Again, God chose to miraculously spare him from what would have been a vicious death by hungry lions.

We find the same principle of obedience to God above obedience to man in Acts as well. The Sanhedrin ordered Peter and John to stop preaching about Jesus Christ. They could not. Peter replied (in classic words), "We must obey God rather than men" (Acts 5:29). Just a chapter earlier, they put it this way: "But Peter and John replied, 'Judge for yourselves whether it is right in God's sight to obey you rather than God'" (Acts 4:19, NIV).

Here is the Christian basis for civil disobedience. We do not practice it when we disagree with the government or do not like a particular law. The principle applies particularly in the context of obedience to God. When the state tries to force us to disobey God, then it is our Christian duty to disobey. The story of Christianity is replete with Christians who paid a major price (sometimes, the ultimate price) for their obedience in the face of a hostile state.

This has even been the case when the prevailing authorities were supposedly Christians. For instance, in the name of Roman Catholicism, Bloody Mary executed Protestants. I was distressed one time when I took a cursory look at *Foxe's Book of Martyrs*, published in 1563. While the first fifty-some pages out of about 300 dealt with the Jews and Romans persecuting the church, the other 85 percent or so of the book dealt with true Christians being persecuted by so-called Christians. As the Reformation unfolded, the kind of persecution that Foxe wrote about in the sixteenth century continued in earnest through the eighteenth century. This kind of persecution in the sixteenth, seventeenth, and eighteenth centuries was the catalyst for many Christians (of different denominations) to come to America in order that they might worship Jesus in the purity of the gospel, as they understood it.

Returning for a moment to the account of Daniel in the lions' den, note how the pagan ruler, King Darius, was impacted by witnessing the effects of God's miraculous delivery of Daniel. He wrote a missive "to all the peoples, nations, and languages that dwell in all the earth" (Daniel 6:25). He recognizes that "the God of Daniel…is the living God, enduring forever; His kingdom shall never be destroyed, and His dominion shall be to the end" (Daniel 6:26).

While earthly kingdoms rise and fall, God's kingdom is forever. Even this pagan king could see that. This notion has implications for those of us who are citizens of both kingdoms. Sometimes those who promote the thesis of America as a Christian nation seem to overstate the case and talk as if America is like God's kingdom on earth. Sadly, America may one day fall. The late Ruth Bell Graham's observation is pertinent: "If America doesn't repent, God will have to apologize to Sodom and Gomorrah." It might be that the first test for American Christians will come through the medical field where doctors might soon be required to perform abortions against their will and conscience.

RENDER UNTO CAESAR

One of the classic statements in the Bible regarding government is in the passage where the religious leaders tried to trap Jesus. They asked Him if they should pay taxes (to the hated Roman oppressors). If He answered yes, then He would lose points with the crowd which suffered heavily under the Romans. If He answered no, then the Romans could seize Him for promoting rebellion. Here is Mark's version:

> [K]nowing their hypocrisy, He said to them, "Why put me to the test? Bring me a denarius and let me look at it." And they brought one. And He said to them, "Whose likeness and inscription is this?" They said to Him, "Caesar's." Jesus said to them, "Render to Caesar the things that are Caesar's, and to God the things that are God's." And they marveled at Him (Mark 12:15-17).

Ultimately, God is the one to whom we are to submit, since even human authority derives its power from Him. Jesus reinforced the notion that human authority comes from divine authority when He appeared before Pilate and said to Him, "You would have no authority over Me at all unless it had been given you from above. Therefore He who delivered Me over to you has the greater sin" (John 19:11).

Submission to Authorites

We continue on the theme of human authority being derived from divine authority. The New Testament's most important passage on government is Romans 13.

> Everyone must submit himself to the governing authorities, for there is no authority except that which God has established. The authorities that exist have been established by God. Consequently, he who rebels against the authority is rebelling against what God has instituted, and those who do so will bring judgment on themselves. For rulers hold no terror for those who do right, but for those who do wrong. Do you want to be free from fear of the one in authority? Then do what is right and he will commend you. For he is God's servant to do you good. But if you do wrong, be afraid, for he does not bear the sword for nothing. He is God's servant, an agent of wrath to bring punishment on the wrongdoer. Therefore, it is necessary to submit to the authorities, not only because of possible punishment but also because of conscience. This is also why you pay taxes, for the authorities are God's servants, who give their full time to governing. Give everyone what you owe him: If you owe taxes, pay taxes; if revenue, then revenue; if respect, then respect; if honor, then honor (Romans 13:1-7, NIV).

Sometimes, this teaching can be deliberately abused, as I noticed in my favorite museum in the world located in Oslo, Norway. This collection of memorabilia is dedicated to honoring the resistance movement against the Nazis during their reign in that country from April 1940 to May 1945. The Nazis expected that their fellow Aryans (Nordics) would welcome their rule. Instead, most Norwegians opposed them every way they could.

The Nazis told the churches what they would say, and they dictated the required curriculum, as they "Nazified"[47] the schools. At one time, all the priests of the Lutheran church (about 3,000 of them) decided to make a stand together against the Germans telling them what they were permitted to say from the pulpit. Virtually all of them were sent to the concentration camps, and only a few of them returned alive after the war. Similarly, the school teachers led a revolt of Christian civil disobedience. They too were dispatched to the camps with few survivors returning afterwards.

In the Oslo museum, they show some of the curriculum the Nazis imposed on the Norwegians. Included in those lessons was Romans 13, what Paul says about our need to submit to the state. When I saw that curriculum, I thought, "Wow. Talk about the devil quoting Scripture!"

Nonetheless, here is the clear teaching of Scripture—that, for the most part, we obey what the government tells us. The only caveat is that we cannot obey the government when it tries to make us violate our Christian conscience, e.g., by trying to force us to worship a false god. The above-mentioned principle of civil government would then apply.

Very similar to Romans 13 is 1 Peter 2. Here we have the pillars of the early church—Peter (in 1 Peter 2) and Paul (in Romans 13)—declaring the need to obey the government, even if it is pagan. Both Peter and Paul were executed by Emperor Nero in about A.D. 64 or 65. They obeyed government to a point, but they would not stop preaching the gospel, though that preaching cost them their lives.

Here is Peter's directive regarding the relationship between Christians and human rulers as found in the second chapter of 1 Peter:

> Be subject for the Lord's sake to every human institution, whether it be to the emperor as supreme, or to governors as sent by him to punish those who do evil and to praise those who do good. For this is the will of God, that by doing good you should put to silence the ignorance of foolish people. Live as people who are free, not using your freedom as a cover-up for evil, but living as servants of God. Honor everyone. Love the brotherhood. Fear God. Honor the emperor (1 Peter 2:13-17).

The witness of the early Church was very powerful. In the face of incredible persecution, they showed their love for Jesus Christ. They stood out like lights in the universe and convinced many to join their cause, even if they had to die for it, which many did.

Christianity does not preach anarchy. It teaches that the normal pattern of the Christian should be submission to the government. However, it does proclaim there is an occasion for civil disobedience. The Biblical principle is that government is willed by and established by God for our good, and civil rulers are also "ministers" of God.

Since this book is attempting to get Americans to remember our nation's Christian roots, what does the Bible say about a people remembering their godly heritage?

Memorial Considerations

One theme that can be found in the Bible is that of creating memorials—visual reminders of what God had done—so that future generations would learn of His works and His faithfulness. For example, an individual or a group would put together some sort of pile of rocks in order to cause them and future generations to remember what God had done in that particular place. Memorials are important. We see that God has acted in some providential way, and we are encouraged to remember Him and give Him thanks. This point is important to our book: We should remember what God has done in the past.

We Americans have memorials, and we need memorials. In one sense, Thanksgiving is a reminder of our nation's Christian heritage. We honor the memory of the Pilgrims and their sacrifice, but we also remember God's providence and how He spared the settlers and founders and helped them create a new nation. Columnist Mark Steyn notes: "Speaking as a misfit unassimilated foreigner, I think of Thanksgiving as the most American of holidays."[48]

Here is a Biblical example of someone remembering God by building a memorial: When Jacob set out to find his uncle, Laban, God appeared to him in a dream, and he saw what we now call *Jacob's ladder.* Here is his reaction:

> Then Jacob awoke from his sleep and said, "Surely the Lord is in this place, and I did not know it." And he was afraid and said, "How awesome is this place! This is none other than the house of God, and this is the gate of heaven." So early in the morning Jacob took the stone that he had put under his head and set it up for a pillar and poured oil on the top of it. He called the name of that place Bethel, but the name of the city was Luz at the first.

> Then Jacob made a vow, saying, "If God will be with me and will
> keep me in this way that I go, and will give me bread to eat and
> clothing to wear, so that I come again to my father's house in
> peace, then the LORD shall be my God, and this stone, which I
> have set up for a pillar, shall be God's house. And of all that you
> give me I will give a full tenth to you." (Genesis 28:16-22).

Jacob named the place "Bethel," meaning God's house. He marked the
sacred place by building a memorial of stones. Jacob's words and actions
evidence the Biblical principle of remembrance.

Here is another example of a memorial: In 1 Samuel 7, during one of
the many conflicts between the Israelites and the Philistines, God brought
His people victory. This happened at a moment of national repentance,
led by Samuel.

> And Samuel said to all the house of Israel, "If you are returning
> to the LORD with all your heart, then put away the foreign gods
> and the Ashtaroth from among you and direct your heart to the
> LORD and serve Him only, and He will deliver you out of the
> hand of the Philistines." So the people of Israel put away the Baals
> and the Ashtaroth, and they served the LORD only.
>
> Then Samuel said, "Gather all Israel at Mizpah, and I will
> pray to the LORD for you." So they gathered at Mizpah and drew
> water and poured it out before the LORD and fasted on that day
> and said there, "We have sinned against the LORD" (1 Samuel
> 7:3-6).

When the Philistines heard that the people of Israel were gathered
together, they came to attack them. Samuel made an offering for the
people, and God gave the Israelites a great victory that day. Here is the
key verse for our point: "Then Samuel took a stone and set it up between
Mizpah and Shen and called its name Ebenezer; for he said, 'Till now
the LORD has helped us'" (verse 12). In future times, and even in future
generations, people could look at that memorial and be reminded of what
God had done. Furthermore, there are two verses in the book of Proverbs
that remind us about commemorating what God has done.

I am not idolatrous toward America, but when I think back to some
of the great memorials in our history, we see God's hand. From my perspective, these memorials remind us of God's intervention to help this
nation become established in the first place. Such items would include

Plymouth Rock, the New England Meeting Hall (symbol of Puritan worship and representative government), the Liberty Bell,[49] the Declaration of Independence,[50] the Constitution,[51] the Lincoln Memorial (which has Scripture verses chiseled on the walls), and the Washington Monument (which has "Praise be to God" in Latin at the very top). Of course, when these symbols are so secularized, as they have been in our day, then they become mere idols that point away from God.

FEASTS OF THE LORD

I believe that the entire ceremonial law of the Old Testament has been fulfilled in the ministry of Jesus Christ—especially His death and resurrection. He is the real scapegoat. He is the real Passover Lamb. Part of the ceremonial laws include the "Feasts of the LORD"—all of which are elaborated in Leviticus 23. Each of these, in their own way, is a day of remembrance, a day to remember some aspect of what God has done for them. These "appointed feasts" are "holy convocations" (Leviticus 23:2). The first is the Sabbath, a weekly reminder that the believer's life belongs to God; the day was to be holy. To the Christian, Sunday, the Lord's Day, is a weekly reminder of the resurrection of Jesus Christ, the cornerstone of the Christian Church. Other feasts mentioned in Leviticus 23 include:

* The Passover, the annual reminder of God's deliverance of His people from slavery in Egypt (5-8);
* The Feast of Firstfruits, a reminder that God gave them the land and that God provides the harvest (9-14);
* The Feast of Weeks, seven weeks after Firstfruits (Pentecost), (15-22);
* The Feast of Trumpets (23-25), which was a memorial proclaimed with blasting of trumpets;
* The Day of Atonement (26-32), the foreshadowing of Christ's death for our sins;
* The Feast of Booths (33-36), an annual reminder that they were once sojourners in the desert before God brought them into the land to dwell in safety.

Each of these feasts had specific regulations as to eating (or not eating), but each was a regular (usually annual) reminder of God's actions on behalf of His people at some point in the past. In their present and in their future, they were not to forget how God had led them in the past.

George Washington reminded us that we as Americans have a lot to be grateful for. As a young man during the French and Indian War, he was miraculously preserved during a massacre against the British and colonial army.[52] Jumping ahead to the Revolutionary War, he felt as if God (whom he often identifies as Providence) had interfered miraculously to help the American cause. For example, when his army was trapped on Brooklyn Heights, they were able to escape—thanks to a fog at just the right time. At another point, the plot involving Benedict Arnold's betrayal of the American cause was exposed just in time. After that incident in 1777, George Washington wrote a letter to a fellow patriot, Thomas Nelson, Jr., in which he marveled at how much the Lord was helping the American cause, "The hand of Providence has been so conspicuous in all this [the colonies' victories in the American War for Independence], that he must be worse than an infidel that lacks faith, and more than wicked, that has not gratitude enough to acknowledge his obligations."[53] When he was first sworn into office, he said this in his First Inaugural Address (April 30, 1789), "No people can be bound to acknowledge and adore the Invisible Hand which conducts the affairs of men more than the people of the United States."[54]

The founding fathers even designed the dollar in such a way to remind us how God had helped America during the Revolution. We find these words on the back of the dollar bill: *Annuit Coeptis,* a Latin phrase meaning "He has favored our undertakings." He refers to God, who the founders felt actively intervened on behalf of the American cause. The eye represents the eye of God, the eye of Providence. This refers to the role of Providence in the founding of America.[55]

This is tricky because we are not saying that Americans as a whole have made a covenant with God, although our founding fathers did so; however, we could at least we could say there is the Biblical precedent that we not forget what God has done in the past.

CONCLUSION

We could elaborate further on other examples of the Bible and government or other instances of the Bible and acts of remembrance (the ultimate example of which is the Lord's Table). Suffice it to say that the Bible does provide some general principles for civil government and the general principle that God's people should not forget how He has helped them in the past. Biblical religion is a history-based religion. Again, America is not the new Israel or the new Promised Land. However, it certainly had uniquely Christian beginnings. Why not pass those on before we lose our heritage altogether, so that, again, the gospel may be proclaimed with total freedom?

CHAPTER 3

Test Your Knowledge of Our Heritage

"[K]nowledge" puffs up, but love builds up.
(1 Corinthians 8:1)

AT this point, let's see how much we know about our nation's Christian heritage. I recommend that any pastor or Sunday school teacher that wants to teach the subject learn to master the kind of information in this quiz.

I developed the following quiz on our godly heritage and handed it to my Sunday school class. Very few people knew the answers, but this is a good way to start. Someone like David Barton[56] or Dr. Peter Lillback[57] or Paul Jehle[58] or author Bill Federer[59] or author Marshall Foster,[60] etc. would likely get all these right. It is helpful, though, to get a feel for how well pastors or Christian teachers know this material.

Even if you do not know five of the following fifty questions, do not get discouraged. Most people, including Christians, do not know this material.

First, I will present the questions. Then we will go back and review the questions and answers one by one. This gives us a good way to get an overview of the material we will be covering in depth later. Bear in mind—there is some overlap in what we find here. In fact, some of the really important points of our heritage are repeated in one way or another throughout this book.

America's
Christian Heritage
Quiz

1. What document says that our rights come from God, and it is the duty of the state not to interfere with that?
   a. The Declaration of Independence
   b. The Articles of Confederation
   c. The Mayflower Compact
   d. The Constitution

2. According to historian David Barton, of the 250 founding fathers, how many were of a skeptical bent (not orthodox, Trinitarian Christians)?
   a. 12
   b. 24
   c. 36
   d. 150

3. When Thomas Jefferson was president, what did he faithfully do every Sunday morning?
   a. Read the newspaper
   b. Attend church (with evangelical preaching)
   c. Attend church (with Unitarian preaching)
   d. Spend time with his family

4. In the early nineteenth century, what took place in the rotunda of the U.S. Capitol building?
   a. A public speaking forum for anyone who wanted to talk
   b. Reading aloud of the recent acts of Congress
   c. Reading aloud of that week's Supreme Court decisions
   d. Evangelical-oriented preaching in a Christian worship service

5. If you visit the U.S. Capitol today, in the rotunda are eight large paintings. How many of the eight contain direct evidence of our Christian heritage?
   a. Two
   b. Three
   c. Four
   d. Five

6. Where was the first Thanksgiving in America?
   a. 1573 in St. Augustine
   b. 1594 in Roanoke
   c. 1619 in Jamestown
   d. 1621 in Plymouth

7. What document opens with "In the name of God. Amen. We whose names are underwritten, having undertaken a voyage for the glory of God and the founding of the Christian religion…"?
   a. The Mayflower Compact
   b. The Baltimore Catechism
   c. The Fundamental Orders of Connecticut
   d. Penn's Frame of Government

8. Roughly how many Pilgrim-Puritan constitutions, charters, compacts, etc., of which the Mayflower Compact is one, led up to THE constitution?
   a. 15
   b. 35
   c. 50
   d. 100

9. Virtually all the settlers were familiar with:
   a. Blackstone's *Commentaries*
   b. The Bible
   c. The writings of John Locke
   d. Plato's *Republic*

10. Who was the main leader of the Puritans (in America)?
   a. Roger Williams
   b. Oliver Cromwell
   c. John Winthrop
   d. John Endicott

11. Who founded Connecticut?
   a. John Endicott
   b. Thomas Hooker
   c. William Duxbury
   d. James Danbury

12. What is significant about the constitution written in Connecticut—the Fundamental Orders of Connecticut?
   a. It includes a bill of rights
   b. It's the first complete constitution written in America
   c. It became the model for the U.S. Constitution
   d. It was written under a tree

13. Who is mentioned in the first paragraph of that Connecticut constitution?
   a. John Calvin
   b. King Charles I
   c. Massasoits
   d. our Lord Jesus

14. What event caused that Connecticut constitution to be written?
   a. It was inspired by a cow kick
   b. It was inspired by a Puritan book
   c. It was inspired by a sermon
   d. It was inspired by a lightning storm

15. Which Puritan minister was banished by the Puritan leadership, to be shipped back to England? Instead, he traveled in the wilderness during winter. God preserved him during this terrible trek; therefore, he named the town he founded in honor of God: Providence (Rhode Island).
   a. Roger Williams
   b. John Endicott
   c. Thomas Hooker
   d. Samuel Fuller

16. Name the four founding documents of the United States:

    a. The Declaration of Independence, the Articles of Confederation, the Constitution, the Northwest Ordinance

    b. The Mayflower Compact, the Declaration of Independence, the Constitution, the Bill of Rights

    c. The Declaration of Independence, the Articles of Confederation, the Constitution, the Bill of Rights

    d. The Mayflower Compact, Penn's Frame of Government, the Declaration of Independence, the Constitution, the Northwest Ordinance

17. How many of these four documents positively mention God or religion in one way or another?

    a. 1

    b. 2

    c. 3

    d. 4

18. Which document states, "Religion, morality, and knowledge being necessary for good government and the happiness of mankind, schools and the means of education shall forever be encouraged…"?

    a. The Declaration of Independence

    b. The Articles of Confederation

    c. The Northwest Ordinance

    d. The Constitution

19. Why is this document significant?

    a. It was written by George Washington

    b. It is the template for new states to follow

    c. It was adopted before the Constitution was ratified

    d. It carefully toes the line between church and state

20. Of the 56 signers of the Declaration of Independence, how many had the eighteenth-century equivalent of seminary degrees?

    a. 6

    b. 13

    c. 24

    d. 37

21. The education of virtually every founding father (approximately 250 men, from 1750–1800) was:

    a. Christian

    b. Secular

    c. Focused on Latin

    d. Focused on classical Greek

22. What document closes with these words, "…we solemnly pledge to each other our mutual cooperation and our lives, our fortunes and our most sacred honor"? [trick question]

    a. The Mecklenburg Declaration (1775)

    b. The Declaration of Independence (1776)

    c. The Articles of Confederation (1777)

    d. The Bill of Rights (1789)

23. What was the name of the man who was technically the first president of the United States of America? [Also tricky]

    a. Elias Boudinot

    b. Patrick Henry

    c. George Washington

    d. John Hanson

24. How many state constitutions mention God?
    a. 50
    b. 43
    c. 26
    d. 11

25. One of the men on our paper money said that the Bible is "the rock upon which our republic rests." On which currency can his image be found?
    a. The $1 bill
    b. The $5 bill
    c. The $10 bill
    d. The $20 bill

26. What document begins, "In the Name of the Most Holy and Undivided Trinity"?
    a. The peace treaty ending the French and Indian War
    b. The peace treaty ending the American Revolution
    c. The peace treaty ending the Civil War
    d. The peace treaty between the U.S. and Japan at the end of WW II

27. Who proposed that the delegates at the Constitutional convention pray?
    a. George Washington
    b. James Madison
    c. John Jay
    d. Ben Franklin

28. According to historian M. E. Bradford, how many of the delegates to the Constitutional convention were practicing, Trinitarian Christians?
    a. 25-27 of 55
    b. 33-35 of 55
    c. 42-43 of 55
    d. 50-52 of 55

29. Of the 55 delegates to the Constitutional convention, how many actually signed the document?
    a. 55
    b. 49
    c. 39
    d. 29

30. Who wrote *The Federalist Papers*, mainly geared toward getting New York State to adopt the Constitution?
    a. Alexander Hamilton
    b. James Madison
    c. John Jay
    d. All of the above

31. What is the essence of tyranny according to James Madison, author of *Federalist #47*?
    a. a runaway king
    b. a runaway judiciary
    c. a runaway president
    d. all three branches of government in the hands of one or a few

32. Which founding father said, "...the rights of the colonists as Christians...are to be found clearly written and promulgated in the New Testament"?
    a. Paul Revere
    b. John Hancock
    c. Samuel Adams
    d. Patrick Henry

33. Which president wrote, "Our constitution was made only for a moral and religious people. It is wholly inadequate to the government of any other"?
    a. George Washington
    b. John Adams
    c. Thomas Jefferson
    d. James Madison

34. Which president wrote, "All men having power ought to be distrusted"?
    a. James Madison
    b. James Monroe
    c. John Quincy Adams
    d. Andrew Jackson

35. Which president stated, "…those nations only are blessed whose God is the Lord"?
    a. George Washington
    b. James Buchanan
    c. Abraham Lincoln
    d. Teddy Roosevelt

36. Which president has all the words of John 11:25-26 spelled out on his tomb, "I am the Resurrection and the Life, sayeth the Lord. He that believeth in Me, though he were dead yet shall he live. And whosoever liveth and believeth in Me shall never die"?
    a. George Washington
    b. John Adams
    c. Abraham Lincoln
    d. Ulysses S. Grant

37. Which president said, "True religion affords to government its surest support"?
    a. George Washington
    b. Abraham Lincoln
    c. Teddy Roosevelt
    d. Franklin D. Roosevelt

38. Which president was named after John Calvin?
    a. Lincoln
    b. Tyler
    c. Coolidge
    d. Hoover

39. Which president said this: "If we ever forget that we are One Nation under God, then we will be a Nation gone under"?
    a. Dwight D. Eisenhower
    b. Richard Nixon
    c. Jimmy Carter
    d. Ronald Reagan

40. Which president said this: "Without God, there could be no American form of government, nor an American way of life. Recognition of the Supreme Being is the first—the most basic—expression of Americanism"?
    a. Dwight D. Eisenhower
    b. Richard Nixon
    c. Jimmy Carter
    d. Ronald Reagan

41. Which president said, "No people can be bound to acknowledge and adore the Invisible Hand which conducts the affairs of men more than the people of the United States"?
    a. George Washington
    b. John Adams
    c. Abraham Lincoln
    d. George W. Bush

42. Which president said the following in a private letter (to a friend after learning of his brother's death): "I must soon follow him, and hope to meet him and those friends who have gone before me in the realms of bliss through the mediation of a dear Redeemer, Jesus Christ"?
    a. James Monroe
    b. John Quincy Adams
    c. Andrew Jackson
    d. Woodrow Wilson

43. Which president said, "I have made it a practice every year for several years to read through the Bible"?
    a. John Quincy Adams
    b. William Henry Harrison
    c. William McKinley
    d. William Taft

44. Which president said, "Hold fast to the Bible as the anchor of your liberty…?
    a. James Buchanan
    b. Abraham Lincoln
    c. Andrew Johnson
    d. Ulysses S. Grant

45. Which president said, "If a man is not familiar with the Bible, he has suffered the loss which he had better make all possible haste to correct"?
    a. Teddy Roosevelt
    b. Woodrow Wilson
    c. Herbert Hoover
    d. Ronald Reagan

46. Which president said, "Of all the systems of morality, ancient or modern, which have come under my observation, none appear to me so pure as that of Jesus"?
    a. John Adams
    b. Thomas Jefferson
    c. Chester Arthur
    d. Woodrow Wilson

47. The Bible verse on the Liberty Bell comes from what book?
    a. Genesis
    b. Exodus
    c. Leviticus
    d. Deuteronomy

48. According to a classic article in *Newsweek* magazine, historians are discovering that something is our real founding document. Can you name that something?
    a. The Declaration of Independence
    b. The Bible
    c. *Common Sense*
    d. The Constitution

49. Which president said, "The foundations of our society and our government rest so much on the teachings of the Bible that it would be difficult to support them if faith in these teachings would cease to be practically universal in our country"?
    a. Calvin Coolidge
    b. Herbert Hoover
    c. Franklin D. Roosevelt
    d. Harry Truman

50. Which president said, "…the rights of man come not from the generosity of the state but from the hand of God"?
    a. Jimmy Carter
    b. John F. Kennedy
    c. Lyndon B. Johnson
    d. Herbert Hoover

Detailed Answers

Do not be discouraged if you did not know a lot of these answers. Most Americans do not. Listed below is the question with the correct answer. In the process of reviewing these questions and answers one at a time, we will learn to build up our knowledge of our Christian heritage.

1. **What document says that our rights come from God, and it is the duty of the state not to interfere with that?**

   a. The Declaration of Independence

   The answer should be obvious to all. It is the Declaration of Independence. Our nation's birth certificate, the Declaration of Independence, mentions God four times.

   - "…the Laws of Nature and of Nature's God…."

   - "All men are created equal, they are endowed by their Creator with certain unalienable rights…."

   - "…appealing to the Supreme Judge of the World for the Rectitude of our Intentions…."

   - "…with a firm Reliance on the Protection of Divine Providence…."[61]

This is quite significant because what it means is that our rights come from God. Period. Not the state. If they came from the state, the state could withdraw them.

What happens when a nation is not based on the notion that our rights come from God? One of the books spawned by the Russian experiment into communism (1917-c. 1991) is Arthur Koestler's *Darkness at Noon*. Koestler was a fellow traveler at one time, but like many others, he became disillusioned by the communists because of Stalin's violence. One of the pro-communist characters in the novel makes a little speech extolling the Revolution and denigrating the only real alternative—a form of government (and human rights) based on Christianity:

> "I don't approve of mixing ideologies," Ivanov continued. "There are only two conceptions of human ethics, and they are at opposite

poles. One of them is Christian and humane, declares the individual to be sacrosanct, and asserts that the rules of arithmetic are not to be applied to human units. The other starts from the basic principle that a collective aim justifies all means, and not only allows, but demands, that the individual should in every way be subordinated and sacrificed to the community—which may dispose of it as an experimentation rabbit or a sacrificial lamb. The first conception could be called anti-vivisection morality, the second, vivisection morality. Humbugs and dilettantes have always tried to mix the two conceptions; in practice, it is impossible. Whoever is burdened with power and responsibility finds out on the first occasion that he has to choose; and he is fatally driven to the second alternative. Do you know, since the establishment of Christianity as a state religion, a single example of a state which really followed a Christian policy? You can't point out one. In times of need—and politics are chronically in a time of need—the rulers were always able to evoke 'exceptional circumstances,' which demanded exceptional measures of defence. Since the existence of nations and classes, they live in a permanent state of mutual self-defence, which forces them to defer to another time the putting into practice of humanism...." [62]

In short, there is a world of difference between those governments, like ours, based on the idea that our rights come from God, versus those whose citizens' rights come from the state.

Most other quiz answers will not be so lengthy. However, since this point is at the heart of this entire book, I have tried to develop this one fully.

2. **According to historian David Barton, of the 250 founding fathers, how many were of a skeptical bent (not orthodox, Trinitarian Christians)?**

a. 12

David Barton argues that the answer is at most only twelve. Here is what he says:

> Of the 250 folks that we would call founding fathers, there may be a dozen, which is about 5 percent, that maybe aren't religious. You could put in there: Franklin, Jefferson, Thomas Paine, and you could throw in Henry Dearborn, Charles Lee, Ethan Allen,

and you could throw in a few others, and that's really it. There's not very many prominent founding fathers among it, and even at that, we're talking maybe a dozen out of 250—so maybe 5 percent of the founding fathers that we can point to and question their religious beliefs.[63]

It is truly amazing that the historical revisionists have taken the exception and made it the rule.

3. **When Thomas Jefferson was president, what did he faithfully do every Sunday morning?**

   b. **Attend church (with evangelical preaching)**

On a regular basis, our third president went to church at the largest nineteenth-century church in Washington, D.C.—the one that met in the rotunda of the Capitol building (until about the 1880s). Here are the remarks of James H. Hutson of the Library of Congress:

> Jefferson was a regular attendant at church services in the House of Representatives during two terms. And we have all kinds of evidence about people seeing him there, and riding a horse through a thunderstorm to get there....
>
> [One time] he was met on the way to church and somebody asked him where he was going. He said, "I'm going to church," and his friend said, "Well, c'mon, you don't believe in that stuff." And, he huffed and puffed and said, "Sir, no government can flourish without religion, and I'm going to give religion the sanction of my appearance and supporting attending church services," something to that effect....
>
> As the head of the executive branch, he permitted church services in the government office buildings and the war office, the treasury building. There are accounts of four-hour communion services in the treasury building during Jefferson's administration conducted by Presbyterian minister named James Lowry who belonged to something called the Associated Presbyterian Church. Whether that still exists, I don't know, but, there were services in the Supreme Court chambers during the early years of the republic. We have eyewitness accounts of those from John Quincy Adams and from others.
>
> I once stated in a book that during the Jefferson administration, the church became the state on Sunday, as it did. You had

church services in all three buildings of all three branches of the government. Madison attended church services in Congress...the services in Congress went on, as far as we know, until the 1880s.[64]

4. **In the early nineteenth century, what took place in the rotunda of the U.S. Capitol building?**

   d. **Evangelical-oriented preaching in a Christian worship service**

5. **If you visit the U.S. Capitol today, in the rotunda are eight large paintings. How many of the eight contain direct evidence of our Christian heritage?**

   c. **Four**

The answer here is "four." These are huge paintings that are as comparable in size to the wall of a normal room. One shows Columbus landing and on the side you can see the planting of the cross. A second painting shows the Christian baptism of Pocahontas. The third shows the Pilgrims with a large open Bible (where you can see, upside down because of the Elder Brewster holding the Bible open, the name of Jesus Christ), having a prayer service aboard the *Mayflower*. The fourth large painting has some Spanish pioneers exploring the interior. One of them has a crucifix on a pole.

6. **Where was the first Thanksgiving in America?**

   c. **1619 in Jamestown**

The answer may surprise the average reader: Jamestown had the first official proclamation for a day of thanksgiving a whole year before the Pilgrims even came over.

7. **What document opens with: "In the name of God. Amen. We whose names are underwritten, having undertaken a voyage for the glory of God and the founding of the Christian religion..."?**

   a. **The Mayflower Compact**

The Mayflower Compact of 1620 was among the most important documents in our history. It was a charter for self-government, and it explicitly declared the Christian motivation of the Pilgrims for their voyage.

8. **Roughly how many Puritan constitutions, charters, compacts, etc.,
of which the Mayflower Compact is one, led up to THE constitution?**

d. 100

This is a really critical point of our nation's history. We are governed by
the Constitution. It is the law of the land. The Constitution is an indirect
outgrowth of the Puritan charters, compacts, frames of government. This
is why *Newsweek* declared on the eve of the Year of the Bible a quarter
century ago that the Bible is our founding document.

9. **Virtually all the settlers were familiar with:**

b. **The Bible**

10. **Who was the main leader of the Puritans (in America)?**

c. **John Winthrop**

If you walk down a certain corridor of the U.S. Capitol (at one of the
entrances), you will pass all sorts of statues. One of the first ones is John
Winthrop, the Puritan leader who was an extraordinary man. He was the
one Ronald Reagan was always quoting in the famous "City on a Hill"
speech. British historian Paul Johnson notes that Rev. Winthrop was "the
first great American."[65]

11. **Who founded Connecticut?**

b. **Thomas Hooker**

The answer is Rev. Thomas Hooker. Also a Puritan, he had a disagreement with fellow Puritans in Massachusetts, so he led a delegation into
the wilderness of what is now Connecticut. He preached a sermon in
1638 on Christian principles of government. Within a year, his followers
put into words the points he made in the sermon and created the nation's
first complete constitution—the Fundamental Orders of Connecticut.
This document mentions how they desired "to maintain and preserve the
liberty and purity of the Gospel of our Lord Jesus which we now profess,
as also the discipline of the churches, which according to the truth of the
said Gospel is now practiced among us."[66]

12. **What is significant about the Connecticut constitution — the Fundamental Orders of Connecticut?**

    b. It's the first complete constitution written in America

    Rev. Hooker's sermon that inspired that constitution was written under a tree — a historic tree commemorated on a special edition twenty-five-cent coin. I once inquired as to the possibility of videotaping that tree, only to discover that it had been destroyed by lightening in the nineteenth century. Another point about the Fundamental Orders of Connecticut is, as Peter Marshall notes, that George Washington had copies of that constitution available to all those who attended the Constitutional Convention in 1787.

13. **Who is mentioned in the first paragraph of that Connecticut constitution?**

    d. Our Lord Jesus

14. **What event caused that Connecticut constitution to be written?**

    c. It was inspired by a sermon

15. **Which Puritan minister was banished by the Puritan leadership, to be shipped back to England? Instead, he traveled in the wilderness during winter. God preserved him during this terrible trek; therefore, he named the town he founded in honor of God: Providence (Rhode Island).**

    a. Roger Williams

    Rev. Roger Williams was an independent-thinking Puritan, who out-Puritaned the Puritans. He was a stickler for details and tried to live out his conscience fully, even if that made him difficult to live with. He angered his fellow Puritans by not going along with certain points, but when he declined to swear an oath of allegiance to the colony, that was the last straw, and they wanted to deport him. Because he was warned in advance, he fled in the wilderness, befriending Indians along the way. Eventually, he founded Rhode Island and made that colony a haven of refuge for theological dissidents.

16. Name the four founding documents of the United States:

 a. The Declaration of Independence, the Articles of
  Confederation, the Constitution, the Northwest Ordinance

According to Dr. Kennedy, these are our nation's founding documents. The first proclaimed why we were independent. The second was the first working constitution of the government. However, this document, the Articles of Confederation, worked so poorly that when the founders held a convention to revise the document, they decided to start all over. They created from scratch a totally new document, the Constitution. Finally, the Northwest Ordinance provided guidelines for any territory in the Northwest (in the Ohio region and beyond) that desired to become a state to join the United States. Thus, the Northwest Ordinance provided the template for new states so that there would be a standardization, a hegemony for each additional state.

17. How many of these four documents positively mention God or religion in some positive way?

 d. 4

We have already covered the Declaration and its fourfold mention of our Creator. The Articles of Confederation was our nation's first working national constitution. It was written in 1777 and ratified in 1781. This constitution mentions God: "And whereas it has pleased the Great Governor of the World to incline the hearts of the Legislatures we respectively represent in Congress, to approve of, and to authorize us to ratify the said Articles of Confederation and perpetual union."[67] But, as mentioned above, the Articles did not work well, and when the founders met together to revise the Articles, they decided to scrap them and start over again.

They created the Constitution, which they signed "in the Year of our Lord."[68] You could argue that this not only mentions God, but recognizes that Jesus is God. One could counter-argue that that reference was a mere formality. However, just two years later, in 1789, the bloody French Revolution began. The French based their revolution on an anti-God, anti-Christian, and anti-Church campaign. They even changed the week from seven days (with its built-in Sabbath rest) to ten-day weeks, and a couple years later, they dropped the Christian calendar, so that "the year of our Lord" would be eliminated. (Jumping ahead about a decade later,

Napoleon changed these things back.) America's revolution recognized God as the source of our liberties. France's revolution erroneously saw God and the Church as antithetical to freedom.

The final key American document to mention is that of the Northwest Ordinance, which provided for the standardization for each new territory that would become a state. This ordinance was written and adopted in 1787 and later re-adopted in 1789. This ordinance stressed the importance of "extending the fundamental principles of civil and religious liberty." It also mentions (Article I): "No person, demeaning himself in a peaceable and orderly manner, shall ever be molested on account of his mode of worship or religious sentiments in the said territory...." Furthermore, this ordinance shows what the founders thought of education and what they thought of the place of religion and morality in education. They thought it was as important (if not more important) than other types of knowledge: "ARTICLE III. Religion, morality, and knowledge being necessary to good government and the happiness of mankind, schools and the means of education shall forever be encouraged."[69] How absurd that modern secularists try to prevent the teaching of any religion or even morality to our children today.

So we see that God and religion (Christianity, by implication) were important to the founding fathers, which they enshrined in our nation's key founding documents.

18. **Which document states, "Religion, morality, and knowledge being necessary for good government and the happiness of mankind, schools and the means of education shall forever be encouraged..."?**

   c. The Northwest Ordinance

We now know that it is the Northwest Ordinance because it has been revealed in the previous answer. However, when you ask these two questions back to back, most people do not know.

19. **Why is this document significant?**

   b. This is the template for new states to follow

The Northwest Ordinance gave the template for new states. In other words, for the whole country, for all time as new states are added, imparting religion and morality and knowledge were the main reasons for education, according to our nation's founders. These were the very same men who gave us the First Amendment, which is today interpreted so as to exclude Christian expression in the schools.

20. **Of the 56 signers of the Declaration of Independence, how many had the eighteenth-century equivalence of "seminary" degrees?**

c. 24

Virtually every founding father received a Christian education based on the Bible. In fact, from the very beginning of Christian settlements in this land, a Christian education was a very important part of colonial life for the average child, both in his formative years and later in college if he attended. Our founding fathers were educated from a Christian worldview. David Barton, author and speaker on America's Christian heritage, points out that more than 40 percent (24 of 56) of the signers of the Declaration of Independence had the eighteenth-century equivalence of seminary degrees.[70] (Technically, seminaries were not founded until 1808.)

21. **The education of virtually every founding father (approximately 250 men, from 1750-1800) was:**

a. **Christian**

The great scholar, Donald S. Lutz, the author of *The Roots of American Constitutionalism*, said:

> Now, many of the founders knew Greek, because that was part of the education they learned at the colleges they attended [which] were usually seminaries. King's College, later to become Columbia, trained ministers. Yale trained ministers, Harvard trained ministers, and so, they spent their time, effectively, in a kind of a pre-minister curriculum. And certainly, they learned the Bible; they learned it down to their fingertips.[71]

22. **What document closes with these words: "…we solemnly pledge to each other our mutual cooperation and our lives, our fortunes and our most sacred honor"? [trick question]**

a. **The Mecklenburg Declaration (1775)**

The Declaration of Independence ends with similar words, but so also does a document reportedly written a year before by a group of Presbyterian elders living in North Carolina.

In 1775, a group of Scotch-Irish Presbyterian elders in Mecklenburg County in Charlotte, North Carolina, indirectly contributed to the Declaration of Independence. They wrote a series of resolves that were later echoed in our nation's birth certificate. Historian George Bancroft writes, "That town had been chosen for the seat of the Presbyterian college, which the legislature of North Carolina had chartered, but which the king had disallowed; and it was the centre [sic] of the culture of that part of the province."[72] The Presbyterians of Mecklenburg declared: "As all former laws are now suspended in this province, and the congress has not yet provided others, we judge it necessary, for the better preservation of good order, to form certain rules and regulations for the internal government of this country, until laws shall be provided for us by the congress." Bancroft adds, "The resolves were transmitted with all speed to be printed in Charleston; they startled the governors of Georgia and North Carolina, who forwarded them to the British government."[73]

Elder Ephraim Brevard, in conjunction with twenty-seven Reformed Christians, one-third of whom were ruling elders in the Presbyterian Church, wrote up these county resolutions. Brevard was a graduate of the College at Princeton, New Jersey (Princeton). Author Lorraine Boettner says of this Presbyterian declaration: "It was the fresh, hearty greeting of the Scotch-Irish to their struggling brethren in the North, and their bold challenge to the power of England."[74] Then they sent them by courier to the Continental Congress. Here's what they resolved:

> We do hereby dissolve the political bands which have connected us with the mother-country, and hereby absolve ourselves from all allegiance to the British crown.... Resolved, That we do hereby declare ourselves a free and independent people; are, and of a right ought to be, a sovereign and self-governing Association, under control of no power other than that of our God and the general government of Congress; to the maintenance of which we solemnly pledge to each other our mutual cooperation and our lives, our fortunes and our most sacred honor.[75]

The Declaration of Independence certainly borrows from some of these phrases. Clearly, these Presbyterian parsons made a contribution to our charter of liberty. Jefferson borrows so freely from the work of these

Presbyterian elders that perhaps he could be accused of plagiarism. Of course, they did not have copyright law back then, and to quote liberally from another source was a genuine compliment to the source. In any event, this is yet another example of Christianity contributing to American liberty.

Consider just how influential the Mecklenburg Declaration was to Thomas Jefferson. Author N. S. McFetridge points out:

> In correcting his first draft of the Declaration it can be seen, in at least a few places, that Jefferson has erased the original words and inserted those which are first found in the Mecklenburg Declaration. No one can doubt that Jefferson had Brevard's resolutions before him when he was writing his immortal Declaration.[76]

23. What was the name of the man who was technically the first president of the United States of America? [Also tricky]

d. John Hanson

The first official government of the United States was under the jurisdiction of the Articles of Confederation, written in 1777 and going into effect in 1781. It stipulated that the president of Congress (a position elected annually) was the president of the whole country. When it went into effect, John Hanson of Pennsylvania was the President of Congress, thus making him the first official president of the country. I have seen his grave in a church in the Philadelphia area. He is listed there as the first president of the United States. The Articles proved unworkable and when a special convention was called in 1787 to revise them, the delegates decided to start all over again, and they created the Constitution. George Washington was our first president under that instrument's rule.

24. How many state constitutions mention God?

a. 50

Every single state constitution mentions God, usually in the preamble. Here are just four examples:

    * "We, the people of the State of Alabama…invoking the favor and guidance of Almighty God…."[77]

* "Preamble. We, the people of Hawaii, Grateful for Divine Guidance...."[78]

* "Preamble. We, the people of Montana, grateful to Almighty God for the blessings of liberty...."[79]

* Vermont's Constitution refers to the "blessings which the Author of existence has bestowed on man."[80] And it declares, "That all men have a natural and Unalienable right to worship Almighty God according to the dictates of their own consciences...."[81]

25. One of the men on our paper money said that the Bible is "the rock upon which our republic rests." On which currency can he be found?

d. The $20 bill

The seventh president, Andrew Jackson, whose portrait is on the $20 bill, made that remark.[82]

26. What document begins "In the Name of the Most Holy and Undivided Trinity"?

b. The peace treaty ending the American Revolution

The agreement for peace ending the American War for Independence was the Treaty of Paris. On the American side, it was negotiated by "D. Hartley, John Adams, B. Franklin, and John Jay." It begins with a recognition of the Christian God in three persons, Father, Son, and Holy Spirit.[83]

27. Who proposed that the delegates at the Constitutional convention pray?

d. Ben Franklin

Ben Franklin was the oldest and among the wisest of the delegates, and yet, he was apparently not an orthodox Christian. Nonetheless, after a couple of frustrating months of endless conflicts among the delegates of the Constitutional convention, Franklin arose to his feet and made an impassioned plea for prayer. A variation of his request was adopted. His whole speech was recorded in the notes by James Madison and is reproduced in the final chapter of this book. (The title of that chapter is a quote from his speech.)

28. **According to historian M. E. Bradford, how many of the delegates to the Constitutional convention were practicing, Trinitarian Christians?**

    d. 50-52 **of** 55

The late Dr. Bradford was a history professor at the University of Dallas. He carefully researched the religion of the delegates to the Constitution and concluded that at least 50, perhaps 52 of the 55 professed to be orthodox believers in Jesus and were members in good standing at Trinitarian churches.

Dr. M. E. Bradford found that there were 28 Episcopalians, eight Presbyterians, 7 Congregationalists, 2 Lutherans, 2 Dutch Reformed, two Methodists, 2 Roman Catholics, and 3 Deists.[84] John Eidsmoe, author of *Christianity and the Constitution*, concludes that at most 5.5 percent of the Constitutional Convention were Deists.[85]

I stress that these were *Trinitarian* men because Unitarianism was beginning to gain a foothold in formerly, staunchly Calvinist New England. At the beginning of the War, New England was strongly Calvinist. Within a generation, Unitarianism had gained a major foothold. A generation or two later, Calvinism virtually collapsed in New England.

29. **Of the 55 delegates to the Constitutional convention, how many actually signed the document?**

    c. 39

There was a great deal of acrimony, especially in conflicts between big states versus little states in how they should be represented. Later there would be conflicts over slavery. By the end, not all who attended the convention signed the document. There was a significant number who refused to sign (or in some cases, who were unable to sign because they had already left Philadelphia). George Mason had problems with the compromise with slavery, which is ironic because he owned two hundred slaves. John Lansing and Robert Yates of New York left with such great disgust early on, that Hamilton became the only New York delegate in favor of the Constitution.

In the end, thirty-nine of fifty-five delegates signed the Constitution, roughly 70 percent of them.

30. Who wrote *The Federalist Papers,* mainly geared toward getting New York state to adopt the Constitution?

    a. Alexander Hamilton

    b. James Madison

    c. John Jay

    d. All of the above

The correct answer is all of the above.

Because New York was such a pivotal swing state in the acceptance of the U.S. Constitution, a series of anonymous letters began to appear in the newspapers there, under a pseudonym. These came to be known as the *Federalist* (sometimes called *The Federalist Papers*). These essays clearly help shed light on what the founders intended by the Constitution. *The Federalist Papers* should be required reading in our law schools, as should be the Constitution.

The Federalist is a collection of eighty-five letters written by someone who called himself "Publius." The real identities of Publius were not known until many years later. The authors were, of course, Alexander Hamilton, James Madison, and John Jay. It is believed that Hamilton wrote fifty-one of the *Federalist* treatises, Madison wrote twenty-six, and Jay wrote five. Author Clinton Rossiter, who wrote the Introduction for the 1961 collection of these classic letters to the editors, observes: "The *Federalist* is the most important work in political science that has ever been written, or is likely ever to be written, in the United States." [86]

All three writers of the *Federalist* were professing Christians. Hamilton may have gone astray for a while, but before he died, he made peace with Jesus Christ.

31. What is the essence of tyranny according to James Madison, author of *Federalist* #47?

    d. All three branches of government in the hands of one or a few

Here is how Madison worded it: "The accumulation of all powers, legislative, executive, and judiciary, in the same hands, whether of one, a few, or many, and whether hereditary, self-appointed, or elective, may justly be pronounced the very definition of tyranny." [87] The founders were in total agreement with the Biblical doctrine of the sinfulness of man.

Thus, they sought for government to protect us from each other—and to protect us from the government.

32. **Which founding father said, "...the rights of the colonists as Christians...are to be found clearly written and promulgated in the New Testament"?**

c. Samuel Adams

Above all, history remembers Sam Adams for his successful role in pushing for our Independence. No one did more than this Christian patriot to secure our liberty under law. His own words reflect his Christian views.

George Bancroft points out that Sam Adams was a very godly man, who valued the heritage of his Puritan forefathers. He not only paid them homage in terms of respect. But he believed their doctrines as well. Bancroft writes, "[H]e may be called the last of the Puritans."[88] He was very devout.

"The Rights of the Colonists" was a historic statement by Sam Adams written in 1772. It is viewed as one of the key forerunners articulating why America should sever its ties to Great Britain. This document included a section entitled, "The Rights of the Colonists as Christians," in which Samuel Adams declared:

> The right to freedom being the gift of God Almighty...the [rights of the Colonists as Christians] may best be understood by reading and carefully studying the institutions of The Great Law Giver and the Head of the Christian Church, which are to be found clearly written and promulgated in the New Testament.[89]

33. **Which president wrote: "Our constitution was made only for a moral and religious people. It is wholly inadequate to the government of any other"?**

b. John Adams

This quote is typical of the fact that the founders intended Americans to be moral and that that morality was rooted in religion. Since the majority religion of Americans at the time was Christian by-and-large, the founders saw an important role for Christianity in society, but always in an unofficial way—not in any way like a state-church.

34. **Which president wrote: "All men having power ought to be distrusted"?**

a. James Madison

The founding fathers believed in the sinfulness of man. I believe that a lot of our freedoms flow from that true understanding of human nature. Because they believed what the Bible and all of history says about man's nature, they built in many safeguards so that power could not be abused.

The answer is James Madison, which is significant. Here one of the chief architects of the Constitution believed in the depravity of man. Madison wrote in *Federalist* #10: "It is in vain to say that enlightened statesmen will be able to adjust these clashing interests and render them all subservient to the public good. Enlightened statesmen will not always be at the helm." Then in *Federalist* #47, Madison spelled out how governmental power had to be divided up between competing forces, lest one group lord it over another.[90]

James Madison, who played a pivotal role at the Constitutional Convention, attended the Presbyterian College of Princeton, New Jersey (Princeton) rather than the Anglican College of William and Mary, where sons of Virginia were expected to attend. He learned directly under Rev. John Witherspoon, who also later turned out to be an important founding father. Perhaps, the most important lesson that James Madison took home from his Princeton education was the firm belief in the Biblical doctrine of man's sinfulness. John Eidsmoe points out: "One thing is certain, the Christian religion, particularly Rev. Witherspoon's Calvinism, influenced Madison's view of law and government."[91]

James Madison was not alone in believing in the Christian doctrine of original sin and spelling out its implications in the new government through an elaborate system of checks and balances. The founding fathers in general knew man was sinful and they could not put power into the hands of any one man or even a group of men. Echoing Scripture, Ben Franklin had written, "There is scarce a king in a hundred who would not, if he could, follow the example of Pharaoh, get first all the peoples' money, then all their lands, and then make them and their children servants forever."[92]

Alexander Hamilton wrote in *Federalist* #6: "Is it not time to awake from the deceitful dream of a golden age and to adopt as a practical maxim for the direction of our political conduct that we, as well as the other inhabitants of the globe, are yet remote from the happy empire of perfect wisdom and perfect virtue?"[93] Hamilton added in *Federalist* #15, "Why has government been instituted at all? Because the passions of men will not conform to the dictates of reason and justice without constraint."[94]

One of *The Federalist Papers* that is attributed to either Hamilton or Madison is #55. Since these were all anonymous initially, it is hard for historians to definitively determine who wrote this particular one—Hamilton or Madison. In any event, *Federalist* #55 shows that the men who gave us the Constitution believed in original sin: "As there is a degree of depravity in mankind which requires a certain degree of circumspection and distrust, so there are other qualities in human nature which justify a certain portion of esteem and confidence. Republican government presupposes the existence of these qualities in a higher degree than any other form. Were the pictures which have been drawn by the political jealousy of some among us faithful likenesses of the human character, the inference would be, that there is not sufficient virtue among men for self-government; and that nothing less than the chains of despotism can restrain them from destroying and devouring one another."[95]

35. **Which president stated, "...those nations only are blessed whose God is the Lord"?**

   c. Abraham Lincoln

Abraham Lincoln said this in one of the most profound speeches of American history. He issued this proclamation for prayer and fasting during the dark days of the Civil War, in the Spring of 1863, when the final outcome was not known (by humans).

Proclamation for a National Day of Fasting

by Abraham Lincoln

March 30, 1863

[I]t is the duty of nations as well as of men to own their dependence upon the overruling power of God; to confess their sins and transgressions in humble sorrow, yet with assured hope that genuine repentance will lead to mercy and pardon; and to recognize the sublime truth, announced in the Holy Scriptures and proven by all history, that those nations only are blessed whose God is the Lord....[96]

36. **Which president has all the words of John 11:25-26 spelled out on his tomb, "I am the Resurrection and the Life, sayeth the Lord. He that believeth in Me, though he were dead yet shall he live. And whosoever liveth and believeth in Me shall never die"?**

   a. George Washington

   This is at Mount Vernon, right behind the stone coffins of George and Martha Washington. I have seen it myself and had the cameraman from Coral Ridge Ministries-TV shoot this plaque.

37. **Which president said, "True religion affords to government its surest support"?**

   a. George Washington

   Again, it was George Washington. He said this in a letter to the Synod of the Dutch Reformed Church in North America, dated October 9, 1789.[97]

38. **Which president was named after John Calvin?**

   c. Coolidge

   It was John Calvin Coolidge. Just knowing we had a president named after such a great Reformer is a fascinating piece of Americana to me. We also had a founding father whose name was an inverse of the other great leader of the Reformation: Luther Martin of Maryland.

39. **Which president said this: "If we ever forget that we are One Nation Under God, then we will be a Nation gone under"?**

   d. Ronald Reagan

   You can hear the wit of Ronald Reagan in the remark.[98]

40. **Which president said this, "Without God, there could be no American form of government, nor an American way of life. Recognition of the Supreme Being is the first—the most basic—expression of Americanism"?**

a. Dwight D. Eisenhower

President Eisenhower noted in 1954 when he signed into law the addition of the phrase "under God" in our Pledge of Allegiance, that this would provide a daily reminder to our nation's children that America was founded under God. A year later, he observed that "Without God, there could be no American form of Government, nor an American way of life."[99]

This is the essence of Americanism. Here again we see the echo of a key point of the Declaration of Independence—our rights come from God, not from the magnanimous hand of the state.

41. **Which president said: "No people can be bound to acknowledge and adore the Invisible Hand which conducts the affairs of men more than the people of the United States"?**

    ### a. George Washington

    Our first president (under the Constitution) said this during his First Inaugural Address.[100]

42. **Which president said the following in a private letter (to a friend after learning of his brother's death): "I must soon follow him, and hope to meet him and those friends who have gone before me in the realms of bliss through the mediation of a dear Redeemer, Jesus Christ"?**

    ### c. Andrew Jackson

    This remarks comes from our seventh president.[101]

43. **Which president said: "I have made it a practice every year for several years to read through the Bible"?**

    ### a. John Quincy Adams

    Like many of our presidents, the Bible was the most important book in the life of John Quincy Adams.[102]

44. **Which president said: "Hold fast to the Bible as the anchor of your liberty...."?**

    ### d. Ulysses S. Grant

Ulysses S. Grant wrote to the Editor of the *Sunday School Times* in Philadelphia:

> My advice to Sunday schools, no matter what their denomination, is: Hold fast to the Bible as the sheet anchor of your liberties; write its precepts in your hearts, and practice them in your lives.
>
> To the influence of this Book are we indebted for all the progress made in true civilization, and to this must we look as our guide in the future. "Righteousness exalteth a nation; but sin is a reproach to any people." [103]

45. **Which president said: "If a man is not familiar with the Bible, he has suffered the loss which he had better make all possible haste to correct"?**

a. **Teddy Roosevelt**

Teddy Roosevelt penned these words.[104] He also noted: "A thorough knowledge of the Bible is worth more than a college education." [105]

46. **Which president said: "Of all the systems of morality, ancient or modern, which have come under my observation, none appear to me so pure as that of Jesus"?**

b. **Thomas Jefferson**

Sometimes it seems as if the ACLU erroneously think they can claim Thomas Jefferson as their patron saint. But, unlike them, he had a very high regard for Jesus Christ—at least for His character and His teaching. (It would be fair to say that he may not have believed the miracles in the Gospels or miracles in general as possible.) Modern ACLU-types see even the most benign public references to God as some sort of assault on the First Amendment. So how shocking, then, to read Jefferson's view that Jesus' morality is without parallel, as reflected in the above quote.[106]

47. **The Bible verse on the Liberty Bell comes from what book?**

c. **Leviticus**

The answer is Leviticus 25:10. On the bell, it says: Leviticus XXV v. X (as in Leviticus 25, v. or verse, 10). "Proclaim liberty throughout the land and to all the inhabitants thereof." I think it is very appropriate that one of the great symbols of America has a Bible verse on it. It is just another reminder of our true heritage.

48. **According to a classic article in Newsweek magazine, what is it that historians are discovering is our real founding document?**

    b. The Bible

Given the nature of this quiz, the answer should be obvious. In December 1982, on the verge of the International Year of the Bible (1983), *Newsweek* magazine did a cover story on the Bible's impact on America, wherein it was stated:

> [F]or centuries [the Bible] has exerted an unrivaled influence on American culture, politics and social life. Now historians are discovering that the Bible, perhaps even more than the Constitution, is our founding document: the source of the powerful myth of the United States as a special, sacred nation, a people called by God to establish a model society, a beacon to the world.[107]

Newsweek may call it a myth. However, given the extraordinary ways that God seemed to have led the way in the creation of the United States, who is to say it is a myth? (Again, we are not saying America is the new Israel or a theocracy, but God does seem to have used this country for the gospel's sake.)

49. **Which president said: "The foundations of our society and our government rest so much on the teachings of the Bible that it would be difficult to support them if faith in these teachings would cease to be practically universal in our country"?**

    a. Calvin Coolidge

Coolidge made this remark in 1923.[108]

50. **Which president said: "The rights of man come not from the generosity of the state but from the hand of God"?**

    b. John F. Kennedy

Probably one of the most secular-minded of our presidents was John F. Kennedy. Although he was our first Catholic president, he ran with the explicit remark that his faith and his politics were completely divorced. Nonetheless, in his Inaugural Address, he reminded us of the fact that God is the source of our rights.[109] Thus, we see again an echo of the Declaration's core principle: our rights come from God; it is the duty of government to recognize that fact.

CONCLUSION

I created this quiz to give people an idea of what we are missing, what we have not been taught about our true heritage. I consider myself a learner in this process. Despite a history degree from a major secular school (Tulane) and an M.A. in communications from a major Christian school (Wheaton), I feel that I had a re-education by joining Dr. Kennedy's church and learning from him. It was not secularism that made the West or America great; it was the gospel of Jesus Christ.

[Sculptor, Richard S. Greenough, 1873. Stands
at Marlborough & Berkeley Streets, in Boston.]

Rev. John Winthrop was the leader of the Massachusetts Bay Colony,
the founder of Boston, and the man who gave the famous "city on a hill"
speech. The actual title of that speech is "A Model of Christian Charity."
Historian Paul Johnson calls Winthrop "the first great American."

PART TWO

The Bible and the Settling of America

*T*HE Bible played a unique role in the settling of America (1607–1774). As one writer put it, many who came and founded colonies came for God, not for gold. Many of them made the Bible the focal point of their colonies, including the chief textbook for education—a practice that lasted through the founding era as well. Many of the settlers used the Biblical principle of covenant to create written documents for self-government that culminated in the writing of the Constitution. Even in this brief description of Part II, we see overlap between what I call the settling era and the founding era.

PHOTO: J. NEWCOMBE

Mayflower II in Plymouth, Massachusetts, an authentic replica of the ship that carried over the Pilgrims in 1620. This group of committed believers helped set a Christian tone to America's foundation.

CHAPTER 4

The Seeds of a Great Nation: The Bible and America's Settlers

*Leave your country, your people and your father's household
and go to the land I will show you.
I will make you into a great nation and I will bless you.*
(Genesis 12:1-2, NIV)

*I*N the Providence of God, many of the original settlers of North America were motivated by the desire to worship Jesus Christ in the purity of the gospel. This was particularly true of the Pilgrims and the Puritans. But it was also true of Huguenots (French Calvinists) and Quakers, and others who came to these shores. It was also partially true of the first permanent North American settlement—Jamestown.

JAMESTOWN

Recently, America celebrated the 400th anniversary of the Jamestown settlement. It was the first permanent British colony in North America. While this was a significant milestone in American history—and surely a cause to celebrate—there are some today who chafe at the idea of rejoicing over this. In 2007, the actual anniversary, we saw political correctness gone amuck. Indeed, much of the official marking of the event was quite negative toward the settlers. One Virginia official said we should not even use the word "celebrate" because "you can't celebrate an invasion." One commentary in the *Virginia Gazette* lamented that Jamestown was not worth a yearlong celebration: "For a whole year or more we shall celebrate the fact that a bunch of British buffoons who knew nothing of what they were doing colonized a swamp for the sake of Christianizing Indians." [110]

Meanwhile, Vision Forum, a Christian group based in Texas, led by Doug Phillips, organized a Christ-centered counter celebration for the 400th anniversary in June 2007. The local paper blasted that group, calling it a cult. I interviewed Doug Phillips for Coral Ridge Ministries. He said: "Well, 2007 marks the quadricentennial of America's founding of Jamestown. But for the first time in the history of America, our officials are not happy about our birthday. In fact, they're ashamed of it. In fact, the official celebration was inaugurated with Governor Tim Kaine introducing Jesse Jackson and Al Sharpton. And on their panel they declared the Jamestown settlers to be guilty of holocaust and lynchings. Now, when I think about that, I'm thinking of Nazis, Klansmen. This is simply a devastation of our history. It's a complete revision and a fabrication of our history. It's grievous." [111]

One of the speakers at Vision Forum's celebration of Jamestown's 400th was John Eidsmoe, retired law professor and author of *Christianity and the Constitution*. He told CRM-TV: "Jamestown hasn't changed; we've changed. And there's been quite a paradigm shift in this nation since the 1907 celebration. Since that time, we've come to view truth as relative, and if that's the case, then leading people to Jesus Christ is no longer important. In fact, it might even be a hate crime. And so, I think for this reason, people have come to regard Jamestown as a source of evil, rather than a positive good in the world. But I think they're neglecting the facts. The plain fact of the matter is: King James, when he gave the charter for the Virginia Company, said it was for the purpose of spreading the gospel to the heathen. And when the Virginia Company gave its report, *A True Report of Virginia*, they said that this is our purpose: to spread the gospel to the heathen and to provide a place where the godly elect from around the world could gather in the New World." [112]

In the late 1500s, Great Britain attempted to settle in Virginia—again, a land named after the Virgin Queen, Elizabeth the First, who reigned at that time. But these attempts failed. Not until Jamestown in 1607 was England able to create a permanent colony. They named it after King James the First, the monarch at that time. King James is best known for the Bible that bears his name. But he was no friend of dissenting Christian groups (the Puritans, Pilgrims, Presbyterians, etc.) He only got involved in the Bible project (King James Bible) in order to provide an alternative to the Geneva Bible—the Pilgrims' and Puritans' Bible of choice. It was the marginal notes (e.g., on Acts 4:19, which says we must obey God rather than men) that really bothered him.

PROPAGATING THE CHRISTIAN RELIGION

As I said earlier, the first charter of Virginia, written in 1606, before they set sail, listed one of the colony's goals as being the "propagating of Christian religion to such people as yet live in darkness and miserable ignorance of the true knowledge and worship of God" [113] Thus, evangelism to the Indians was part of the goal for the Jamestown settlement.

The Jamestown settlers were instructed by a letter they had received back in England, which they were to open upon their arrival in the New World. One of the statements in that letter reminded them that unless they did things God's way and unless He helped them, the colony would be in vain. "...When it shall please God to send you on the coast of Virginia, you shall do your best endeavour to find out a safe port in the entrance of some navigable river.... In all your passages you must have great care not to offend the naturals [natives], if you can eschew it; and imploy some few of your company to trade with them for corn and all other...victuals if you have any; and this you must do before they perceive you mean to plant among them; for not being sure how your own seed corn will prosper the first year, to avoid the danger of famine, use and endeavour to store yourselves of the country corn.... Lastly and chiefly the way to prosper and achieve good success is to make yourselves all of one mind for the good of your country and your own, and to serve and fear God the Giver of all Goodness, for every plantation which our Heavenly Father hath not planted shall be rooted out." [114]

If you visit Jamestown today, you can see that critical last sentence emblazoned on an obelisk that was erected in 1907, on the 300th anniversary of the settlement. Whatever shortcomings of the Jamestown colony, this principle was foundational: "every plantation which our Heavenly Father hath not planted shall be rooted out." [115]

A CONTRAST WITH THE SPANISH MODEL

Dan Ford, author of *In the Name of God, Amen*, also spoke at the Christian celebration of Jamestown: "Our obligation in America is to return to the principles that founded the colony, to know what they believed. We are to hold to that because they were there. They knew what they did, and we see the fruit of what they produced.... Well, the idea of bringing Christianity to America, which already existed in the Spanish model was self-consciously different with the English. To bring Christianity to them meant evangelizing, but it meant much more than evangelizing.... The English model was to bring the families, as well as the gospel. You evangelize, but you plant plantations, and those plantations have to be built on family and family life. You'll find a marked difference between the Spanish style and motive of evangelizing, and the English style and motive. The Spanish had a concept called 'The Crusade,' which goes back to the Middle Ages. And a lot of the reformers cursed them for that approach. You don't bring Christ's dominion with a sword. You bring your sword for defense, but you don't propagate with a sword. The English model was to plant plantations, that is to develop a dominion through economic investment and home building that would bless their new neighbors. So when they said, 'For the sake of the Indians…' they were quite literally competing with Spain, the Spanish model. And men such as Sir Edwin Sandys, who was the treasurer of the London Company of Virginia, who had been educated in Geneva, wrote a book on the relations of the religions of the Western part of Europe. And in that book, he specifically criticized the Spanish model. He said Spain was weakening itself. It's interesting that Spain would be weakening itself at the expense of the king's riches gained by the plunder of America. Spain was sending its best and brightest young men to America, taking them away from their families, taking them away from potential brides, and weakening Spain…the English anticipated that the Spanish model would be short-lived because it was based on an unbiblical model." [116]

The First Act: Planting a Cross

The first thing the Jamestown colonists did when they landed in the New World was to plant a cross (at Cape Henry) and claim the new land for Jesus Christ. Dr. Peter Lillback is the president of The Providence Forum, with whom I had the privilege to co-write a massive book on the Christian faith of George Washington. Dr. Lillback was another speaker at the recent event. He says, "It is most remarkable that when these British settlers came to this new place, it was going to be called Jamestown—

a place where England was advanced. However, they didn't put up a picture of the king. They put up an emblem of the King of Kings, the cross of Jesus Christ. That cross is a symbol of the Christian faith, and they were recognizing they were advancing the cause of the gospel when they arrived in the New World."[117]

One of the most colorful and resourceful and able of the colonists was the fearless Captain John Smith, whom God used to save the colony from perishing. John Smith was very courageous and decisive. Dr. Paul Jehle, author and pastor, notes that Smith helped save the colony by applying a Biblical principle: "The year that he was president, he gave his famous speech that if you do not work you're not going to eat, from the Biblical injunction [2 Thessalonians 3:10]. And individuals who were going to be lazy and let other people work for them were not going to get any food. This helped bring order into Jamestown very quickly."[118]

At one point, John Smith was captured by the Indians and almost clubbed to death, but Pocahontas, the teenage daughter of the Indian chief, intervened and spared his life. Later Pocahontas came to faith in Jesus Christ, was baptized—as represented in a huge painting in the rotunda of the U.S. Capitol building—and adopted Rebekkah as her Christian name. Pocahontas later married colonist John Rolfe.

THE STARVING TIME

The Jamestown Colony encountered incredible difficulties, premature deaths, and conflicts with the Indians. This was especially true after John Smith was forced to leave the colony permanently and seek treatment in England in 1609 after a gunpowder accident. This initiated the "starving time" of 1609 and 1610. Jehle notes that the settlement shrank from 500 colonists in 1609 when Smith left the colony down to sixty. In less than ten months, more than 400 had died. Jehle says: "Now, that's burying more than one a day."[119] Eidsmoe notes: "By this time, 500 men had come to Jamestown. By the end of that winter, only sixty were left. That's a death rate of nearly 90 percent."[120]

They decided to abandon the whole colony in 1610 at the height of the starving time. They buried their cannons, buried their armor, burned the fort down, and embarked on a ship to leave. But then something miraculous took place—another ship came. Dr. Lillback states: "They had given up. And just as they were getting ready to sail—at that very moment in time—in the starving times, a ship from England [led by Lord de la Warr, later spelled Delaware] arrived. It supplied all of their needs. And that's how close Jamestown came to closing their doors and just disappearing. They looked back at that, the settlers themselves, and said, 'God's providential intervention kept us as a colony.'"[121]

THE CHURCH: HOME OF THE FIRST LEGISLATURE

In Jamestown, they practiced the first representative government—the first colonial legislature. This took place in the church. Writing in 1619, colonist John Pory wrote: "The most convenient place we could find to sit in was the choir of the church...forasmuch as men's affairs do little prosper where God's service is neglected, all the burgesses took their places in the choir, till a prayer was said by Mr. Bucke, the minister, that it would please God to guide and sanctify all our proceedings to His own glory, and the good of this plantation."[122] They began their meetings with prayer and thanksgiving. John Eidsmoe points out that this was the first English Legislature in the Western hemisphere.

As historian Paul Johnson notes: "Thus, within a decade of its foundation, the colony had acquired a representative institution on the Westminster model. There was nothing like it in any of the American colonies, be they Spanish, Portuguese, or French, though some of them had now been in existence over a century."[123]

In the same year, 1619, for the first time in America, a colony declared a day of Thanksgiving—to God. Captain John Woodlief declared on December 4th of that year: "We ordain that the day of our ship's arrival at the place assigned for plantation in the land of Virginia shall be yearly and perpetually kept holy as a day of Thanksgiving to Almighty God."[124]

Because of the permanence of Jamestown, a small group of Christian Separatists—the Pilgrims—decided to settle in what they called the northern parts of Virginia. Dr. Lillback notes: "The Pilgrims came to build on the foundation of Christian civilization and European civilization from England in Virginia, and so, because that civilization was here, they were ready to cross the ocean. It's highly unlikely that they would have gone to just unreached areas as discoverers, because they were a civilized people that wanted to advance a Christian cause."[125] The Pilgrims came, and, after them, thousands of Puritans, creating a Christian tone for the burgeoning nation. Paul Jehle notes: "There's no question that both Jamestown and Plymouth become the key parent colonies for America. They contribute unique things that made America what it was. Jamestown was a replica of England; the Pilgrims were Separatists. They had separated from the Church of England. So, the Pilgrims were a purer form of the Reformation that came later on in spiritual aspects of Christians following the Scriptures.... That became very critical to the history of New England.... In the south Jamestown had become more of a replica of England, but also a key aspect in the national area where we were going to be one nation. That came out of Jamestown, somewhat prophetically; whereas, in New England it came out that we are going to be individuals that are self-governed by the Bible and Christianity. So certainly, Jamestown and Plymouth, when you take them together, you see a foundation for America that all thirteen colonies begin to express at the time of the Revolution." [126]

THE SEEDS OF A GREAT NATION

The seeds of a great nation were planted in Jamestown 400 years ago. But it would seem that America today has all but forgotten her Christian roots. Nonetheless, to properly understand her present and her future, a nation should also remember her past.

On the 400th anniversary of Jamestown, Dr. Paul Jehle said, "It's a time to celebrate, a time to worship, a time to look back at our roots, and as the original visitor guide of 1907 said at the tourist centenary celebration, 'When any tourist goes by these sacred shrines to our forefathers, because of their Christianity, we should thank God we're Americans.'" [127]

THE PILGRIMS

The Pilgrims helped set the tone for America's uniquely Christian heritage. Each year, we have an annual reminder of our Christian roots in the celebration of Thanksgiving.

The late Dr. D. James Kennedy once observed that America essentially began as a church-relocation project. This is because the Pilgrims, who landed at Plymouth Rock in 1620, were a single congregation that had begun in Scrooby, England, then moved to Leyden, Holland, and finally to Plymouth, Massachusetts.

The Pilgrims began their congregation secretly in 1606 (some say 1604) with a spiritual covenant—before God, the congregation committed one man to another. That spiritual commitment was later politicized in the Mayflower Compact, the first step in American constitutionalism.

The Pilgrims and other Christian non-conformists were persecuted by King James I (1566-1625), although he was outwardly Protestant. He once declared of Pilgrim, Puritan, and Presbyterian types, "I will make them conform themselves, or else I will harry them out of the land, or else do worse!" He once declared of Presbyterians, who had a strong presence in Scotland: "Presbytery agreeth with monarchy like God with the Devil." The Pilgrims suffered miserably under King James, and so they decided to emigrate to Holland, for religious tolerance—about a year after they formed. Even that was difficult to arrange, and they experienced major persecution along the way.

But they finally made it to Holland and, at first, things worked well. At least they experienced religious toleration. However, they had to work long, hard hours. After a while, it became obvious that they were beginning to lose some of their young people to the influences of the worldly Dutch youth. The Pilgrims felt that if they were to remain pure in their mission as a congregation, they might do best to settle down in the New World.

They deliberated as to where they might move and decided—now that Jamestown was a permanent settlement—to try and emigrate to the northernmost parts of Virginia. At that time, that would have been roughly where New York City is now.

By this time, the congregation numbered about 500 people. Their pastor was Rev. John Robinson, who, like the members of his flock, were all strict Calvinists. In fact, Rev. Robinson represented the Calvinist side in a series of deliberations in Holland about Calvinism (God saves the sinner, whom He has chosen, through faith in Christ) versus Arminianism (the sinner is saved through faith in Christ—faith which originated in the sinner's own heart). At this Council of Dordt, the Calvinist side handily defeated the Arminian side.

Rev. Robinson was a very loving man who promoted democratic ideals. God was supreme, but each man was not to exalt himself above another. As Robinson shepherded the flock, and as they decided to plant their congregation in America, the plan was to send over a fraction of their number initially and eventually all go over, voyage by voyage, as soon as it was feasible. The first group was comprised of about fifty Pilgrims (nearly half the passengers) in the voyage of the *Mayflower*. Initially, it was going to be more Pilgrims coming over in 1620 because they had an additional boat, the *Speedwell*, but that did not prove seaworthy. So they had to downsize the number. Also, they lost precious time, as the storm clouds gathered over the Atlantic.

All of the details of the amazing story of the Pilgrims have been preserved for us by William Bradford, one of their leaders. In the New World, he was elected year after year as governor of the colony. His classic book is *Of Plymouth Plantation*.

Only one person died on the voyage over—a cursing, unkind crew member who hated the Pilgrims. How come only one died, in an age when death was relatively common in that type of voyage? A little-known fact about the *Mayflower* answers the question. The *Mayflower* was normally a wine cargo boat, and the wine from previous voyages had soaked some of the beams and essentially acted as a disinfectant. *God works in mysterious ways. . . .*

The *Mayflower* had to contend with some severe storms, yet they still made it over. In fact, the storms were so bad (and remember, because of the delays involving the *Speedwell*, they had gotten a late start), some considered the possibility of turning back to England. Cotton Mather said, ". . . they met with such terrible storms, that the principal persons on board had serious deliberations upon returning home again. . . ."[128]

During the storm, catastrophe struck. Amidst a terrible storm, the main beam of the mast cracked. Death was certain for the crew and passengers if this couldn't be repaired. The whole Pilgrim adventure could easily have ended up on the bottom of the Atlantic. Providentially, one of the Pilgrims had a large iron screw on board—some historians argue it was a jack for lifting roofs onto houses, others that it was part of a printing press. Whatever it was, the main beam was secured with this large screw, and so the *Mayflower* was saved.

When they finally landed in mid-November, they were too far north. But any attempt to sail south (to the northern parts of Virginia) was impossible to do safely. They took this as a sign of God's Providence, and they settled in Plymouth. But first they did something so significant that we will dwell on it in depth in a later chapter: writing up the Mayflower Compact, a forerunner of the U.S. Constitution.

The winter proved deadly. About half of their numbers died. But when the Spring of 1621 came and the *Mayflower* sailed back to England, no

Pilgrim was on board. They all were committed to persevering with their new colony.

The Clearing of the Land

The Indians in that area were very hostile, yet most of them had died off in a plague that swept through there a few years before the Pilgrims arrived. Again by God's providence, they didn't have to contend with fierce Indians, which was a constant problem for settlers in other regions.

Years before the Pilgrims ever disembarked the *Mayflower* at Plymouth, there was a Frenchman caught by the Indians in those parts. Presumably, he was part of a fishing expedition in those parts of the New World. The Indians abused him and were about to kill him, so he sought to put the fear of God into them. He prophesied, according to Cotton Mather, "that God being angry with them for their wickedness, would not only destroy them all, but also people the place with another nation, which would not live after their brutish manners." They responded that God could not kill them. After this, they died in such horrible numbers that "our first planters [the Pilgrims] found the land almost covered with their unburied carcasses."

Not *all* of the territory was barren wilderness having to be cleared, as there were already some cultivated fields that had been used and left by the Indians, who, again, had been stricken by a strange illness a few years before the Pilgrims came. The number of Indians killed off by the plague was per capita 19 in 20.[129]

The First Thanksgiving

Also in the spring of 1621, an Indian came to their colony. He spoke English and helped them survive in the New England wilderness. His name was Squanto.

Although life in their colony was very difficult at first, after a while, it was obvious that God was allowing them to survive. Squanto taught them how to survive in that barren wilderness. Because of what Squanto taught them and because of the peace treaty with the Indians he was able to negotiate in conjunction with them, this small colony in the wilderness slowly began to survive and eventually prosper.

And before they were even a vibrant community, they decided to set aside a time for Thanksgiving to the Lord for all His goodness to them. The Pilgrims celebrated three days of Thanksgiving and invited the Indians to celebrate with them, a tradition we celebrate to this day.

So out of humble beginnings, a great nation was begun in this "errand in the wilderness." Not too bad for a church-relocation project. The Pilgrims set the tone for the new nation. They began the whole venture "In the Name of God. Amen," the opening words of the Mayflower Compact.

THE PURITANS

After the earlier Pilgrims, probably *the* single greatest influence in the settling of America, paving the way for the founding of America, was a group of stalwart, Bible-centered Christians known as the Puritans.

The Puritans' vision was well encapsulated in a sermon. This is one of the great Christian speeches echoing down through the centuries, although it is not necessarily that well-known. On board the America-bound ship, the *Arbella*, Rev. John Winthrop delivered his sermon "A Model of Christian Charity," which included the classic line: "For we must consider that we shall be like a City upon a Hill; the eyes of all people are on us."[130] To this day, presidents, politicians, commentators, pastors, and authors cite this classic line from the early days of America.

For instance, President Ronald Reagan said in his final Radio Address to the Nation:

> I've often recalled one group of early settlers making a treacher-
> ous crossing of the Atlantic on a small ship when their leader,
> a minister, noted that perhaps their venture would fail and they
> would become a byword, a footnote to history. But perhaps, too,
> with God's help, they might found a new world, a city upon a
> hill, a light unto nations.[131]

John Winthrop served as the great leader of the first major wave of Puritans who came to our shores. These were not your "huddled masses, yearning to breathe free." These men and women were among the cream of society; they were the well-educated and the well-to-do, but they were religious nonconformists. All they wanted was the freedom to worship Christ according to the Bible. The Scriptures were at the very heart of their movement. John Palfrey, author of *A History of New England,* which was published in 1859, said, "The Puritan searched the Bible, not only for principles and rules, but for mandates,—and, when he could find none of these, for analogies,—to guide him in precise arrangements of public administration, and in the minutest points of individual conduct."[132]

Because the Puritans desired to pursue a more pure form of New Testament Christianity, they were discriminated against and persecuted. Winthrop and other students at Cambridge University made a covenant with each other, committing themselves to God first and then to each other.

Again, the Puritans had disagreed with Separatists like the Pilgrims. How could they leave the Church to form their own? Wouldn't it be better to stay and purify the Anglican Church of England from within?

Ideally, that's what the Puritans believed. But, by the 1620s, the king and the Anglican Church made things intolerable for religious nonconformists. King James died in 1625, and Charles I ascended to the throne. Charles got into so many conflicts with Puritan nonconformists in his realm that it eventually led to England's Civil War. (Charles lost and was beheaded in 1649, in what is now known as *regicide*.)

Meanwhile, the persecution against the Puritans was such that they decided to leave England. Seeing that the Pilgrims, their spiritual first cousins, had gained a foothold in New England, the Puritans decided to follow suit. Although they disagreed with the Pilgrims of Plymouth and other Separatists, they could not argue with the success the Plymouth colony was beginning to enjoy.

Beginning in 1628, and especially from 1630 to 1642, more than 20,000 Puritans came into Massachusetts—about forty miles up the coast from Plymouth.

"ERRAND INTO THE WILDERNESS"

The godly men and women who settled New England—the Pilgrims and then the Puritans—were on an "errand into the wilderness," according to Rev. Cotton Mather (1663-1728), a prolific Puritan divine, from whom we learn so much about their settlements. Mather's large, two-volume set, *The Great Works of Christ in America*, first published in 1702, provides an early account of so much from that era. Mather says of his godly ancestors, "wherever they sat down, they were so mindful of their errand into the wilderness, that still one of their first works was to gather a church into the covenant and order of the gospel."[133]

This was not easy. The shores were inhospitable, as were the winters, which proved so fatal at first. The Indians were hostile. Many things were going against the Puritans. Nonetheless, God blessed their efforts. Mather writes, "Never was any plantation [New England at large] brought unto such a considerableness, in a space of time so inconsiderable! an howling wilderness in a few years became a pleasant land, accommodated with the necessaries—yea, and the conveniences of humane life; the gospel has carried with it a fulness of all other blessings...."[134]

John Winthrop had a sizable estate, which he spent to help further the colony. Mather tells us, "Many were the afflictions of this righteous man! He lost much of his estate in a ship, and in an house, quickly after his coming to New England, besides the prodigious expense of it in the difficulties of his coming hither."[135]

This uprooting from their homes and their wider families must have been traumatic, but it was all worth it. For example, months later, when the Puritans finally were beginning to settle in the New World, Winthrop wrote his wife, who had been unable to come with them initially because she was pregnant. Here is what he said to her, despite a harsh winter that was killing off many of their numbers and despite all the difficulties that they faced: "We here enjoy God and Jesus Christ, and is not this enough?"[136] This one statement speaks volumes about the Puritans and their dedication to our Lord.

The Puritan's philosophy of church government differed from that of the Plymouth Pilgrims. They did not want to do away with the old ideas and the Anglican Church; they wanted a state-run religion, and their views were quite consistent with the monarchy.

Dr. Kennedy points out that one of the Pilgrims—their doctor—helped soften the Puritans' view of a state-church. In that first year, many Puritans, like the Pilgrims ten years before, were deathly sick. They called on the Plymouth Pilgrims for help who responded by sending their physician, Dr. Samuel Fuller, to stay with the Puritans for the entire winter. Fuller told the Puritan's first governor, John Endicott, about the Pilgrim's church and civil government in Plymouth, and the governor and the other settlers in Boston were greatly moved. The Puritans eventually decided to emulate the freedom and government of the tiny group of Plymouth Pilgrims and separate themselves from the Anglican Church in England. In short, the Pilgrims, so vastly overwhelmed in number, had a major influence on the Puritans by showing them the excellence of the congregational way. This meant that each congregation would decide important matters for itself, which was a key stepping stone to American democracy.

Dr. Kennedy says of Dr. Fuller's input:

> If that had not been true, we would not have had the religious freedom we have today in America, since the Puritans soon outnumbered the original Pilgrims by the thousands. It is conceivable that if it were not for Samuel Fuller, the ideas of the Pilgrims might have been completely overwhelmed by the loud chorus of the Puritans, and we might have a state religion and a monarchy. So when we talk about William Bradford and William Brewster and Edward Winslow, we should also remember Dr. Samuel Fuller.[137]

Modern secularists malign the Puritans for not separating the church from the newly founded state, but they don't realize that this practice actually came from a renegade Puritan, Rev. Roger Williams. Williams came into conflict with the rest of the Puritans and, as a result, was banished from Massachusetts. He was to be sent back to England, but instead he fled to the wilderness and founded Rhode Island, which he created to be a place where, under God, men and women could practice whatever religious tradition they chose. The state would not interfere with their beliefs. Historian Paul Johnson calls Roger Williams "the second great American."[138] To take Williams out of the realm of the Puritans is inaccurate. So even the practice of separating the institution of the church from the institution of the state (for the protection of the church) came from one branch of Puritans.

Above all, these Puritans desired to serve Christ and to see other people come to know Him. They desired that the New World would be *a city set on a hill, a shining city to the glory of Christ.*

"THE FIRST GREAT AMERICAN"

"The first great American," according to British historian and prolific writer Paul Johnson, was John Winthrop.[139] And Paul Johnson is not alone in his praise of John Winthrop. Cotton Mather calls Winthrop "the American Nehemiah." Furthermore, Mather said that Winthrop had a "Mosaic spirit."[140]

Johnson sums up Winthrop's great accomplishment—leading thousands of fellow Puritans to build a new society in the wilderness: "Moreover, it has to be said, on his behalf, that he implemented this system of government firmly in American soil, so that at the end of twenty years the colony had been built up from nothing to a body politic which was already showing signs of maturity, in that it was reconciling the needs of authority with the needs of liberty." [141]

THE PAPER TRAIL

Paul Johnson notes a unique characteristic of America's founding: we still have all the paperwork, including the charters, covenants, compacts, and so on: "These early diaries and letters, which are plentiful, and the fact that most important documents about the early American colonies have been preserved mean that the United States is the first nation in human history whose most distant origins are fully recorded." And the overall point of the settlement of America by the Puritans? Johnson notes, "...the overwhelming thrust was religious."

Furthermore, the first elections held were to choose the ministers. Johnson observes, "In a sense, the clergy were the first elected officials of the new American society, a society which to that extent had a democratic element from the start...." [142]

WHO IS BOSTON'S "PATRON SAINT"?

Under Rev. John Winthrop's leadership, the Puritans founded Boston in 1630. Like all the Puritan settlements, Boston began as a Bible commonwealth. Cotton Mather wrote, "The dispensations of the gospel were never enjoyed by any town with more liberty and purity for so long a while together." [143]

Furthermore, in a sermon, Cotton Mather pointed out that Catholic countries and territories often named cities after saints who became the patron saint of that city. So St. Augustine would be the patron saint of St. Augustine, Florida; St. Francis of Assisi, that of San Francisco; and so on. What about Boston, which was named for Boston in England, Mather asked. According to him, the protector of Boston is Jesus Christ, not a patron saint. [144]

Rev. Mather pointed out that Boston had been threatened many times, but God always spared the city. Ten times fire "made notable ruins among us." A French warship threatened them. Famine stared the town in the face. But God always provided for them at the last minute. Four times there was an outbreak of small-pox.[145] In all these difficulties, God pulled them through.

And the impact of the gospel on Boston and New England in those days? A man from London said of Massachusetts (as recorded in Mather's book from 1702): "I have lived in a country where in seven years I never saw a beggar, nor heard an oath [a cuss word], nor looked upon a drunkard."[146]

As Cotton Mather said, "It may be there never was any region under heaven happier than poor New-England hath been in Magistrates, whose true piety was worthy to be made the example of after-ages."[147]

THE COLONIAL CHARTERS

An important way to grasp the Christian character of the early settlers of America is by quickly reviewing the charters of many of the colonies. Both the charters and the state constitutions provide further evidence of the Christian heritage of America. Virtually every one of these historic documents state the aim of glorifying God. Some of this material we have already noted, but here it comes by way of review.

Our chief guide for this point will be David Brewer, who served as an Associate Justice on the U.S. Supreme Court from 1890-1910 and wrote the *Trinity* decision—an important decision we will explore in the Appendix. Brewer wrote a book entitled, *The United States: A Christian Nation*, in which he spells out the evidence for our Christian heritage from the various colonial charters.

VIRGINIA'S GRANT

David Brewer pointed out that the various charters for the very first permanent, British settlement in North America mentioned God. I refer to the charter of the settlement named after the Virgin Queen, Elizabeth I:

> The first colonial grant, that [was] made to Sir Walter Raleigh in 1584, was from "Elizabeth, by the grace of God, of England, France and Ireland, queen, defender of the faith," etc; and the grant authorizing him to enact statutes for the government of the proposed colony provided that "they be not against the true Christian faith now professed in the Church of England." The first charter of Virginia, granted by King James I in 1606, after reciting the application of certain parties for a charter, commenced the grant in these words: "We, greatly commending, and graciously

accepting of, their Desires for the Furtherance of so noble a Work, which may, by the Providence of Almighty God, hereafter tend to the Glory of His Divine Majesty, in propagating of Christian Religion to such People as yet live in Darkness and miserable Ignorance of the true Knowledge and Worship of God, and may in time bring the Infidels and Savages, living in those parts, to human Civility, and to a settled and quiet Government; Do, by these our Letters-Patents, graciously accept, and agree to, their humble and well intended Desires."

Language of similar import may be found in the subsequent characters of that colony, from the same king, in 1609 and 1611; and the same is true of the various charters granted to the other colonies. In language more or less emphatic is the establishment of the Christian religion declared to be one of the purposes of the grant.[148]

CHARTER OF NEW ENGLAND

In 1620, the same year the Pilgrims sailed off and ended up in Plymouth on their attempt to get to the "northern parts of Virginia," King James granted a charter for the whole region—a small portion of which the Pilgrims settled in (by happenstance). David Brewer writes:

> The charter of New England, granted by James I in 1620, after referring to a petition, declares: "We, according to our princely inclination, favoring much their worthy disposition, in hope thereby to advance the enlargement of Christian religion, to the glory of God Almighty."[149]

CHARTER OF MASSACHUSETTS

The charter of Massachusetts was to become very controversial. The authorities in England would grant one, then abolish it, then re-grant a similar one, only to withdraw later. One of the twenty-eight complaints against King George III in the Declaration of Independence touches on this. The king was guilty of "taking away our Charters, abolishing our most valuable Laws, and altering fundamentally the Forms of our Governments."[150] Going back to the seventeenth century, the Puritans set out to guard their original charter zealously, observes Brewer:

> The charter of Massachusetts Bay, granted in 1629 by Charles I, after several provisions, recites: "Whereby our said people inhabitants,

there, may be so religiously, peaceably, and civilly governed as their good life and orderly conversation may win and incite the natives of the country to their knowledge and obedience of the only true God and Saviour of mankind, and the Christian faith, which in our royal intention and the adventurers free profession, is the principal end of this plantation," which declaration was substantially repeated in the charter of Massachusetts Bay granted by William and Mary, in 1691.[151]

THE FUNDAMENTAL ORDERS OF CONNECTICUT

From Massachusetts, a group of Puritans was to go further inland and create the settlement of Connecticut. The Fundamental Orders of Connecticut, a forerunner to the U.S. Constitution, mentioned that their goal *as a colony* was "to maintain and preserve the liberty and purity of the gospel of our Lord Jesus which we now profess, as also the discipline of the Churches, which according to the truth of the said gospel is now practiced amongst us."[152]

RHODE ISLAND'S 1638 SETTLEMENT

Although Rev. Roger Williams' colony of Rhode Island allowed for different points of view, even non-Christian ones, notice how the settlement was clearly Christian in origin. Again, we hear from David Brewer:

> In 1638, the first settlers in Rhode Island organized a local government by signing the following agreement: "We whose names are underwritten do here solemnly in the presence of Jehovah incorporate ourselves into a Bodie Politick and as He shall help, will submit our persons, lives and estates unto our Lord Jesus Christ, the King of Kings and Lord of Lords and to all those perfect and most absolute laws of his given us in His holy word of truth, to be guided and judged thereby. Exod. 24:3, 4; 2 Chron. 11:3; 2 Kings 11:17."[153]

Finding Scripture in an American colonial charter is common, because the Bible is the book that made America.

RHODE ISLAND'S OFFICIAL 1663 CHARTER

When Oliver Cromwell died, doubt was cast on the Rhode Island charter. Therefore, Rev. Williams traveled to England to secure a new one, which he was able to accomplish in 1663. This new charter also mentions the importance of Christianity. Brewer summarizes:

> The charter granted to Rhode Island, in 1663, naming the petitioners, speaks of them as "pursuing, with peaceable and loyal minds, their sober, serious and religious intentions, of godly edifying themselves and one another in the holy Christian faith and worship as they were persuaded; together with the gaining over and conversion of the poor, ignorant Indian natives, in these parts of America, to the sincere profession and obedience of the same faith and worship."[154]

The phrase "as they were persuaded" shows how freedom of conscience was important to Roger Williams.

THE CHARTER OF MARYLAND

Catholics were the first official settlers of Maryland (named after Maria, the wife of Charles I). But they were not the only founders and settlers of the colony. By the time of the Revolutionary War, the Catholic population in Maryland was less than 10 percent of the total. Listen to the goals they articulated for the new settlement in 1632:

> Charles, by the Grace of God, of England, Scotland, France, and Ireland, king, Defender of the Faith, &c...being animated with a laudable, and pious Zeal for extending the Christian Religion, and also the Territories of our Empire, hath humbly besought Leave of us, that he may transport, by his own Industry, and Expense, a numerous Colony of the English Nation, to a certain Region, herein after described, in a Country hitherto uncultivated, in the Parts of America, and partly occupied by Savages, having no knowledge of the Divine Being, and that all that Region, with some certain Privileges, and Jurisdiction, appertaining unto the wholesome Government, and State of his Colony and Region aforesaid, may by our Royal Highness be given, granted and confirmed unto him, and his Heirs.[155]

THE CHARTER OF CAROLINA

Two states were eventually to emerge from one territory, that of Carolina. Brewer points out that the Christian faith was also important in that charter: "The charter of Carolina, granted in 1663 by Charles II, recites that the petitioners, 'being excited with a laudable and pious zeal for the propagation of the Christian faith.'"[156]

Pennsylvania's Frame of Government

William Penn, a man of God and a Quaker, set out to provide a haven for Christian nonconformists. The government Penn set up found its freedom for all under God:

> In the preface of the frame of government prepared in 1682 by William Penn, for Pennsylvania, it is said: "They weakly err, that think there is no other use of government than correction, which is the coarsest part of it; daily experience tells us that the care and regulation of many other affairs, more soft, and daily necessary, make up much of the greatest part of government; and which must have followed the peopling of the world, had Adam never fell, and will continue among men, on earth, under the highest attainments they may arrive at, by the coming of the blessed second Adam, 'the Lord from heaven.' And with the laws prepared to go with the frame of government, it was further provided 'that according to the good example of the primitive Christians, and the ease of the creation, every first day of the week, called the Lord's Day, people shall abstain from their common daily labor that they may the better dispose themselves to worship God according to their understandings.'"[157]

The *Frame of Government* applied not only to Pennsylvania, but at the time, it applied to the region that would eventually break away into the state of Delaware. Before he gained possession of Pennsylvania, William Penn helped write the *Concessions of New Jersey.* The original Seal of the Province of New Jersey (1697) had inscribed on it Proverbs 14:34: "Righteousness exalteth a nation."[158]

Charter of Georgia—1732

Like so many colonies of North America, Georgia began as a haven for Protestant refugees.[159] The original charter of Georgia declared that the "prosperous success" of this proposed colony depends first of all upon "The blessing of God." They also declared freedom of worship for all Protestants: "...there shall be a liberty of conscience allowed in the worship of God, to all persons inhabiting, or which shall inhabit or be resident within our said provinces and that all such persons, except papists, shall have a free exercise of their religion, so they be contented with the quiet and peaceable enjoyment of the same, not giving offence or scandal to the government...."[160]

FRENCH SETTLEMENTS

One could argue that one of the goals for the French territories in North America included the Christianizing of the Indians. At one point, the French had more land mass in North America than the British did. When the United States made the Louisiana Purchase from the French in 1803, it was the largest sale of land in the history of the world. One of the French goals was the Christianization of the Indians. Perhaps they were more successful than the Protestant British at converting the native-Americans. It was a slow work for both groups. In any event, we see a Christian aspect of the settlement of this land. Brewer writes:

> From the very first, efforts were made, largely it must be conceded by Catholics, to bring the Indians under the influence of Christianity. Who can read without emotion the story of [Jacques] Marquette, and others like him, enduring all perils and dangers and toiling through the forests of the west in their efforts to tell the story of Jesus to the savages of North America?[161]

Historian George Bancroft adds:

> Religious enthusiasm colonized New England; religious enthusiasm took possession of the wilderness on the upper lakes and explored the Mississippi. Puritanism gave New England its worship and its schools; the Roman church and Jesuit priests raised for Canada its altars, its hospitals, and its seminaries. The influence of Calvin can be traced in every New England village; in Canada, not a cape was turned, nor a mission founded, nor a river entered, nor a settlement begun, but a Jesuit led the way.[162]

David Brewer also mentions the Christian motivation of the Protestant refugees persecuted by Catholic France, the Huguenots:

> The Huguenots, driven from France by the Edict of Nantes, sought in the more southern colonies a place where they could live in the enjoyment of their Huguenot faith. It is not exaggeration to say that Christianity in some of its creeds was the principal

cause of the settlement of many of the colonies, and cooperated with business hopes and purposes in the settlement of the others. Beginning in this way and under these influences it is not strange that the colonial life had an emphatic Christian tone.[163]

CALVIN'S INFLUENCE IN THE FOUNDING ERA

People think that the influence of the Puritans collapsed sometime in the eighteenth century so that by the time America was founded, the Enlightenment was more important to the framers of our government than Puritanism. This is not so. (The writings of John Locke, Sir William Blackstone, and Montesquieu reflected the Biblical views of the founding fathers, but that was very different from the atheistic views of Enlightenment philosophers like Rousseau and Voltaire.)[164]

The vast majority of Americans at the time of the founding era were still Calvinists, just as the Puritans and the Pilgrims were all Calvinists.

Dr. Lorraine Boettner (a man), author of many important books, including *The Reformed Doctrine of Predestination*, writes:

> It is estimated that of the 3,000,000 Americans at the time of the American Revolution, 900,000 were of Scotch or Scotch-Irish origin, 600,000 were Puritan English, and 400,000 were German or Dutch Reformed. In addition to this the Episcopalians had a Calvinistic confession in their Thirty-nine Articles; and many French Huguenots also had come to this western world. Thus we see that about two-thirds of the colonial population had been trained in the school of Calvin. Never in the world's history had a nation been founded by such people as these. Furthermore these people came to America not primarily for commercial gain or advantage, but because of deep religious convictions. It seems that the religious persecutions in various European countries had been providentially used to select out the most progressive and enlightened people for the colonization of America.
>
> Furthermore, Bancroft writes: "The Revolution of 1776, so far as it was affected by religion was a Presbyterian measure. It was the natural out growth of the principles which the Presbyterianism of the Old World planted in her sons, the English Puritans, the Scotch Covenanters, the French Huguenots, the Dutch Calvinists, and the Presbyterians of Ulster."[165]

THE PRESBYTERIANS AND THE AMERICAN REVOLUTION

Several historians point out the link between Presbyterians and the American War for Independence. Here again, we see the influence of John Calvin at work, as he is the grandfather of Presbyterianism—John Knox being its father. Before the war, there were the "Sons of Liberty," men like Samuel Adams or James Otis. These patriots of independence were labeled "the Presbyterian junto," according to the royalists (those loyal to Great Britain in the brewing conflict).[166]

Lorraine Boettner writes:

> So intense, universal, and aggressive were the Presbyterians in their zeal for liberty that the war was spoken of in England as "The Presbyterian Rebellion." An ardent colonial supporter of King George III wrote home: "I fix all the blame for these extraordinary proceedings upon the Presbyterians. They have been the chief and principal instruments in all these flaming measures. They always do and ever will act against government from that restless and turbulent anti-monarchial spirit which has always distinguished them everywhere."[167]

Therefore, prominent members of Parliament and of the king's council blamed the Presbyterians for the American Revolution. Paul Carlson, author of *Our Presbyterian Heritage,* describes what happened one day in Parliament:

> Horace Walpole rose from his seat in the British House of Commons to report on the "extraordinary proceedings" which had lately occurred in the far-off colonies of the New World.
>
> "There is no good crying about the matter," said Walpole sadly. "Cousin America has run off with a Presbyterian parson, and that is the end of it."
>
> That "Presbyterian parson" was none other than the Reverend Dr. John Witherspoon, president of the College of New Jersey (now Princeton University)...."[168]

By the time the British surrendered at Yorktown, every colonel but one in the American army was an elder in the Presbyterian Church and on top of that, half of all the officers and soldiers in the colonial army were Presbyterians.[169]

Author and speaker Marshall Foster said this about the Presbyterians and the War for Independence: "About one-fourth of the colonists were

Scotch-Irish Presbyterians, and they made up about 80 percent of George Washington's Officer Corps and about 50 percent of his army. And those Scots knew how to hate the English, ever since the days of William Wallace. So, you know why we won the Revolution; there's one of the biggest reasons."[170]

THE PILGRIMS, THE PURITANS, THE PRESBYTERIANS

To recap—the Pilgrims got a toehold in the New World. The Puritans came next in wave after wave of migration. By the end of the seventeenth century, the Puritans outnumbered the Pilgrims and the two were practically indistinguishable.

Then the Presbyterians, also followers of Jesus Christ via the teachings of John Calvin and John Knox, came in great waves, in the footsteps of the Puritans before them—although they settled up and down the Atlantic Coast, not just in one area. The numbers of Presbyterians that came in the eighteenth century is in the hundreds of thousands. (Some have said as few as 250,000 in a land of 3,000,000; others as many as 600,000.) All of this works inexorably toward the conclusion of free Christian people, worshiping Jesus Christ according to the dictates of their conscience, with a Biblically based charter for self-government. This is why we say America always was and will be one nation under God.

CONCLUSION

As John Winthrop looked out over the sea and back at his fellow travelers, he continued with the sermon that included the famous line, "We shall be as a city on a hill." I will close this chapter with portions of his message.

He declared, "... the Lord will be our God and delight to dwell among us as His own people. He will command a blessing on us in all our ways, so that we shall see much more of His wisdom, power, goodness, and truth than we have formerly known." Then he added—and here is the context of his famous "city on a hill" remark: "We shall find that the God of Israel is among us, and ten of us shall be able to resist a thousand of our enemies. The Lord will make our name a praise and glory, so that men shall say of succeeding plantations: 'The Lord make it like that of New England.' For we must consider that we shall be like a City upon a Hill, the eyes of all people are on us...."

John Winthrop concluded that when Moses stood before the people, he said that the choice was theirs—life or death. "Beloved, there is now set before us life and good, death and evil, in that we are commanded this day to love the Lord our God, and to love one another; to walk in His ways and to keep His commandments and His ordinance, and His laws, and the articles of our covenant with Him, that we may live and be multiplied...."

Then Winthrop gave his dramatic close, based on the words of Deuteronomy: "Therefore, let us choose life that we and our seed may live; by obeying His voice, and cleaving to Him, for He is our life and prosperity."[171] These words applied not only to the Puritans who founded Boston, but also to many of the early settlers of North America up and down the Atlantic sea coast. These words are worth our remembering—and heeding—today.

PHOTO: J. NEWCOMBE

The New England Primer taught millions of Americans basic grammar and deep Biblical truths. It was used from 1692 to after 1900.

In Adam's fall
We sinned all.

Thy life to mend,
This Book attend.

The Cat doth play,
And after slay.

A Dog will bite
A thief at night.

An Eagle's flight
Is out of sight

The idle Fool
Is whipt at school.

As runs the Glass,
Man's life doth pass.

My Book and Heart
Shall never part.

Job feels the rod,
And blesses God.

Proud Korah's troops
Were swallowed up.

The Lion bold
The lamb doth hold.

The Moon shines bright
In time of night.

Nightingales sing
In time of spring.

The sturdy Oak, it was
the tree,
That saved his royal ma-
jesty.

Peter denies
His Lord, and cries.

Queen Esther comes in
royal state,
To save the Jews from
dismal fate.

Rachel doth mourn
For her first born.

Samuel anoints
Whom God appoints.

Time cuts down all,
Both great and small.

Uriah's lovely wife
Made David seek his life.

Whales in the sea
God's voice obey.

Xerxes the great did die,
And so must you and I.

Youth's forward slips
Death soonest nips.

Zaccheus did climb the
tree,
His Lord to see.

CHAPTER 5

The Bible and Education

The fear of the LORD *is the beginning of knowledge.*
(Proverbs 1:7)

*T*HE secular media does not understand Christianity. One of the
most unforgettable mistakes made by anyone against Christians
was made in a front-page story in 1993 by *Washington Post* writer Michael
Weisskopf. He said: "Corporations pay public relations firms millions of
dollars to contrive the kind of grass-roots response that Jerry Falwell or
Pat Robertson can galvanize in a televised sermon. Their followers are
largely poor, uneducated and easy to command [emphasis mine]."[172] The *Post*
ended up apologizing soon after. But the fact that the statement made
it into print shows what many of our nation's elite class really think of
Christians: that we are largely uneducated.

Well, to paraphrase the late Dr. D. James Kennedy on that subject: Tell
the Rev. John Harvard that Bible-believing Christians are ignorant—or
the Puritan Elihu Yale or the Presbyterian elders who founded the college
that came to be known as Princeton. Generally, Christianity and education go hand in hand.[173]

At one time, America was one of the best-educated nations in the world.
In New England, after generations of Puritan influence, John Adams
remarked that finding an illiterate man in New England was as rare as a
comet. As we have moved away from our Christian roots, we have also
moved away from literacy. The founders understood that our experiment

in self-government could only be maintained by a well-educated populace. James Madison, one of the key architects of the Constitution, once noted: "A well-instructed people alone can be permanently a free people."[174]

Long before James Madison was born, education was critically important to the Christian experiment in self-government that so many of the settlers of North America were trying to conduct. The reason was simple: so that children could read the Bible for themselves. The purpose of this chapter is to show that during the settling and founding eras of America, the Bible played a pivotal role in shaping the worldview of those who created this land. No other book played a role even remotely close.

Please note that while this chapter appears in the section on the Bible and the Settling of America, it could just as well appear in the section on the Bible and the Founding of America. Because there was an unbroken succession of Bible-based education that began with the Puritans and continued even through the nineteenth century, including, therefore, the founding era.

THE OLD DELUDER SATAN ACT

The first law passed in America related to education was an act in the Puritan colony of Massachusetts in 1642 and revised in 1647. While it could be called the Massachusetts School Law, it is best known as "The Old Deluder Satan Act." This act mandated schools for the masses so that children would learn the Scriptures, lest they go astray. Here is how that legislation begins:

> It being one chief project of that old deluder Satan to keep men from the knowledge of the Scriptures, as in former times by keeping them in an unknown tongue, so in these latter times by persuading from the use of tongues, that so at least the true sense and meaning of the original might be clouded by false glosses of saint-seeming deceivers, that learning may not be buried in the grave of our fathers in the church and commonwealth, the Lord assisting our endeavors.
>
> It is therefore ordered that every township in this jurisdiction, after the Lord has increased them to the number of fifty householders, shall then forthwith appoint one within their town to teach all such children as shall resort to him to write and read....[175]

In other words, the Puritans were concerned that Satan not get the victory with the Puritan children by keeping them ignorant of the Bible. Therefore, schools were to be established so that children could read and write. The blessing of literacy is a by-product of Christianity.

This reminds me of what Dr. Samuel Blumenfeld, an expert on American education, had to say. He wrote a book in 1985 probing the question, *Is Public Education Necessary?* As he investigated the roots of education for the masses, he found that John Calvin, in particular, was quite prominent. (Of course, the Puritans were committed Calvinists, as were many other American colonists.) Blumenfeld writes:

> The modern idea of popular education—that is, education for everyone—first arose in Europe during the Protestant Reformation when papal authority was replaced by Biblical authority. Since the Protestant rebellion against Rome had arisen in part as a result of Biblical study and interpretation, it became obvious to Protestant leaders that if the reform movement were to survive and flourish, widespread Biblical literacy, at all levels of society, would be absolutely necessary.[176]

America was settled by men and women who were committed to the Bible.

The New England Primer

When children were taught their ABC's in Puritan New England, they were also taught a great deal of theology. Beginning in 1692, thousands of New England children were taught basic reading skills through a small blue book, *The New England Primer.* This book was quite influential, and all the founding fathers from New England (and beyond) were weaned on Biblical principles, in part, through this little book. This would include Benjamin Franklin, John Adams, Sam Adams, John Hancock, and so on.

David Barton, a walking encyclopedia on America's Christian heritage, gave me a copy of *The New England Primer* that his ministry reproduced in 1991. What a great service, to make this powerful little book available to Christian schools and home-schools everywhere.

*The New England Prime*r taught Biblical truths to generations of early Americans. It included all 107 questions and answers of the Shorter Catechism of the Westminster Confession of Faith (1646), which were the stated beliefs of Calvinists everywhere. (That would include the Pilgrims, the Puritans, the Huguenots, the Presbyterians, and even many of the

Anglicans.) Here is probably the most well-known Q & A from that catechism (as reprinted in *The New England Primer*):

> Quest. What is the chief end of man?
> Ans.   Man's chief end is to glorify God and enjoy Him forever.

In one of the many reprints of *The New England Primer* (this one coming from 1843), they explain the value of the Shorter Catechism:

> Our Puritan Fathers brought the Shorter Catechism with them across the ocean and laid it on the same shelf with the family Bible. They taught it diligently to their children.... If in this Catechism the true and fundamental doctrines of the Gospel are expressed in fewer and better words and definitions than in any other summary, why ought we not now to train up a child in the way he should go?—why not now put him in possession of the richest treasure that ever human wisdom and industry accumulated to draw from?

The 1900 reprint of *The New England Primer* tells how God used this very small book:

> *The New England Primer* was one of the greatest books ever published. It went through innumerable editions; it reflected in a marvelous way the spirit of the age that produced it, and contributed, perhaps more than any other book except the Bible, to the molding of those sturdy generations that gave to America its liberty and its institutions.

Let us consider for a few minutes what *The New England Primer* actually taught the children. Early on, we have "A Lesson for Children."

Pray to God.	Call no ill names.
Love God.	Use no ill words.
Fear God.	Tell no lies.
Serve God.	Hate Lies.
Take not God's	Speak the Truth.
Name in vain.	Spend your Time well.
Do not Swear.	Love your School.
Do not Steal.	Mind your Book.
Cheat not in your play.	Strive to learn.
Play not with bad boys.	Be not a Dunce.

I cannot imagine anyone teaching such things today. But wouldn't we be better off if we did?

The children learned their ABCs with these great theological truths:

A
In ADAM's Fall
We sinned all.

B
Heaven to find;
The Bible Mind.

C
CHRIST crucify'd
For sinners dy'd.

D
The Deluge drown'd
The Earth around.

E
ELIJAH hid
By Ravens fed.

F
The judgment made
FELIX afraid.

G
As runs the Glass,
Our Life doth pass.

H
My Book and Heart
Must never part.

J
JOB feels the Rod, —
Yet blesses GOD.

K
Proud KORAH's troop
Was swallowed up.

L
LOT fled to Zoar,
Saw fiery Shower
On Sodom pour.

M
MOSES was he
Who Israel's Host
Led thro' the Sea.

N
NOAH did view
The old world & new.

O
Young OBADIAS,
DAVID, JOSIAS,
All were pious.

P
PETER deny'd
His Lord and cry'd.

Q
Queen ESTHER sues
And saves the Jews.

R
Young pious RUTH,
Left all for Truth.

S
Young SAM'L dear,
The Lord did fear.

T
Young TIMOTHY
Learnt sin to fly.

V
VASHTI for Pride
Was set aside.

W
Whales in the Sea,
GOD's Voice obey.

X
XERXES did die,
And so must I.

Y
While youth do chear
Death may be near.

Z
ZACCHEUS he
Did climb the Tree
Our Lord to see.

The New England Primer went on to teach
the children these Biblical truths:

Who was the first man?
Adam.

Who was the first woman?
Eve.

Who was the first Murderer?
Cain.

Who was the first Martyr?
Abel.

Who was the first Translated?
Enoch.

Who was the oldest Man?
Methuselah.

Who built the Ark?
Noah.

Who was the Patientest Man?
Job.

Who was the Meekest Man?
Moses.

Who led Israel into Canaan?
Joshua.

Who was the strongest Man?
Sampson.

Who killed Goliah?
David.

Who was the wisest Man?
Solomon.

Who was in the Whale's Belly?
Jonah.

Who saves lost Men?
Jesus Christ.

Who is Jesus Christ?
The Son of God.

Who was the Mother of Christ?
Mary.

Who betrayed his Master?
Judas.

Who denied his Master?
Peter.

Who was the first Christian
Martyr?
Stephen.

Who was chief Apostle of the
Gentiles?
Paul.

Furthermore, *The New England Primer* went on to teach children even a simple grace before a meal and after:

BLESS me, O Lord,
and let my food strengthen me to serve thee,
for Jesus Christ's sake.
AMEN.

I Desire to thank God
who gives me food to eat
every day of my life.
AMEN.

The New England Primer contained many other Biblical teachings that we do not have space to reproduce here. It also contained the Apostles Creed, with its declaration of belief in the Trinity:

"I BELIEVE in God the Father . . .
in Jesus Christ his only Son our Lord . . .
I believe in the Holy Ghost. . . ."

Our founding fathers were weaned on these beliefs. Furthermore, the primer contained a wealth of prayers and hymns. By today's standards, the *Primer* seems geared to an older audience. But back then, it was for teaching children. It also taught glimpses of Church history, such as this nugget:

MR. JOHN ROGERS, minister of the gospel in London, was the first martyr in Queen MARY's reign, and was burnt at Smithfield, February 14, 1554. His wife with nine small children, and one at her breast following him to the stake; with which sorrowful sight he was not in the least daunted, but with wonderful patience died courageously for the gospel of JESUS CHRIST.

Some few days before his death, he wrote the following

Advice to his Children.

GIVE ear my children to my words
Whom God hath dearly bought,
Lay up His laws within your heart,
and print them in your thoughts.

I leave you here a little book
for you to look upon,
That you may see your father's face
when he is dead and gone:
Who for the hope of heavenly things,
While he did here remain,
Gave over all his golden years
to prison and to pain.
Where I, among my iron bands,
inclosed in the dark,
Not many days before my death,
I did compose this work:
And for example to your youth,
to whom I wish all good,
I send you here God's perfect truth,
and seal it with my blood.
To you my heirs of earthly things:
which I do leave behind,
That you may read and understand
and keep it in your mind.
That as you have been heirs of that
that once shall wear away,
You also may possess that part,
which never shall decay.
Keep always God before your eyes
with all your whole intent,
Commit no sin in any wise,
keep His commandment....
I know I am a sinner born,
from the original,
And that I do deserve to die
by my fore-father's fall:
But by our SAVIOUR's precious blood,
which on the cross was spilt,
Who freely offer'd up His life,
to save our souls from guilt;
I hope redemption I shall have,

and all who in Him trust,
When I shall see Him face to face,
and live among the just.
Why then should I fear death's grim look
since CHRIST for me did die....
Farewell my children to the world,
where you must yet remain;
The LORD of hosts be your defence,
'till we do meet again.[177]

We have quoted *The New England Primer* at length, but this is because this powerful little book wielded such great influence on school children for generations. It was extremely influential and was exported beyond the borders of the northeastern colonies. Because of the *Primer* and other Bible-based materials, so many of the American colonists (including the founders) had a Biblical worldview.

THE EDUCATION OF CHILDREN

One of the great Puritan divines was Cotton Mather, who at one time had the record of being the youngest man to ever enter Harvard (at the age of twelve). Cotton Mather wrote many books, including the two-volume classic, *The Great Works of Christ in America.* He wrote a short piece called "The Education of Children." Among the many things he declared was this purpose of education:

> The Minster that shall give his Neighbours No Rest, until they have agreeable Schools among them, and that shall himself also at some Times inspect and Visit the Schools, will therein do much towards Fulfilling that part of his Ministry, Feed my Lambs; and his Neighbours under his Charge will (whatever they think of it!) have cause to Bless God, for this Expression of his Faithfulness.[178]

Suffice it to say that education was of high value to the Puritans, who helped set the tone for the founding of America.

THE MOST QUOTED BOOK

A number of years ago, two political science professors, Charles S. Hyneman and Donald S. Lutz, conducted a ground-breaking, massive study. They carefully examined about 15,000 political documents, including several thousand books, monographs, and pamphlets written during America's founding era. These books, etc. were written between 1760 and 1805. They found 3,154 citations or references to other sources. What sources were being cited by the founding fathers and others writing on politics during the founding era?

The Bible was the number one source cited or quoted. In fact, four times more than any human source, the political writers during the founding era of America were quoting the Scriptures. Specifically, during that particular half century, 34 percent of political literary citations came from the Bible.[179]

After the Bible, the top three sources cited in the political writings during the founding time period, were Baron Charles Louis Joseph de Secondat Montesquieu, who accounted for 8.3 percent of the citations; Sir William Blackstone with 7.9 percent; and John Locke with 2.9 percent.[180] All three of these men were professing Christians whose views on politics, government, and law were influenced directly and positively by the Scriptures.

One time I got to meet Dr. Donald S. Lutz, one of those professors involved in that major study. Dr. Lutz has written many books and has served as professor of political science at the University of Houston. I got to interview him for our ground-breaking Coral Ridge Ministries documentary, *One Nation Under God*.

Dr. Lutz said this:

> During the Founding Era, the late 1700s, there were no magazines, newspapers had a very small circulation, there was no television, there was no internet, what did people do for entertainment? They would read pamphlets.... Now, of all the pamphlets published during the last part of the 1700s, more than 80 percent of them were reprinted sermons. And these reprinted sermons didn't just cite the Bible, they cited all kinds of things. So, for example, John Locke—the reason John Locke was even cited is because these ministers thought that John Locke was a good Christian, and what he had to say was commensurate with the Bible.[181]

Thus, the Bible was well-known up and down the Atlantic seacoast at the time of the settling and the founding of America.

NOAH WEBSTER

When we consider America and education, we should not neglect Noah Webster (1758-1843), whom one scholar calls the "Founding Father of American Scholarship and Education."[182] The name of Noah Webster is now synonymous with "dictionary" since he created such important lexicons. The way words are spelled in this book (and any twenty-first-century book for that matter) has been directly impacted by Webster. *The Encyclopedia of American Biography* says, "Webster's American dictionary was a scholarly achievement of the first rank, winning critical acclaim at home and abroad."[183] History professor Richard J. Moss explains, "We know Webster, perhaps as well as any name from the early republic, because he wrote a dictionary."[184] He is the father of a crowning achievement in American history. And this we owe to the Bible. Webster wrote the following testimony about the moment he gave his life to Christ:

> My mind was suddenly arrested...fastened to the awakening and upon my own conduct. I closed my books, yielded to this the influence which could not be resisted or mistaken, and was led by a spontaneous impulse to repentance, prayer, and entire submission and surrender of myself to my Maker and Redeemer.[185]

Noah Webster wanted our young nation to distinguish its language from that of its progenitor England. Harvard professor Oscar Handlin explains, "The language of the new nation was not the same as that of England, and he would ultimately compile a dictionary to prove it."[186] Of this achievement, Professor Handlin wrote, "His efforts...[had] the effect of standardizing the national language in written if not altogether in spoken form."[187]

Noah Webster labored long and hard and produced the monumental *American Dictionary of the English Language* in 1828. It is such a great book that reprints of this huge volume are still available. About one-third of the definitions in that book contain references to the Bible — showing how a Biblically literate man was writing for a Biblically literate audience. I just opened my copy of this huge book at random and found a Bible verse (Acts 2:46) used to amplify the definition of the word "gladness": "they...did eat their meat with *gladness* and singleness of heart." [emphasis his]

Aside from direct references to the Bible, Webster manages to squeeze in some thoughts of his own. For example, under the word "love" we find, "The christian [*sic*] *loves* his Bible. In short, we *love* whatever gives us pleasure and delight, whether animal or intellectual; and if our hearts are right, we *love* God above all things...."

The dictionary penned by Webster was a great gift to America. To this, the codification of our nation's language, we are in debt to the Bible. Professor Moss sums up, "The dictionary that he published in 1828 was written by the light of the Bible."[188]

The Scriptures played a pivotal role in the education of America during the settling era, the founding era, and even the first century or more of the republic. Secularism dominating American education is more of a Johnny-come-lately than vice versa. With it has come a wave of illiteracy—even more, "functional illiteracy."

UNIVERSITIES IN AMERICA

Those North American colonies that made the Bible the focal point of their settlements placed a high premium on education. For example, the Puritans settled Boston in 1630 and within the year made plans for the establishment of a college to train ministers of the gospel. That college was born in 1636. Its name? Harvard, which took up John 17:3 as its first goal: "And this is life eternal, that they know Thee to be the only very God and Jesus Christ, whom thou has sent" (The Geneva Bible).

Even to this day, etched in stone, is the original goal of Harvard:

> [O]ne of the next things we longed for and looked after was to advance learning and perpetuate it to posterity; dreading to leave an illiterate ministry to the churches, when our present ministers shall lie in the dust.[189]

Harvard was named after Rev. John Harvard, who died young of tuberculosis. He donated books and money for the founding of the new college the Puritans wanted to build in the Boston area. Even today, there is a large statue in the school's quad of Rev. Harvard seated with a gigantic book open on his lap. It is, of course, the Bible. The original motto of Harvard was (in Latin): Truth for Christ and the Church. In the twentieth century, when Harvard became more secularized, they cut the last part of the phrase, so that the motto is only Truth (Veritas). It was not secularism that produced Harvard, but Christianity.

In the "Harvard College Laws" of 1642 (from "New England's First

Fruits"), they quote a few Scriptures to show what the point of all their study is: to know God better. For example, they write:

> 2. Let every student be plainly instructed and earnestly pressed to consider well the main end of his life and studies is *to know God and Jesus Christ which is eternal life* (John 17:3).... And seeing the Lord only gives wisdom, let everyone seriously set himself by prayer in secret to seek it of Him (Prov. 2:3).

> 3. Everyone shall so exercise himself in reading the Scriptures twice a day that he shall be ready to give such an account of his proficiency therein, both in theoretical observations of the language and logic, and in practical and spiritual truths, as his tutor shall require, according to his ability; seeing *the entrance of the word giveth light, it giveth understanding to the simple* (Psalm 119:130).[190]

Harvard was essentially Christian longer than it was pagan. There is still some Christianity present, but it is not the dominant force by any means. But, again, paganism did not produce this great institution, the religion of Jesus did.

In the mid-1600s, some Puritans broke away from the Massachusetts colony and formed their own Bible-based settlement in Connecticut, beginning in the Hartford area. By the turn of the eighteenth century, some Puritans settled in New Haven. In 1700, ten clergymen stood around a table and donated their books so that a new college could be started in order to train future ministers. Each minister said, "I give these books for the founding of a college in this colony."[191] A year later, the General Assembly of Connecticut established a charter for the school.

It was named after a wealthy Puritan who made his fortune in international trade. Philanthropist Elihu Yale (1649-1721) made generous donations to "churches, schools, and missionary societies."[192] Mr. Yale had been born in Boston, but had been uprooted to England when he was three. He donated books and other valuable resources to the Congregationalists of Connecticut. For this endowment, the school was named after him.

Yale College and University was outwardly Christian for the first two and a half centuries of its existence. There are still some Christian remnants there. My mother's first cousin, William F. Buckley, Jr., caused quite a scandal in the early 1950s when he wrote a book, *God, Man, and Yale*, essentially documenting that Yale had largely jettisoned its

Christian roots. This was news to some people; hence, the uproar.

Liberals generally do not start these institutions. They only take them over like parasites and de-Christianize them, one step at a time. They do what Jesus warned the Pharisees against. To paraphrase Him: Woe to you, for you shut the kingdom of heaven in men's faces. You yourselves won't go in, and you prevent others from going in. A lot of these secularizing men and women at these once-great Christian institutions will have much to give an account for on Judgment Day.

Princeton is another great school with thoroughly Christian origins. It, too, has been Christian longer than it has been pagan. Princeton was founded by Presbyterian elders. The first president of Princeton was Rev. Jonathan Dickinson. He once noted (echoing the truths of Paul in Romans 1) that God has revealed truths about Himself so clearly in nature that "to call these into Question is not only Weakness and Ignorance; but the height of Stupidity and Madness." Thus, atheism, according to the first president of Princeton was "the height of stupidity and madness."[193] The motto of Princeton was "Under God's Power, She Flourishes." Dickinson once said, "Cursed be all that learning that is contrary to the cross of Christ."[194]

At the time of the American Revolution, Rev. John Witherspoon, a native of Scotland, was the president of Princeton. He was a strong Presbyterian. Scholar John Eidsmoe describes him as a key educator of key founding fathers, including James Madison, known as the Father of the Constitution. Says Eidsmoe: "John Witherspoon is best described as the man who shaped the men who shaped America. Although he did not attend the Constitutional Convention, his influence was multiplied many times over by those who spoke as well as by what was said."[195]

In 1776, New Jersey had elected John Witherspoon to the 1776 Continental Congress. Congress called for a national day of fasting and prayer on May 17, 1776. John Witherspoon was called upon to preach the sermon for that day. His topic was "The Dominion of Providence over the Affairs of Men."

Theologically, Princeton led the field for a century or two. Some of the greatest theological minds have taught at that school. For example, Jonathan Edwards was once the president of Princeton. Later, there were a father and son who were both brilliant, A. A. Hodge and his son Charles Hodge, two of the greatest theological minds this country ever produced. In the early part of the twentieth century, B. B. Warfield taught at Princeton. Later came Bruce Metzger, who until his recent death, was probably the most respected New Testament scholar alive. While he was not conservative on all points, he certainly believed the Bible is the Word of God, that Jesus is the divine savior who died for sinners, and that He rose again on the third day. Unfortunately, one with Dr. Metzger's views—no matter how well-qualified—could likely not get a job there today because his views are too conservative. Again, liberals don't create institutions. They just take them over. Out of the ashes of Princeton was born Westminster Theological Seminary in the 1920s. I count it a privilege to know personally the current president of Westminster, a diplomatic man who has worked hard at maintaining Biblical integrity at that school, Dr. Peter Lillback. I had the privilege of helping him write *George Washington's Sacred Fire* (Providence Forum, 2006), which documents the Christian faith and practice of George Washington.

We could go on and on about the Christian origins of these various colleges. William and Mary was founded by Christians for Christian purposes, as were Dartmouth, Brown, the University of Pennsylvania, New York University, and so on. In fact, the late D. James Kennedy pointed out that nearly every one of the first 123 colleges and universities founded in America were Christian in origin. Their very reason-for-being was the spread of the gospel of Jesus Christ.

In fact, Dr. Lutz, who is Roman Catholic, elaborates on how the founders had a thoroughly Christian education, beginning with an example of a key founding father:

> James Madison, who was...important for the writing of the Constitution, went to school at what is now Princeton in New Jersey, stayed an extra year, a fifth year, and...during which he studied...the Hebrew language. And so, he read could the Bible in the original. That was his goal, and he did. He had already learned Greek his first four years. And of course, the Bible was written in its original manifestation in Greek and [Hebrew]. So, by learning [Hebrew], he knew the Biblical languages, and he could go back and he could read it in the original, which he did—James Madison.
>
> Now, many of the founders knew Greek, because that was part of the education they learned, as the colleges they attended were usually seminaries. King's College, later to become Columbia, trained

ministers. Yale trained ministers, Harvard trained ministers, and so, they spent their time, effectively, in a kind of a pre-minister curriculum. And certainly, they learned the Bible—they learned it down to their fingertips. You know, we Catholics are jealous of this often. The Bible rolled off of their lips, easily. It was in their thoughts.... They all understood covenant theology. They all, in a sense, practiced covenant theology, by helping to write covenants.[196]

Author and speaker David Barton would concur. Barton has researched the founding fathers' own writings and actions as much as anyone I know of who is alive. I have had the privilege of interviewing him about half a dozen times for Coral Ridge or on the radio. I have visited the headquarters of Wallbuilders in Aledo, Texas (outside of Fort Worth) where he has collected tens of thousands of original and reprinted books, monographs, and proclamations—documenting our nation's Christian roots. Here is what David Barton said about the founding fathers and education:

The founding fathers all had a Christian worldview, at least by way of education. There is not a one of them—raised in home school, or in parochial schools with some of them, or in private schools with others, or in public schools with others, they went to all forms of education—that did not have a Biblical worldview or Christian approach to Christianity. There [are] none of them that were not raised on *The New England Primer*. And *The New England Primer* teaches students the Shorter Catechism, all 200 questions, takes them through Bible verses. That was the public school textbook of America until 1900. The founding fathers, themselves, reprinted that textbook that they had used for their own kids. In 1777-1795, people like Ben Franklin and Noah Webster and Sam Adams reprinted that book, so that is a great indication of what we learned at the elementary level. Then as you move on into university and college, you will find that as students prepared to go to Harvard, or to Yale, or to Princeton, and John Quincy Adams, or [John] Hancock, or any, they could not get into those schools until they had mastered the Greek language, because their freshman project at all those universities—William and Mary, and Dickenson, and Dartmouth, everything—was to make a handwritten translation of the Greek New Testament into English. And so, that was part of going to school, it was making that handwritten [translation]. And on average, young boys went to university between the ages of eleven and fourteen. So on average, they were making a translation of the Greek New Testament into English by the time they were eleven—eleven, twelve, thirteen. So there is, clearly, a Biblical approach to education that was taught, both in lower elementary and in secondary, and in graduate work, if you will, in universities.[197]

Therefore, anyone who continues to insist that Christianity and ignorance go hand in hand does not know what he or she is talking about.

CONCLUSION

When the Bible was the chief textbook of America, the country was predominately literate. Today, the Bible is not allowed in schools for the most part. What has been the result? Illiteracy. Crime. Ignorance of our past. Decline of basic decency and manners.

This chapter is in the section on the Bible and settling of America— i.e., the pre-founding era. However, there is a type of seamless garment between the two eras. That garment is made all the more seamless by the Great Awakening. Certainly, not all of the founders of our country were regenerate. But the vast majority were, and even the ones who were not had been weaned on Biblical truths.

Thus, the Bible helped shape and make America by being the chief textbook in one way or another in both the settling and founding eras of our nation.

EMBARKATION OF THE PILGRIMS   ROBERT W. WEIR
OIL ON CANVAS, 12' x 18'; COMMISSIONED 1837; PLACED IN THE U.S. CAPITOL ROTUNDA IN 1844.

The Mayflower Compact, November 11, 1620, was the forerunner of the U.S. Constitution. It begins as did America, "in the name of God. Amen."

CHAPTER 6

The Biblically Based Covenants: Forerunners to the Constitution

I will confirm my covenant between Me and you
and will greatly increase your numbers.
(God to Abraham, Genesis 17:2, NIV)

*T*HE American Constitution was not just written in 1787 through the genius of the founding fathers. It was in the making from 1620, when the Mayflower Compact was written, through the time the founders met in Philadelphia almost one-hundred-fifty years later. There were about a hundred or so Biblically based compacts, frames of government, charters, and so on, that paved the way for our key founding document. All of these documents were Christian. Most of these documents were produced by Puritans.

Please note something that applies to this whole book: We are not saying that some churchmen should rule America with *their* interpretation of the Bible. Heaven forbid. What we are saying is that America's best governing principles come from the Bible directly or indirectly, including the Biblical notion of covenant which gave rise to our Constitution.

Dr. Donald S. Lutz, author of *The Origins of American Constitutionalism*, is a key guide to this point. We will hear often in this chapter from this professor of political science at the University of Houston. He points out that the Bible provided the concept of the covenant. The Biblical notion of covenant was put into place by the early settlers, paving the way toward our national constitution. He said, "Indeed, the concept of federalism—the creation of a new unified entity that is indissoluble yet

117

preserves the freedom and integrity of its constituent parts—derives from the Biblical notion of covenant, which the dissenting Protestant colonists understood so well." [198] The old slogan, "E pluribus unum," which means "out of the many, one," meant to the founders: federalism—out of the many states, one government. Today it is usually misinterpreted as symbolic of pluralism, and multi-culturalism.

Recently, I spent a year teaching my adult Sunday school class at Coral Ridge Presbyterian Church on the Christian roots of America. I said repeatedly, "If you only remember one thing from this class, please remember this: the American Constitution is a by-product of the Biblical concept of the covenant." The chief mediators of this were the Puritans and their spiritual cousins, the Pilgrims.

THE MAYFLOWER COMPACT

How did America begin? "In the name of God. Amen." [199] Those are the opening words of the Mayflower Compact. The compact was an agreement for self-government that the Pilgrims wrote up to provide cohesion to their colony. In 1620, when they set out to settle in the northern parts of Virginia. At that time, this would have been in the New York City area, but they had been blown off course and they found themselves in the Cape Cod region. They were providentially hindered, on threat of their lives, from sailing further south, so the Pilgrim leaders had to act decisively to make sure that the colony stayed together as one.

Let me provide some background information. Of the approximately one hundred passengers onboard the *Mayflower*, about fifty were Pilgrims; two dozen were crew members and the rest "strangers," who were by default members of the English state church, the Church of England (which the Pilgrims were not). They did not share the Pilgrims' unique Biblical worldview, but were generally sympathetic toward them. Each crew member had a specific talent or skill and was hired for that particular role. For instance, Miles Standish the soldier was hired for protection; John Alden was hired for his cooperage (barrel-making) skills.

It was rumored that because the colony-to-be was now in unchartered territory and technically under no government's jurisdiction, some of the strangers on board were considering striking out on their own. The Pilgrims knew that would be disastrous for the colony, so they wrote up a political agreement for self-government. This was a political restating of the spiritual covenant they had made with each other, under God, when the congregation began about fourteen years earlier in Scrooby, England.

They wrote up a covenant statement which declared the Christian reason for their colony. It called upon God as a witness to their becoming an official political entity—"a civil body politic"—words we still use today:

> In the name of God, Amen. We whose names are underwritten, the loyal subjects of our dread sovereign lord, King James,…having undertaken for the glory of God, and advancement of the Christian faith, and the honor of our king and country, a voyage to plant the first colony in the northern parts of Virginia; do by these presents, solemnly and mutually in the presence of God and one of another, covenant and combine ourselves together into a civil body politic, for our better ordering and preservation, and furtherance of the ends aforesaid.[200]

Author on America's Christian heritage, Marshall Foster, notes: "They set up the Mayflower Compact, which was the first covenantal compact theory of government ever written down and lived out in a free society in the history of mankind. I think that's a rather unique accomplishment."[201] The great nineteenth-century historian, George Bancroft, writes: "In the cabin of the *Mayflower,* humanity recovered its rights, and instituted government on the basis of 'equal laws' enacted by all the people for 'the general good.'"[202] British historian Paul Johnson, author of *A History of the American People*, points out that the Mayflower Compact was "the single most important formative event in early American history, which would ultimately have an important bearing on the crisis of the American Republic."[203]

The Mayflower Compact was the first step toward the American Constitution, and it was based on the Biblical notion of covenant.

Pilgrim expert, Paul Jehle, notes this about the Mayflower Compact:

> This is very significant, and many historians have looked at this and recognized that this was, in essence, a parallel…a miniature Declaration of Independence. It was a declaration of dependence upon God. And what happened was this preamble, so to speak, this charter, The Mayflower Compact, though it was not respected by England…. England actually brought over the Pierce Patent one year later to make the Pilgrims licit or licensed by England, even though the Pilgrims were governed by The

Mayflower Compact, a self-governing document. And one must realize that the body of laws, the by-laws, so to speak, of that Mayflower Compact, compiled by 1636...the Pilgrim constitution in essence, linked together like the Declaration of Independence and the Constitution today, are very clear phrases of law.[204]

Marshall Foster notes how the Pilgrims had a positive influence on the politics of their spiritual cousins, the Puritans:

The Pilgrims were the foundation of our government upon that covenantal, compact theory of government where men elect their representatives based upon their character. So, also, our form of government with the three branches of government. They were Congregationalists. When the Puritans came over ten years later, they were Episcopalians. They believed in top-down, church-controlled church state. Well, do you know that the Pilgrims, especially their doctor [Dr. Samuel Fuller], converted the Puritans when they came over because of his love for them. He went and helped them as they were dying of the same diseases that the Pilgrims had endured ten years before. And he helped John Winthrop and the Puritans understand not only Christian love and charity, but he helped them understand the congregational way. And they gave up their Episcopal form of government and became Congregationalists. And that had tremendous ramifications on our form of government. For if we would have had the king's charter over all of the colonies, if the Episcopal church had been the state church of America, from the very beginning, which it would have been had the Puritans maintained their dominant Episcopal approach, there would have been no religious liberty in America. And there would have never been a Congress with a Senate and a House of Representatives and a President; it would have been a top-down Episcopalian type of government. Remember: a church government, the church polity always precedes a governmental polity. Your religious polity—whatever religion you are, whether it's Hindu, Buddhist, Islamic, whatever the church polity or structure is of your church community—will be the structure of your governmental community. So you look, for example, at the Islamic communities of the world. What is the structure of their religion? Top-down. Mohammed said, you know, this is what the mullahs say, and you obey or die, okay? Well, what form of government does that roll into, in their state?

> It rolls into a totalitarian dictatorship. You will find no democra-
> cies among the Islamic states, true democracies. Why? Because
> of their religious presuppositions.[205]

Thus, we see the important theological views play not only for one's religious convictions, but even for their politics.

The Puritans modified their church-government over time to the
Congregational model. In the eighteenth century, with the immigration of
hundreds of thousands of Presbyterians, that representative form of church
government became the model and base for our republican (lowercase "r")
form of government.

We call the Separatists who formed Plymouth "the Pilgrims" because
of 1 Peter 2:11, where they viewed themselves as pilgrims and sojourners
on this earth. This group uniquely set the tone for this nation. Despite
our intense secularism today, we pay the Pilgrims indirect homage by
recognizing the Constitution as the supreme law of the land. They wrote
its precursor and began the whole process.

WINTHROP'S "MODEL OF CHRISTIAN CHARITY"

We heard in a previous chapter about Rev. John Winthrop's classic
sermon, "A Model of Christian Charity." This was the "city on a hill"
sermon, preached on board the *Arbella*, before about a thousand Puritan
immigrants on seventeen ships on their way to the New World. Dr. Paul
Jehle, a pastor in Plymouth, author, and an expert on American history,
notes that that sermon was really a treatise on covenant theology. Dr.
Jehle observes:

> This "Model of Christian Charity" was really a dissertation on
> taking covenant theology, that the Puritans had believed from the
> Reformation, and applying it to a new plantation. So, the entire
> sermon and then the written version was a [summary] of what it
> meant to walk in covenant with God and walk in covenant with
> one another and to be accountable.

The Puritans set up local towns. These, too, were held together by covenants.
This covenant concept is key to understanding America. A covenant involved
three parties—God, and the citizens of the community one to another.
The Declaration of Independence was, in a sense, a declaration of depend-
ing on God, as well as independence from England. Dr. Jehle goes on:

"I would say that the idea of covenant is one of the strongest elements from the Puritan community that we have embraced in American society."[206]

Some people have totally discredited anything related to the Puritans because of the Salem witchcraft trials. Those trials became a disaster because they neglected to follow the Biblical mandates, not because they followed them. The Puritan leader, Increase Mather, was away in England during the witch mess. When he returned, he was greatly upset, and he insisted that the colony return to the Biblical practice that every accusation be secured by *two* witnesses. Once this principle was applied, the trials came to a screeching halt, and there was no more hysteria. Amazingly, the leaders repented soon after for the twenty people that had been unjustly executed for allegedly being witches. It was an ugly chapter in the American Puritan story. Thankfully, it was not representative of their contribution to American constitutionalism—as their covenants were.

PURITANS AND COVENANTS

The Puritans attempted to create the New Jerusalem in the New World. In this, they failed. Nonetheless, they became the midwives to our liberties. How so? They gleaned the Word of God, looking for principles of government, law, education, and so on. In 1865, John Palfrey, author of *History of New England*, wrote: "The Puritan searched the Bible, not only for principles and rules, but for mandates, and, when he could find none of these, for analogies, to guide him in precise arrangements of public administration, and in the minutest points of individual conduct."[207] One of the key areas of importance of the Puritans were the Biblically-based covenants—their *political* charters, which is the focus of this chapter.

All of the Puritan settlements were Bible commonwealths. They tried to base their church practices, their laws, their customs, their style of government—everything—on the Scriptures. As Paul Johnson put it, "But authority lay in the Bible, not the minister and, in the last resort, every man and woman decided 'in the light which Almighty God gave them' what the Bible meant." Johnson goes on to say, "It explains why New England religion was so powerful a force in people's lives and of such direct and continuing assistance in building a new society from nothing."[208]

The Puritans began by making spiritual covenants with each other before God. They had done this in England before they came here, but they also made covenants here. For example, on August 6, 1629, the Puritans who arrived and settled Salem entered into a "holy covenant" to form their "Church State." Here is the context of that, as described by America's first great historian, nineteenth century, George Bancroft:

> In the last days of June, the band of two hundred arrived at Salem.... They were not so much a body politic as a church in the wilderness, seeking, under a visible covenant, to have fellowship with God, as a family of adopted sons.... The governor was moved to set apart the twentieth of July to be a solemn day of humiliation, for the choice of a pastor and a teacher at Salem....

They voted on this, and Bancroft comments: "Such is the origin of the use of the ballot on this continent...." One of the first elections in America was by Puritans to choose their minister.

Bancroft continues: "[T]he church, like that of Plymouth, was self-constituted, on the principle of the independence of each religious community. It did not ask the assent of the king, or recognize him as its head; its officers were set apart and ordained among themselves; it used no liturgy; it rejected unnecessary ceremonies, and reduced the simplicity of Calvin to a still plainer standard." [209]

When the Puritans founded Salem, they did so by forming a covenant. Puritan divine Cotton Mather quotes the Salem covenant:

> We covenant with our Lord, and one with another; and we do bind our selves in the presence of God, to walk together in all his ways, according as he is pleased to reveal himself unto us in his blessed word of truth; and do explicitly, in the name and fear of God, profess and protest to walk as followeth, through the power and grace of our Lord Jesus Christ. [210]

SAMPLES OF PURITAN COVENANTS

Here are just a few samples of additional Puritan covenants of New England:

⋆ The Covenant of the Charles-Boston Church (1630)

> In the Name of our Lord Jesus Christ, and in Obedience to his holy Will and Divine Ordinance, We whose Names are here under written, being by his most wise and good providence brought together

into this part of America in the Bay of Massachusetts, and desirous to unite ourselves into one Congregation or Church under the Lord Jesus Christ our Head, in such sort as becometh all those whom he hath redeemed, and sanctified to himself, DO hereby solemnly and religiously (as in his most holy Presence) promise and bind ourselves, to walk in all our ways according to the Rule of the Gospel, and in all sincere Conformity to his holy Ordinances, and in mutual Love and Respect each to other, so near as God shall give us Grace.[211]

★ The Dedham Covenant, 1636

...We whose names are here unto subscribed do, in the fear and reverence of our Almighty God, mutually and severally promise amongst ourselves and each to profess and practice one truth according to that most perfect rule, the foundation whereof is ever lasting love.[212]

★ Covenant of Exeter, New Hampshire, July 5, 1639

...considering with ourselves the holy will of God and our own necessity, that we should not live without wholesome laws & government amongst us, of which we are altogether destitute; do in the name of Christ & in the sight of God combine ourselves together, to erect & set up amongst us such government as shall be to our best discerning, agreeable to the will of God, professing ourselves subjects to our Sovereign Lord King Charles, according to the Liberties of our English Colony of the Massachusetts & binding ourselves solemnly by the grace & help of Christ & in his name & fear to submit ourselves to such godly & Christian laws as are established in the realm of England to our best knowledge....[213]

The founders of Connecticut also created a very significant charter for self-government, The Fundamental Orders of Connecticut. Have you ever wondered why Connecticut calls itself the Constitution state? The U.S. Constitution was written in Pennsylvania. But in 1639, the Puritan founders of Connecticut wrote up the first complete constitution in the New World. It was based on a 1638 sermon of their founder, Rev. Thomas Hooker. Notice these references to God and His Son in the preamble to the Fundamental Orders of Connecticut:

★ "...it has pleased Almighty God by the wise disposition of His divine providence...."

* "...the Word of God requires...."

* "...an orderly and decent government established according to God...."

* "...the liberty and purity of the Gospel of our Lord Jesus which we now profess, as also the discipline of the churches, which according to the truth of the said Gospel is now practiced among us...."[214]

Based on this godly foundation, they all covenanted and combined themselves together as a united group. This constitution was signed on January 14, 1639, almost one-hundred and fifty years before the U.S. Constitution was drafted. It has been called "the first written constitution...in the history of nations."[215] Like the Mayflower Compact, the Fundamental Orders of Connecticut vests the authority in the consent of the people. "We the People" in the U.S. Constitution of 1787 articulates the same radical concept.

In his *Beginnings of New England* (1889), John Fiske points out that the Fundamental Orders of Connecticut "marked the beginnings of American democracy, of which Thomas Hooker deserves more than any other man to be called the father. *The government of the United States today is in lineal descent more nearly related to that of Connecticut than to that of any of the other thirteen colonies....*"[216] [emphasis mine]

I disagree with Fiske in that John Calvin should be given that honor. Hooker was a Calvinist, but so also were the Pilgrims, the Puritans, the Huguenots, the Presbyterians, and so on. This is why some historians have called John Calvin, "the virtual founder of America."[217] The first great historian of America was a Unitarian, not a Calvinist: George Bancroft. But he once said that he who will not honor the memory of John Calvin knows little of the origins of American liberty.

The link between the Puritans' constitutionalism and the American Constitution is no minor point. Their governing documents were political versions of their spiritual covenants. And all of these political compacts and constitutions paved the way for the Constitution. Modern secularists like to point out that the Constitution doesn't mention God (although it does: "in the year of our Lord..."). But regardless of that, Constitutionalism as enjoyed by Americans is a major contribution of the Puritans, who were unquestionably committed Christians. The framework for America's liberty under law was created by Christianity.

THE NEW ENGLAND ARTICLES OF CONFEDERATION

After so many of these colonies in New England created their political charters, representatives of several of the colonies met in 1643 and wrote up the New England Articles of Confederation. They stated why they had emigrated in the first place:

> Whereas we all came into these parts of America with one and the same end and aim, namely, to advance the Kingdom of our Lord Jesus Christ and to enjoy the liberties of the Gospel in purity with peace....[218]

It was the gospel of Jesus Christ that gave birth to America.

THEIR "PERFECT TECHNOLOGY"

The aforementioned Dr. Donald S. Lutz, author of *The Origins of American Constitutionalism*, has researched and written extensively on the link between the Biblical-type covenant and the Constitution. I interviewed Dr. Lutz in 2005 for Coral Ridge Ministries for our television special, *One Nation Under God*, hosted by the late Dr. D. James Kennedy. It documents the Christian roots of the nation. Dr. Lutz remarked to our television audience that the tools the Pilgrims, the Puritans, and other dissenting Protestants brought were not effective, but one "tool" they brought was effective. That was covenant-making, which they learned from the Scriptures. Said Dr. Lutz:

> These poor people came to the New World, they had the wrong technologies, their plows would not work, their houses that they constructed were inappropriate for the weather. All their technology was wrong, except for one technology they brought with them, which was the ability to use covenants to create communities. It was the perfect technology. It was the technology that mattered, that allowed them to survive all up and down the coast.[219]

When Dr. Lutz first began to study the Constitution and its sources many years ago, he began to see that its roots lay in the Puritan covenants long before it, which, in turn, got back to the teaching about covenants in the Bible:

> Our search takes us to the earliest state constitutions, then to colonial documents of foundation that are essentially constitutional such as the Pilgrim Code of Law, and then to proto-constitutions

such as the Mayflower Compact. The political covenants written by English colonists in America lead us to the church covenants written by English colonists in America lead us to the church covenants written by radical Protestants in the late 1500s and early 1600s, and these in turn lead us back to the Covenant tradition of the Old Testament. The American constitutional tradition derives in much of its form and content from the Judeo-Christian tradition as interpreted by the radical Protestant sects to which belonged so many of the original European settlers in British North America.[220]

Dr. Lutz also notes that the Biblical notion of covenant, as mediated by Calvinists, is a major key to understanding the early governments in colonial America—beyond just Puritan New England. He said this, "…essentially Calvinist sects predominated in New England, most of the central colonies (including the Dutch, Swedish, and German settlers), and the piedmont [sic] region of the South." It was this particular strain of Christianity that helped produce these political arrangements. Lutz writes: "Wherever dissenting Protestantism went, so, too, went their church covenants."[221]

COVENANTAL VIEWS

The Christian dissidents in America—most notably the Puritans—that established Christian covenants were creating on this soil what their Calvinistic brethren were creating back in Europe in certain places. God Himself was viewed as the source of the covenant. Dr. Marshall Foster observes:

> God began the covenant concept and talks about it in Scripture with His covenant with His Son, where He gave the world to His Son in covenant and in relationship in an agreement. A covenant is an arrangement where there are stipulations that one party does something and the other party does something and they agree to accomplish a task. And this is what we see throughout Scripture in God's relationship with man. He does it again and again through various covenants. This is also true, taking it to the governmental level, of our relationship man to man. A covenant then is a relationship in which both parties are accountable to come together; they sign an agreement and that agreement is that "I will do this, and you will do this, and we will accomplish this

task." Our form of government is a covenant, compact theory of government based upon the original Protestant views of covenant government that were developed all the way back to the times of Calvin…right through the Declaration of Independence, which is a Christian resistance document actually. It's a document that says [in effect], 'We have the right to take this king and de-king him, because he has lost his authority before God and man, because there are [twenty-eight] reasons that we are going to state how he has broken his covenant with his people.' So the Declaration of Independence itself is a covenant document in which the covenant has been broken and a new covenant is being developed, and the new covenant says, 'This king broke his covenant, so now we must have a covenant, one with another, for a new nation.' And they were rationalizing or reasoning with the nations of the world by saying, 'This is why we must do this.' And that's what the whole Declaration was about. And it ended with the covenant statement, didn't it? That 'with firm reliance upon Divine Providence, we pledge our lives, our fortunes and our sacred honor.' That is the stamp of a covenant.[222]

I believe one cannot truly understand American history without understanding its Biblical roots.

The Christian Motivation for the First Secular Compact

God was always a witness for these covenants. But the first colony that chose not to mention Him did so because they were super-religious. They did not want to take His name in vain. Lutz notes, "Ironically, the first secularized compact in colonial history originated in a colony whose members were so religious that taking oaths was regarded as tantamount to taking God's name in vain. Calling upon the Lord as witness amounted to an oath, so the people of Providence (Rhode Island) produced a covenant-derived compact, the Providence Agreement of August 20, 1637." Who was sovereign in this? The people. Lutz writes: "…the signers are sovereign. This is the first explicit use of popular sovereignty in America."[223] God only is ultimately sovereign. Thus, the people are answerable to God in their consciences. The American Christian idea of political sovereignty, here, as elsewhere, was toward other men and otherwise limited and under God's authority.

The Bible was the source of all this. Lutz writes, "The tribes of Israel shared a covenant that made them a nation. American federalism originated, at least in part, in the dissenting Protestants' familiarity with the Bible."[224] And so, while common law was an important part of British tradition,[225] what the Americans were creating here—by using the Scriptures as their guide—was breaking with these traditions, or rather amending them upon an even greater Biblical understanding. Lutz writes, "But in the American constitutional tradition, what *replaced* common law was a new political technique, the written constitution."[226] By the time the founders of America wrote the Constitution, they had a rich well to draw from.

THE MASSACHUSETTS BODY OF LIBERTIES

An important document in the history of America and its founding was the Massachusetts Body of Liberties. This was a list of legal rights and civil liberties that were based on the Bible and English common law. They were compiled by a minister who was also a lawyer, Rev. Nathaniel Ward. Bruce Frohnen is the editor of a massive book of early important American documents, entitled, *The American Republic: Primary Sources*. He says this about Ward's document: "The Massachusetts Body of Liberties is generally seen as an important source of rights recognized in the first ten amendments to the American Constitution, or Bill of Rights."[227] Dr. Jehle says this about the Massachusetts Body of Liberties:

> So, you have two key elements in the Massachusetts Body of Liberties that became permanent parts of American society by the time the Constitution was ratified. One, that civil government had a limited purpose to administer justice, and was a minister of God, accountable to God. And two, that the individual, also, had liberties given by God that government was to respect. So, you had this twofold idea, which you can see today in the Constitution and the Bill of Rights, and particularly, because the Bill of Rights is dealing with the liberties that the people have that government must respect, and the idea that the civil government, itself, has a specific ordained ministry. And, of course, the idea that civil government is a minister of God is implied and stated in the Declaration of Independence, the charter of America; whereas, the Constitution is more like the by-laws that administer that charter. So, you see these elements in Puritan New England coming through clearly later on—a hundred years later.

These principles get back to the Magna Carta, which was based on Biblical principles, as Dr. Jehle notes:

> From the inception of the Magna Carta in 1215, this idea from the Scriptures that trial by jury, innocent till proven guilty, the idea of your liberties and private property being protected, that no property can be taken without consent of the individual, was a legacy brought by the Puritans to New England and embodied in the Massachusetts Body of Liberties, as well as the Fundamental Orders of Connecticut, and many other documents preceding the Declaration of Independence and the Constitution....[228]

WILLIAM PENN

Although the Puritans were the main mediators of the Biblical-type covenant, there were others also influenced by the Calvinistic stream. For example, William Penn, the Quaker minister, learned much from the French Huguenots when he was in France early in his life. Dr. Peter Lillback, president of Westminster Theological Seminary and the founder/ director of Providence Forum, notes:

> There was William Penn, a Quaker minister, who realized that religious coercion always failed, and he provided for religious liberty for everyone who settled there. In fact, his Charter of Privileges in 1701, begins and ends with the same language, "Religious liberty is absolutely necessary for a person to be happy. It will never be in any way limited, coerced, or taken away, as long as people live here." So, he said it twice, because he wanted everyone to remember how important it was. And so, all the religions, Protestant, Catholic, the independents, they all could come to Pennsylvania and have religious liberty.[229]

Here is what Penn said in the "the Great Law," the first Legislative Act in the Colony of Pennsylvania:

> Whereas the glory of Almighty God and the good of mankind is the reason and end of government, and, therefore, government itself is a venerable ordinance of God, and forasmuch as it is principally devised and intended by the Proprietary and Governor and freemen of Pennsylvania and territories thereunto belonging, to make and establish such laws as shall best preserve true Christian and civil liberty, in opposition to all unchristian, licentious, and

unjust practices, whereby God may have his due, Caesar his due, and the people their due....[230]

What is government to the Christian? It is our civil duty before God.

CONCLUSION

Dr. Donald S. Lutz said that Americans "invented modern Constitutionalism and bequeathed it to the world."[231] That is quite a gift. In fact, the U.S. Constitution has become the prototype for most of the nations of the world that have a written charter for self-government.

It all gets back to the Bible, which inspired different colonies with slightly different variations in theology, to write up a simple document that captured that colony's relationship between God and the colonists. Thus, Dr. Lutz could conclude:

> The United States Constitution was the culmination of a constitutional experience already one hundred fifty years old, and it derived from but was significantly different from that of Englishmen in the mother country.[232]

In short, no Bible, no Puritan covenants. No Puritan covenants, no U.S. Constitution. This is a history lesson most of us have never learned. It is a lesson that America by and large has forgotten. The Bible thus played a critical role in the shaping of America by teaching this concept of covenants, which has been enshrined for all time by the Constitution.

This whole thing stopped working when God was taken out of the equation. People no longer consider themselves accountable to God. We are fast approaching the condition of ancient Israel under the Judges, where every man did that which was right in his own eyes. Without accountability, there can be no covenant—just an agreement between people that can be broken.

The founding fathers met in Independence Hall in Philadelphia, where they declared independence in 1776, and created a constitution in "the year of our Lord," 1787.

PART THREE

The Bible and the Founding of America

*S*OME thinkers today will acknowledge that Christianity and the Bible may have been important to some of the original colonists—certainly, the Pilgrims and the Puritans—but when they speak of the founding era, they argue that the founders were largely secularists. Were the founding fathers Deist by and large, and did they intend America to be a secular nation? What does the evidence actually show? Also, considering America's shortcomings, including those during the founding era, how can we talk about the nation having ever been "Christian"?

Patrick Henry (VA), John Rutledge (SC), and
George Washington, (VA)

LIBRARY OF CONGRESS

PAINTED BY T. H. MATTESON, 1849

On September 7, 1774, when the founding fathers first met, they had a lengthy prayer meeting, led by the Rev. Jacob Duché. He read from Psalm 35, which was encouraging to them, as the British were clamping down. Congress has been praying ever since, though not as fervently.

CHAPTER 7

The Bible and the Founders of America

Your word is a lamp to my feet and a light to my path.
(Psalms 119:105)

THERE is no book that had more influence on the founding fathers of America than the Bible. The purpose of this chapter is to look at more of the evidence for this. Some of the people listed below were *not* believers in Jesus Christ or the Bible, although the vast majority of them were. Yet they all appealed to the Bible.

As Dr. Donald Lutz once put it, the founders knew the Bible "down to their fingertips."[233] Consider these various leaders in the founding era of our country and consider what they said about God, His Son, or the Bible. These include signers of the Declaration of Independence and signers of the Constitution. Most of the entries that follow are men, but on occasion I have listed alphabetically critical institutions from the founding era.

★ **John Adams** (1735-1826), who was a leading founding father, was the one who suggested that George Washington should lead the Continental Army. This ultimately led to our victory over the British and to Washington presiding over the Constitutional convention and serving as our first president. John Adams also wrote the oldest, longest-lasting constitution in the world, that of his native state of Massachusetts in 1780.[234] In 1775, John Adams said this: "I would ask by what law the parliament has authority over America? By the law in the Old and New Testament it has none; by the law of nature and nations it has none.... The two characteristics of this people, religion and humanity, are strongly marked in all their proceedings. We are not exciting a rebellion. Resistance by arms against usurpation and lawless violence is not rebellion by the law of God or the land. Resistance to lawful authority makes rebellion." [235]

Adams believed that religion and morality were indispensable to our national prosperity (a sentiment shared by George Washington). Adams declared: "We have no government armed with power capable of contending with human passions unbridled by morality and religion. Avarice, ambition, revenge, or gallantry would break the strongest cords of our Constitution as a whale goes through a net. Our Constitution was made only for a moral and religious people. It is wholly inadequate to the government of any other." [236]

Adams wrote a letter to Thomas Jefferson after both were out of office, in which he declared:

> The general principles, on which the Fathers achieved independence, were the only Principles in which that beautiful Assembly of young Gentlemen could Unite.... And what were these general Principles? I answer, the general Principles of Christianity, in which all these Sects were United: And the general Principles of English and American Liberty, in which all those young Men United, and which had United all Parties in America, in Majorities sufficient to assert and maintain her Independence.
>
> Now I will avow, that I then believed, and now believe, that those general Principles of Christianity, are as eternal and immutable, as the Existence and Attributes of God; and that those Principles of Liberty, are as unalterable as human Nature and our terrestrial, mundane System. [237]

★ **Samuel Adams** (1722–1803) was one of the greatest of the founding fathers. He constantly pushed for American independence. He has been described accurately as the lightning rod of the American War for Independence. America's first great historian, nineteenth-century author, George Bancroft, said of Sam Adams: "...no one man had done so much to bring about independence as the elder Adams...." [238] Bancroft adds: "He was the first who asserted the independency of the colonies upon the supreme authority of the kingdom."[239] He played a key role in the Boston Town Meeting, which played a key role in independence. He organized the "Committees of Correspondence," which David Barton points out was an alternative media for the colonists seeking independence.

Samuel Adams was a devout man who committed his life to Christ while a young man at Harvard, as the Great Awakening was sweeping through at that time. He once called himself "the last of the Puritans."[240] In 1775, Adams said: "Call me an enthusiast...this union among the colonies and warmth of affection can be attributed to nothing less than the agency of the Supreme Being. If we believe that he superintends and directs the affairs of empires, we have reason to expect the restoration and establishment of the public liberties."[241]

Adams said: "Has the king of Great Britain ever yet discovered the least degree of that princely virtue, clemency? It is my opinion that his heart is more obdurate, and his disposition toward the people of America more unrelenting and malignant, than was that of Pharaoh toward the Israelites in Egypt. No foreign power can consistently yield comfort to rebels, or enter into any kind of treaty with these colonies, till they declare themselves independent."[242] We see here a common practice of the founders—an appeal to Scripture and Scriptural themes. They were all Biblically literate, even the few unbelievers amongst them.

Historian George Bancroft also said of Adams: "The austere purity of his life witnessed the sincerity of his profession. Evening and morning his house was a house of prayer; and no one more revered the Christian sabbath. He was a tender husband, an affectionate parent."[243]

Author Robert Flood notes: "Samuel Adams had been telling his countrymen for years that America had to take her stand against tyranny. He regarded individual freedom as 'the law of the Creator' and a Christian right documented in the New Testament."[244]

On March 20, 1797, in a Proclamation of a Day of Fast, Samuel Adams, as the Governor of Massachusetts, declared: "I conceive we cannot better express ourselves than by humbly supplicating the Supreme Ruler of the world...that the confusions that are and have been among the nations may be overruled by the promoting and speedily bringing in the holy and happy period when the kingdoms of our Lord and Saviour Jesus Christ may be everywhere established, and the people willingly bow to the sceptre of Him who is the Prince of Peace."[245]

Furthermore, Samuel Adams wrote "The Rights of the Colonists," a historic 1772 statement—one of the key forerunners articulating why America should sever its ties to Great Britain. In this document, Adams included a section entitled, "The Rights of the Colonists as Christians," in which he declared:

> The right to freedom being the gift of God Almighty.... The rights of the Colonists as Christians...may best be understood by reading and carefully studying the institutions of The Great Law Giver and the Head of the Christian Church, which are to be found clearly written and promulgated in the New Testament.[246]

Thus, the Bible and the Christian faith were critical to the life and beliefs of our nation's key founders.

★ **Samuel Chase** (1741-1811), was a signer of the Declaration of Independence, who served as a U.S. Supreme Court Justice, 1796-1811. In 1799, in *Runkel v. Winemiller,* he wrote: "Religion is of general and public concern, and on its support depend, in great measure, the peace and good order of government, the safety and happiness of the people. By our form of government, the Christian religion is the established religion; and all sects and denominations of Christians are placed upon the same equal footing, and are equally entitled to protection in their religious liberty."[247]

★ **Chaplains in America** are older than the nation. This includes military chaplains and legislative chaplains. In fact, when the ACLU challenged the chaplain program in the early 1980s, the Supreme Court ruled against them because of the historical reality of the whole chaplaincy program, which predated the writing of the Constitution in 1787. George Bancroft said during the time of the Revolutionary War: "Eloquent chaplains kept alive the custom of daily prayer and weekly sermons."[248] Also during the war, some were encouraged to serve as chaplains, if they were not inclined to soldier. Bancroft writes, "For the relief of scrupulous consciences in the army, it was made an instruction that dissenting clergymen might act as chaplains."[249]

When George Washington first received a copy of the Declaration of Independence on July 9, 1776, he made an order to hire chaplains in every regiment. These were to be "persons of good Characters and exemplary lives." Washington said, "The blessing and protection of Heaven are at all times necessary but especially so in times of public distress and danger." And he added, "The General hopes and trusts, that every officer and man, will endeavour so to live, and act, as becomes a Christian Soldier, defending the dearest Rights and Liberties of his country."[250] Thus, chaplains have been important in the history of America from the very beginning.

★ **The Continental Congress** often called for days of prayer. Even the very first time they met in 1774, the first question was on the subject: Should they open in prayer? They voted in the affirmative, so on the first official day of Congress, they had a lengthy prayer service. George Bancroft notes: "At the opening of congress, Washington was present, standing in prayer, and Henry and Randolph and Lee and Jay and Rutledge and Gadsden; and by their side the Presbyterians and Congregationalists; the Livingstons, Sherman, Samuel Adams, John Adams; and others of New England, who believed that a rude soldiery were then infesting the dwellings and taking the lives of their friends...the minister, with the earnestness of the best divines of New England, unexpectedly burst into an extempore prayer for America, for the congress, for Massachusetts, and especially for Boston."[251] Here are the founding fathers meeting together as a group for the first time, and what do they do? Conduct a lengthy prayer meeting.

Samuel Adams was the first leading colonist to have called for congress in the first place—representatives from all the thirteen colonies to meet in a location somewhat mid-point: Philadelphia. George Bancroft describes what happens when he returned to his native state: "The congress of Massachusetts, though destitute of munitions of war, armed vessels, military stores, and money, had confidence that a small people, resolute in its convictions outweighs an empire. On the return of Samuel Adams, they adopted all the recommendations of the Continental Congress. They established a secret correspondence with Canada. They entreated the ministers of the gospel in their colony 'to assist in avoiding that dreadful slavery with which all were now threatened.'

"With such words they adjourned, to keep the annual Thanksgiving which they themselves had appointed, finding occasion in their distress to rejoice at 'the smiles of Divine Providence on the union in their own province and throughout the continent.'"[252]

Bancroft notes: "From the sermons of memorable divines, who were gone to a heavenly country, leaving their names precious among the people of God on earth, a brief collection of faithful testimonies to the cause of God and his New England people was circulated by the press, that the hearts of the rising generation might know what had been the great end of the plantations, and count it their duty and their glory to continue in those right ways of the Lord wherein their fathers walked before them." What was the make-up of the colonists at this time? Bancroft observes, "The thirteen colonies were all Protestant; even in Maryland the Catholics formed scarcely an eighth, perhaps not more than a twelfth part of the population; their presence in other provinces, except Pennsylvania, was hardly perceptible."[253] Researcher Benjamin Hart noted that as late as 1776, 99.8 percent of the people in this country claimed to be Christian (98.4 percent claiming to be Protestants and 1.4 percent Catholic).[254]

How did freedom-loving British leaders view the Congress? William Pitt (whose name has been immortalized in the city name of Pittsburgh), who became the Earl of Chatham, said to Ben Franklin: "The congress... is the most honorable assembly of statesmen since those of the ancient Greeks and Romans in the most virtuous times."[255]

★ **John Dickinson** (1732-1808), was a signer of the United States Constitution, who also wrote the first draft of the forerunner to the Constitution, i.e., The Articles of Confederation in 1776. Author Bill Federer notes that John Dickinson is best remembered as "The Penman of the Revolution."[256] During those difficult days, he encouraged the colonists to trust in the Lord: "But, above all, let us implore the protection of that infinitely good and gracious Being 'by whom kings reign, and princes decree justice...' [Proverbs 8:15]."[257]

Regarding the country's rights, he also noted:

> A communication of her rights in general, and particularly of that great one, the foundation of all the rest—that their property, acquired with so much pain and hazard, should be disposed of by none but themselves—or to use the beautiful and emphatic language of the sacred Scriptures "that they should sit every man under his vine, and under his fig-tree, and NONE SHOULD MAKE THEM AFRAID...." [Micah 4:4] [emphasis his][258]

Thus, the Bible provided the ideal to which the penman of the Revolution appealed. His readers would agree.

⋆ **Ben Franklin** (1706-1790) signed both the Declaration of Independence and the Constitution. From his own writings, he was not an evangelical; however, he was not a atheist either. For example, Ben Franklin included when he wrote the cornerstone inscription of Pennsylvania Hospital: "In the year of Christ, 1755."[259] Perhaps, most significantly, during the Constitutional convention, when the whole proceeding was grinding to a halt, he provided the turning point by giving an impassioned plea for prayer. I have reproduced some of that classic speech in a later chapter, named after a phrase from that speech ("Can an Empire Rise without His Aid?").

Years earlier, as the storm clouds of war were gathering, Ben Franklin declared: "The eyes of all Christendom are now upon us, and our honor as a people is become a matter of the utmost consequence. If we tamely give up our rights in this contest, a century to come will not restore us in the opinion of the world; we shall be stamped with the character of dastards, poltroons, and fools; and be despised and trampled upon, not by this haughty, insolent nation only, but by all mankind. Present inconveniences are therefore to be borne with fortitude, and better times expected."[260]

⋆ **Alexander Hamilton** (1755?-1803) was a signer of the Constitution. He was the architect of America's financial success. That's why his face is on the ten dollar bill. He was the author of most of the lengthy letters that comprise *The Federalist Papers.* Hamilton said, "The Supreme Intelligence who rules the world has constituted an eternal law, which is obligatory upon all mankind, prior to any human institution whatever. He gave existence to man, together with the means of preserving and beautifying that existence; and invested him with an inviolable right to pursue liberty and personal safety. Natural liberty is a gift of the Creator to the whole human race. Civil liberty is only natural liberty, modified and secured by the sanctions of civil society. It is not dependent on human caprice; but it is conformable to the constitution of man, as well as necessary to the well-being of society."[261]

After the completion of the Constitutional Convention of 1787, Alexander Hamilton stated:

For my own part, I sincerely esteem it a system which without the finger of God, never could have been suggested and agreed upon by such a diversity of interests.[262]

Hamilton also wanted to see a religious organization. He wrote, "Let an association be formed to be denominated "The Christian Constitutional Society," its object to be first: the support of the Christian religion; second: the support of the United States."[263]

★ **John Hancock** (1737-1793) was the president of the Continental Congress that declared independence from Great Britain in July 1776. On April 15, 1775, the Massachusetts Provincial Congress declared a Day of Public Humiliation, Fasting and Prayer, signed by the President of the Provincial Congress, John Hancock:

> In circumstances dark as these, it becomes us, as Men and Christians, to reflect that, whilst every prudent Measure should be taken to ward off the impending Judgements.... All confidence must be withheld from the Means we use; and reposed only on that GOD who rules in the Armies of Heaven, and without whose Blessing the best human Counsels are but Foolishness—and all created Power Vanity;
>
> It is the Happiness of His Church that, when the Powers of Earth and Hell combine against it...that the Throne of Grace is of the easiest access—and its Appeal thither is graciously invited by the Father of Mercies, who has assured it, that when His Children ask Bread He will not give them a Stone....
>
> RESOLVED, That it be, and hereby is recommended to the good People of this Colony of all Denominations, that THURSDAY the Eleventh Day of May next be set apart as a Day of Public Humiliation, Fasting and Prayer...to confess the sins...to implore the Forgiveness of all our Transgression...and a blessing on the Husbandry, Manufactures, and other lawful Employments of this People; and especially that the union of the American Colonies in Defence of their Rights (for hitherto we desire to thank Almighty GOD) may be preserved and confirmed.... And that AMERICA may soon behold a gracious Interposition of Heaven.

By Order of the Provincial Congress,
John Hancock, President.[264]

Hancock later became governor of Massachusetts and, in 1791, he declared a statewide proclamation of public thanksgiving to Almighty God. He thanked God for all sorts of blessings that He had poured out, but above all he was thankful to God for sending His Son, and he longed for the earthly kingdom of Christ to be established. We thank God for many blessings, writes Hancock, "but the great and most important Blessing, the Gospel of Jesus Christ: And together with our cordial acknowledgments, I do earnestly recommend, that we may join the penitent confession of our Sins, and implore the further continuance of the Divine Protection, and Blessings of Heaven upon this People...that all may bow to the Scepter of our LORD JESUS CHRIST, and the whole Earth be filled with His Glory" [emphasis his].[265] I never learned things like that about our founding fathers in school.

⋆ **Patrick Henry** (1736-1799) was the great orator of the American Revolution. During his impassioned "Give me liberty or give me death" speech in March 1775 (just one month before the Battle of Lexington, when it all began), Henry declared: "We must fight! I repeat it, sir, we must fight! An appeal to arms and to the God of Hosts is all that is left us! Besides, sir, we shall not fight our battles alone. There is a just God who presides over the destinies of nations, and who will raise up friends to fight our battles for us."[266]

Patrick Henry was a student of the Bible. Holding up his copy he said:

> This book [the Bible] is worth all other books which have ever been printed, and it has been my misfortune that I have never found time to read it with the proper attention and feeling till lately. I trust in the mercy of Heaven that it is not yet too late.[267]

One time, Patrick Henry declared in a speech in a courtroom:

> I know, sir, how well it becomes a liberal man and a Christian to forget and forgive. As individuals professing a holy religion, it is our bounden duty to forgive injuries done us as individuals. But when [to] the character of Christian you add the character of patriot, you are in a different situation. Our mild and holy system of religion inculcates an admirable maxim of forbearance. If your enemy smite one cheek, turn the other to him. But you must stop there. You cannot apply this to your country. As members of a

social community, this maxim does not apply to you. When you consider injuries done to your country your political duty tells you of vengeance. Forgive as a private man, but never forgive public injuries. Observations of this nature are exceedingly unpleasant, but it is my duty to use them.[268]

★ **John Jay** (1745-1829) was indisputably a devout evangelical. A lawyer from New York, he was a co-author (along with Hamilton and Madison) of *The Federalist Papers*. He was also the first chief justice of the Supreme Court. Historian George Bancroft writes, "Descended from Huguenot refugees, educated in the city at its college, of the severest purity of morals, an able writer, and a ready speaker, his superior endowments, his activity, and his zeal for liberty, were tempered by a love for order."[269]

Here is what John Jay said in his will: "Unto Him who is the Author and Giver of all good, I render sincere and humble thanks for His merciful and unmerited blessings, and especially for our redemption and salvation by his beloved Son. He has been pleased to bless me with excellent parents, with a virtuous wife, and with worthy children. His protection has accompanied me through many eventful years, faithfully employed in the service of my country; and His providence has not only conducted me to this tranquil situation, but also given me abundant reason to be contented and thankful. Blessed be His Holy Name. While my children lament my departure, let them recollect that in doing them good, I was only the agent of their Heavenly Father, and that He never withdraws His care and consolations from those who diligently seek Him."[270]

★ **Thomas Jefferson** (1743-1826) was not an orthodox Christian, yet he was neither an atheist nor agnostic. His political writing was influenced by a reverence for Almighty God—the source of our liberties. He was asked by the Continental Congress (July 6, 1775) to write "the Declaration of the Causes and Necessity for Taking Up Arms." This was a year before the Declaration of Independence and the purpose was to explain why some colonists were picking up arms and going to the Boston area, where the British were imposing closure of the port and had many warships in the harbor. Jefferson wrote,

> But a reverence for our great Creator, principles of humanity,
> and the dictates of common sense, must convince all those who

reflect upon the subject, that government was instituted to promote the welfare of mankind, and ought to be administered for the attainment of that end...we most solemnly, before God and the world, declare, that, exerting the utmost energy of those powers, which our beneficent Creator hath graciously bestowed upon us...being with one mind resolved to die freemen rather than to live slaves.... With a humble confidence in the mercies of the Supreme and impartial Judge and Ruler of the Universe, we most devoutly implore His divine goodness to protect us happily through this great conflict, to dispose our adversaries to reconciliation on reasonable terms, and thereby to relieve the empire from the calamities of civil war.[273]

Of course, he was the chief author of the Declaration of Independence. This key document, our nation's birth certificate, mentions God four times and declares that our rights come from God alone. Therefore, man cannot take them away.

Jefferson also made some great affirmations that arise from the Judeo-Christian tradition (as opposed to a Zoroastrian, Islamic, Buddhist, Hindu, or atheistic base):

"The God who gave us life, gave us liberty at the same time."[274] Also, he once declared:

"Indeed, I tremble for my country when I reflect that God is just."[275] These last two statements are chiseled in stone at the Jefferson Memorial in Washington, D.C.

★ **John Langdon** (1741-1819) was a signer of the United States Constitution. He served as a U.S. Senator as the governor of New Hampshire. As Governor, he made an official Proclamation for a General Thanksgiving to the State on October 21, 1785 (a common phenomenon during that time): "recommending to the religious Societies of every Denomination, to assemble on that Day, to celebrate the Praises of our divine Benefactor; to acknowledge our own Unworthiness, confess our manifold Transgressions, implore his Forgiveness, and intreat the continuance of those Favours which he had been graciously pleased to bestow upon us; that he would inspire our Rulers with Wisdom, prosper our Trade and Commerce, smile upon our Husbandry, bless our Seminaries of Learning, and spread the Gospel of his Grace over all the Earth."[271]

* **Richard Henry Lee** (1732-1794) of Virginia was a signer of the Declaration of Independence. Author Bill Federer points out that on November 1, 1777, as recorded in the Journals of Congress, on November 1, 1777, Lee and Samuel Adams and Gen. Daniel Roberdeau recommended a resolution for a day of prayer: "Thursday, the 18th of December next, for solemn thanksgiving and praise, that with one heart and one voice the good people may express the grateful feelings of their hearts, and consecrate themselves to the service of their Divine Benefactor; and that, together with their sincere acknowledgments and offerings, they may join the penitent confession of their manifold sins, whereby they had forfeited every favor, and their humble and earnest supplication that it may please God, through the merits of Jesus Christ, mercifully to forgive and blot them out of remembrance."[272]

* **The Liberty Bell** is an icon of American Freedom. Bill Federer notes that in 1752, it "was cast in England by an order of the Pennsylvania Assembly to commemorate the fiftieth anniversary of the colony's existence.... The Liberty Bell got its name from being rung at the first public reading of the Declaration of Independence, July 8, 1776. It cracked as it rang at the funeral for Chief Justice John Marshall, 1835." This icon of American liberty has a Bible verse on it, which was chosen by Isaac Norris, the Speaker of the Pennsylvania Assembly. The verse is Leviticus 25:10: "proclaim liberty throughout all the land unto all the inhabitants thereof; it shall be a jubilee."[276]

Here is a true story about the Liberty Bell. About ten years ago, our choir director (at Coral Ridge Presbyterian) and his wife led one of their annual tours for students in the high school youth choir. They went to Philadelphia and ministered in churches throughout the area. Our daughter was a member of that choir. Upon returning home, she said the trip was fine, except she had this complaint: "I couldn't believe it. One time, we were really close to the second largest mall in the country, and instead we had to go see some stupid bell with a crack in it!" We hope that as she gets older, she grows to appreciate our nation's Christian roots.

* **William Livingston** (1723-1790) served in the first and second Continental Congresses, as well as the Constitutional Convention. This founding father declared: "I believe the Scriptures of the Old and New

Testaments, without any foreign comments or human explanations...
I believe that he who feareth God and worketh righteousness will be
accepted of Him.... I believe that the virulence of some...proceeds not
from their affection to Christianity, which is founded on too firm a basis
to be shaken by the freest inquiry, and the Divine authority of which I
sincerely believe without receiving a farthing for saying so."[277]

* **James Madison** (1751-1836) played a critical role during the Constitutional Convention; he wrote the notes of the proceedings. He also served
as our nation's fourth president. George Bancroft notes that Madison
was "bred in the school of Presbyterian dissenters under Witherspoon
at Princeton, trained by his own studies, by meditative rural life in the
Old Dominion, by an ingenuous indignation at the persecution of the
Baptists, and by the innate principles of right, to uphold the sanctity of
religious freedom."[278]

In his "A Memorial and Remonstrance," a classic treatise on religious
liberty from 1785, James Madison stated:

> It is the duty of every man to render to the Creator such homage,
> and such only, as he believes to be acceptable to Him. This duty
> is precedent both in order of time, and degree of obligation, to
> the claims of Civil Society.
>
> Before any man can be considered as a member of Civil So-
> ciety, he must be considered as a subject of the Governor of the
> Universe.[279]

Thus, like virtually all the founding fathers, Madison saw strong political
implications in the fact that God would one day hold all human beings
accountable.

* **Luther Martin** (1748-1826) attended the Constitutional Convention as
a delegate from Maryland. Martin said that he was committed to what
he called the "sacred truths of the Christian religion."[280]

* **The Massachusetts Congress** in 1775 declared, "Resistance to tyranny
...becomes the Christian and social duty of each individual. Fleets,
troops, and every implement of war are sent into the province, to wrest
from you that freedom which it is your duty, even at the risk of your

lives, to hand inviolate to posterity. Continue steadfast, and, with a proper sense of your dependence on God, nobly defend those rights which heaven gave, and no man ought to take from us."[281]

* **James McHenry** (1753-1816) was a signer of the Constitution. He served as the first president of the Bible society in Baltimore. Note what he said about the difference the distribution of the Word of God makes in society:

> In vain, without the Bible, we increase penal laws and draw intrenchments around our institutions. Bibles are strong intrenchments. Where they abound, men cannot pursue wicked courses, and at the same time enjoy quiet conscience.
>
> Consider also, the rich do not possess aught more precious than their Bible, and that the poor cannot be presented by the rich with anything of greater value. Withhold it not from the poor. It is a book of counsels and directions, fitted to every situation in which man can be placed. It is an oracle which reveals to mortals the secrets of heaven and the hidden will of the Almighty....
>
> It is an estate, whose title is guaranteed by Christ, whose delicious fruits ripen every season, survive the worm, and keep through eternity. It is for the purpose of distributing this divine book more effectually and extensively among the multitudes, whose circumstances render such a donation necessary, that your cooperation is most earnestly requested.[282]

* **The Minutemen** played a key role in the War for Independence. They were given their name because they could enter battle at a minute's notice if they had to. What is not well known is that they were generally deacons and elders of the churches. The American Revolution began on April 19, 1775, when British troops...on their way to secure gunpowder in Concord, Massachusetts,...encountered some of the men from the Lexington church, whose pastor was the patriotic Jonas Clark. Bancroft writes of that church: "How often in that building had they, with renewed professions of their faith, looked up to God as the stay of their fathers and the protector of their privileges!" Continuing, Bancroft says, "The ground on which they trod was the altar of freedom, and they were to furnish the victims."[283] In one sense, these were the first Minute Men, and they were the first casualties of the war.

The battle began in Lexington and moved to nearby Concord. Bancroft notes: "The people of Concord, of whom about two hundred appeared in arms on that day, derived their energy from their sense of the divine power. This looking to God as their sovereign brought the fathers to their pleasant valley; this controlled the loyalty of the sons; and this had made the name of Concord venerable throughout the world." "...William Emerson of Concord, late chaplain to the provincial congress..." wrote up the events of Lexington: "'From the nineteenth of April 1775,' said Clark, of Lexington, on its first anniversary, 'will be dated the liberty of the American world.'"[284] Bancroft adds, "'We conjure you,' they wrote, 'by all that is dear, by all that is sacred; we beg and entreat, as you will answer it to your country, to your consciences, and above all, to God himself, that you will hasten and encourage by all possible means the enlistment of men to form the army, and send them forward to head-quarters at Cambridge with that expedition which the vast importance and instant urgency of the affair demands.'"[285]

A year before the Battles of Lexington and Concord (1774), notes Bill Federer, Minutemen were already beginning to enlist in the brewing conflict: "[T]he Massachusetts Provincial Congress reorganized the Massachusetts militia, providing that over one-third of all new regiments be made up of 'Minutemen'." That congress told the Minutemen: "You...are placed by Providence in the post of honor, because it is the post of danger.... The eyes not only of North America and the whole British Empire, but of all Europe, are upon you. Let us be, therefore, altogether solicitous that no disorderly behavior, nothing unbecoming our characters as Americans, as citizens and Christians, be justly chargeable to us."[286]

★ **Gouverneur Morris** (1752-1816) was not only a signer of the Declaration, but he is credited with writing some of the Constitution, including the preamble ("We the people"). Morris spoke more on the floor during the Constitutional Convention than anyone else. He said this about the link between religion and morality: "Religion is the only solid basis of good morals; therefore education should teach the precepts of religion, and the duties of man toward God."[287]

★ **Constitutional signer John Rutledge** (1739-1800), president of South Carolina's congress, said: "...my most fervent prayer to the omnipotent

Ruler of the universe is, that under his gracious providence the liberties of America may be forever preserved."[288]

* **George Washington** (1732–1796) has been called the Father of our Country. He played a critical role in the founding of a nation. In recent times, some writers have questioned his Christianity. But the fact is, he was a devout eighteenth-century Anglican, orthodox in his stated beliefs. I have had the privilege of co-writing with Dr. Peter Lillback a very thick book on his Christian faith, *George Washington's Sacred Fire*. In that book, we point out: "His Biblical literacy suggests that he read the Scriptures regularly, and we can also show that he used the 1662 *Book of Common Prayer* from the Church of England, which was a very orthodox guide for Christian worship of the Trinity. In fact, the *Book of Common Prayer* is more theologically sound than the average book available in a Christian bookstore today."[289]

Washington's first order made during the war reflected his religious convictions. He felt that it would be wrong for our soldiers to curse or gamble or do anything to displease God. Thus, on July 4, 1775, he gave his first order (speaking of himself in the third person):

> The General most earnestly requires and expects a due observance of those articles of war established for the government of the army, which forbid profane cursing, swearing, and drunkenness. And in like manner he requires and expects of all officers and soldiers, not engaged in actual duty, a punctual attendance on Divine service, to implore the blessing of Heaven upon the means used for our safety and defence.[290]

Washington once said, "true religion affords to government its surest support." He also said in a letter to the governors of the states after we won the war that our nation will not be happy if we do not imitate Jesus Christ, whom he called the divine author of our religion: "I now make it my earnest prayer that God would have you and the State over which you preside in his holy protection…and that he would most graciously be pleased to dispose us all to do justice, to love mercy, and to demean ourselves with charity, humility, and pacific temper of mind, which were the characteristics of the Divine Author of our blessed religion; without a humble recognition of whose example, in these things, we can never hope to be a happy nation."[291]

In 1779, George Washington was asked by a group of Indians, who were seeking to educate their children in the ways of the Englishmen. He said, "You do well to wish to learn our arts and ways of life, and above all, the religion of Jesus Christ."[292] Washington said in his Farewell Address: "Of all the dispositions and habits which lead to political prosperity, religion and morality are indispensable supports. In vain would that man claim the tribute of patriotism, who should labor to subvert these great pillars of human happiness.... And let us with caution indulge the supposition that morality can be maintained without religion."[293] What does that last statement mean? It means that religion is the means of maintaining morality. When the Founding Fathers spoke of "religion," they were speaking of Christianity, in a nation which at the time was 99.8 percent Christian.[294]

★ **James Wilson** (1742-1798), who signed the Declaration of Independence, spoke of the God-given law that man instinctively knows because God has made it known to us: "As promulgated by reason and the moral sense it has been called natural; as promulgated by the holy Scriptures, it has been called revealed law.... But it should always be remembered, that this law, natural or revealed, made for men or for nations, flows from the same divine source; it is the law of God.... Human law must rest its authority, ultimately, upon the authority of that law, which is divine."[295] Thus, God's law is above man's law. Let not the laws of men contradict the laws of God.

★ **John Witherspoon** (1723-1794) was a Presbyterian minister and the President of College of New Jersey, now Princeton University, as well as a delegate to the Continental Congress of 1776 from New Jersey. He pointed out that our trust should be in God, not in man:

> While we give praise to God, the Supreme Disposer of all events, for His interposition on our behalf, let us guard against the dangerous error of trusting in, or boasting of, an arm of flesh...he is the best friend to American liberty, who is most sincere and active in promoting true and undefiled religion, and who sets himself with the greatest firmness to bear down profanity and immorality of every kind. Whoever is an avowed enemy of God, I scruple not to call him an enemy of his country.[296]

This is not too subtle. Witherspoon also said, "The character of a Christian must be taken from Holy Scriptures...the unerring standard."[297]

CONCLUSION

We could go on and on with other examples and quotes.

I could even include rank non-believers in this. For example, Thomas Paine (1737-1809) was a founding father who definitely lost whatever faith he may have had. By no stretch of anyone's imagination was he a Christian by the end of his life. However, early in his life, when he was helpful to the American cause, this son of a Quaker wrote *Common Sense* (1776), which helped galvanize the colonists toward independence. He declared "In the early ages of the world, mankind were equals; the heathen introduced government by kings, which the will of the Almighty, as declared by Gideon and the prophet Samuel, expressly disapproved." We see in Thomas Paine's *Common Sense* a respect for God and His Word: "But where, say some, is the king of America? I'll tell you, friend, he reigns above, and doth not make havoc of mankind like the royal brute of Great Britain. Yet that we may not appear to be defective even in earthly honors, let a day be solemnly set apart for proclaiming the charter; let it be brought forth placed on the divine law, the Word of God; let a crown be placed thereon, by which the world may know, that so far as we approve of monarchy, that in America the law is king."[298] In *Common Sense*, Thomas Paine also wrote: "...we claim brotherhood with every European Christian, and triumph in the generosity of the sentiment." Paine further declared: "The distance at which the Almighty hath placed England and America is a strong and natural proof that the authority of the one over the other was never the design of heaven. They belong to different systems—England to Europe, America to itself. Everything short of independence is leaving the sword to our children."[299] Later, the disappointments of life soured Mr. Paine, making him bitter not better, and he vented his anger against the Almighty and the Bible in some of his vitriolic writings, such as *The Age of Reason*—which was rejected by George Washington, Ben Franklin, and other American leaders. Thomas Paine was helpful to the American cause for liberty when he was pro-Bible, not when he was against the book that made America.

Here is an example of a non-believing founding father who had had faith earlier in life, but apparently not later. Ethan Allen (1738-1789) played a critical role during the Revolution. He and his men surprised the British commander of the fort at Ticonderoga. Allen declared: "Deliver to me the fort instantly." The commander asked: "By what authority?" Allen replied, "In the name of the great Jehovah, and the Continental Congress!" The British commander noticed that Allen had his hand cocked and in it was his drawn sword, aimed at the commander's head. So the commander gave up the fort and ordered his men to drop their arms.[300] However, somewhere along the line, Allen lost his faith and fervor. Nonetheless, when his country needed him, his faith in God was strong.

Let me close with the words of our second president. John Adams said this about the Scriptures: "I have examined all [religions], as well as my narrow sphere, my straightened means, and my busy life would allow; and the result is, that **the Bible is the best Book in the world. It contains more of my little philosophy than all the libraries I have seen.**" [emphasis mine][301] Thus, we see that the Bible shaped the men that made America.

The author at the new Capitol Visitor Center in Washington, D.C. This is the new way people visit the U.S. Capitol. Unfortunately it is given over to political correctness. The history books have been rewritten, and God has been erased. This is a far cry from the intent of the founding fathers, as is clear by their words and deeds.

CHAPTER 8

The Intent of the Founding Fathers

He has shown you, O man, what is good;
And what does the LORD require of you
But to do justly, To love mercy,
And to walk humbly with your God?
(Micah 6:8, NKJV)

ALMOST a decade ago, liberal judges unleashed a national debate that gets at the heart of our nation's history. Are we one nation under God? The specific question was: Is the phrase "under God" in the Pledge of Allegiance unconstitutional? Some judges have said as much. In the summer of 2002, Americans were shocked when two circuit court judges took it upon themselves to declare the phrase impermissible in a school setting because of the first amendment. I think this decision was a wake-up call to millions of Americans. President George W. Bush called the decision "ridiculous" and said it was out of step with our traditions, including the Declaration of Independence, which acknowledges God. Politicians—even the more liberal ones—were falling all over themselves to see who could get to a microphone first to decry the decision. They raced to the television cameras to get seen saying the Pledge of Allegiance, including the banned phrase under God. Here's what some of the politicians had to say immediately after the decision became known:

* Senator Christopher Bond, (R) Missouri: "Our founding fathers must be spinning in their graves. This is the worst kind of political correctness run amok."

* Tom Daschle, (D) South Dakota, Senate leader at the time, said the decision was just plain "nuts."

* Dennis Hastert, (R) Illinois, the then leader of the House, remarked: "Obviously, the liberal court in San Francisco has gotten this one wrong." [302]

The reaction startled the chief judge in the decision, who chose to put his own ruling on hold the very next day.

The fall-out from the decision probably startled even many liberals. In some ways, as obnoxious as the decision was, it didn't surprise me. Why not? Because this decision was the natural out-working of the faulty view of "the separation of church and state," which liberal judges have been holding for years. Decades, in fact.

Even now, the pledge decision is worming its way back into the courts, beginning at the 9th Circuit Court of Appeals.

THE MISUNDERSTANDING OF "SEPARATION OF CHURCH AND STATE"

There is probably no area with more confusion in our society than the whole matter of "separation of church and state," which began with very liberal courts and has now filtered down to ridiculous decisions.

For example, recently I heard about a case in Byron, Illinois, in a rural part of the state about two hours west of Chicago, where there was an egregious violation of a Christian's civil liberties because the young man was allegedly violating "the separation of church and state."

Joshua Hendrickson, a junior in a public high school, is blind. He has a Braille Bible, which he was reading to himself silently in the lunchroom. Some of his friends asked him to read aloud. He did so. (He happened to be reading the Old Testament book of Isaiah.) The principal found out, and he suspended the boy for three days, putting this on the boy's permanent record. Thankfully, the Christian Law Association of Seminole, Florida, got involved and successfully showed the school how wrong this principal was. This provides an excellent illustration of the fact that the assault against Christians has even reached Main Street, Small-town America.

Suppose the boy wasn't blind, and he was turning the pages of a *Playboy* or some other pornographic magazine. Would he be suspended for three days and have this on his permanent record? It's almost as if the Bible is X-rated in our public schools.

The tragedy is that this story typifies the great misunderstanding of the "separation of church and state" in our society today.

Is this what the founders intended? Absolutely not.

Did the founding fathers give us any kind of clue as to what they envisioned for America as to the relationship between any public expression of religion (specifically Christianity) and the state? The answer is "Yes." And it's not at all hard to find; it is a matter of public record. In this chapter, I propose to demonstrate that the founders did not intend us to have "state-sanctioned atheism," which seems to be the goal of the American Civil Liberties Union (ACLU), the People for the American Way, Americans United for the Separation of Church and State, and all the other legal groups that are suing to completely remove our Christian heritage. I also want to address the liberal judges they have managed to persuade. Our history is rich with examples that the modern-day purge of Christianity from the public square is not at all what the founders had in mind.

The founding fathers said in Article 6 of the Constitution that "no religious Test shall ever be required as a Qualification to any Office or public Trust under the United States."[303] Some people on the left interpret that to mean that religious people need not apply toward government office; they have interpreted that to be a secular requirement. Not at all. First of all, that prohibition was at the federal level, not the state level—at a time when some states, e.g., Delaware, had in their constitutions that one could not hold office unless they believed in Jesus Christ.[304] Secondly, it spelled freedom for Christians of all denominations. (Then eventually it spelled freedom for non-Christians as well.) If a religious test were allowed, and only Anglicans could apply for public office, then religious freedom would be denied to the Presbyterians. Our founders struck a careful balance allowing for religious freedom on a voluntary basis, while always publicly recognizing that God is the source of our liberties.

"ONE INDISSOLUBLE BOND"

The late Dr. Kennedy once asked a group if they could guess what John Quincy Adams, the sixth president of the United States, considered the highest glory of the American Revolution? Dr. Kennedy went on to suggest that Adams was considering: That the revolution secured our independence from England? Or that it got rid of the Stamp Tax? Or the Tea Tax? Or that the Revolution dissolved our bonds with Parliament and the king? No, not any of those. What was the highest glory of the American

Revolution, according to this president? Listen well. According to J. Wingate Thornton, John Quincy Adams said, "The highest glory of the American Revolution was this: it connected in one indissoluble bond, the principles of civil government with the principles of Christianity."[305]

"One indissoluble bond"—Government and Christianity! Well, today there are those who have come with their solvents of unbelief, skepticism, atheism, Marxism, humanism, and secularism and are doing everything in their power to totally dissolve that indissoluble bond. Someone will say, "Yes, but doesn't the First Amendment say there should be a wall of separation between church and state?" I wonder how many still believe that. If you do, let me remind you of something: The First Amendment never mentions "a wall," it never mentions "separation," it never mentions the "church," and it never mentions the "state." The First Amendment says, "Congress shall make no law respecting an establishment of religion, or prohibiting the free exercise thereof...."

Thomas Jefferson, in a *private* letter to the Danbury Baptists, used the phrase "a wall of separation between Church and State."[306] Again, as Dr. Kennedy points out, a wall inhibits people equally on both sides while the First Amendment inhibits only the Congress: "*Congress* shall make no law respecting an establishment of religion...*Congress* shall make no law prohibiting the free exercise thereof."[307] The First Amendment says absolutely nothing about what Christians or people adhering to any religion, or ministers, or clergymen, or churches may or may not do.

Furthermore, Mr. Jefferson, though one of our most noteworthy founding fathers, was thousands of miles away in France when both the Constitution and the Bill of Rights were written. Modern courts have mistakenly made him *the* authority on the matter, and misquoted *him* at that. David Barton asks, Where are their quotations from George Washington, James Madison, Alexander Hamilton, Gouverneur Morris—the founding father who spoke the most times at the Constitutional Convention—to settle the matter? What has happened in American jurisprudence in the last several decades has been very dishonest.

Built on the Foundation of Roger Williams

Our founders intended a separation of the institution of the Church from the institution of the State. However, they never intended state-sanctioned atheism, which is where we are heading today. They never intended for ACLU attorneys, acting as the high priests of atheism, to make sure little Johnny would never say a prayer in school—or that little Johnny's teacher would never utter a Judeo-Christian sentiment in the classroom.

The separation of church and state means many things to many people. Felix Morley pointed out, as far back as 1960, that "The separation is today outrageously interpreted to mean that Christianity shall not be taught in the public schools of a Christian nation."[308]

The founders did not want a national denomination. While they gleaned some positive input from the Puritans (e.g., the covenants, the civil liberties, etc.), they did not want a national state church. They did not want to repeat what the Puritans had tried to do in Massachusetts.

A dissident Puritan leader helped clarify church-state understandings, insisted that the force of government should never be used to coerce religious opinion. Roger Williams' great contribution was freedom of conscience and a clarion call against using the force of the state to enforce correct doctrine.

A century before Williams, Martin Luther said: "I will preach, speak, write the truth, but will force it on no one, for faith must be accepted willingly, and without compulsion." Also, he said about those who light the wooden sticks to burn heretics at the stake: "If fire is the right cure for heresy, then the [heretic-] burners are the most learned doctors on earth; no need we study any more; he that has brute force on his side may burn his adversary at the stake."[309]

Truth is the cornerstone of Christianity. Jesus calls the Holy Spirit the Spirit of truth and when Jesus prayed for unity within the Church he prayed, "Sanctify them in the truth; Your word is truth" (John 17:17). Christians are sanctified by the truth, and if we abide by Jesus' teaching, the truth shall set us free (John 8:32).

Thus, the sword has no power to unify or protect the true Church. Religious differences are not to be solved by the carnal sword. Instead, declared Roger Williams: "...they are only to be fought against with that sword which is only (in soul matters) able to conquer, to wit, the sword of God's spirit, the Word of God."[310] So Roger Williams was trying to remind his Christian brethren who desired to return to New Testament Christianity in its purity of another facet of the New Testament to which we also need to return: We serve the Prince of Peace, and those who live by the sword shall die by the sword.

The Bloody Tenet of Persecution

Roger Williams wrote *The Bloody Tenet of Persecution* in 1644. He sets forth twelve conclusions to sum up his beliefs. We will consider just a few of them:

> First, that the blood of so many hundred thousand souls of Protestants and Papists, spilt in the wars of present and former ages, for their respective consciences, is not required nor accepted by Jesus Christ the Prince of Peace.

This seems so obvious today, but it wasn't so obvious then. Sadly, we as Christians have to admit that many have mistakenly taken up the sword in some cases to squelch heresy or disagreement from our viewpoint. Roman Catholics and Protestants are both guilty, although, in fairness, the former much more significantly than the latter. After making other arguments against using the sword to enforce religious conformity, Williams notes this:

> Seventhly, the state of the Land of Israel, the kings and people thereof in peace and war, is proved figurative and ceremonial, and no pattern nor [precedent] for any kingdom or civil state in the world to follow.

Here Williams is pointing out that the theocracy of Israel is gone. We are not living under a theocracy any longer.

> Eighthly, God requireth not a uniformity of religion to be enacted and enforced in any civil state; which enforced uniformity (sooner or later) is the greatest occasion of civil war, ravishing of conscience, persecution of Christ Jesus in his servants, and of the hypocrisy and destruction of millions of souls.

Persecution by "Christians" to enforce uniformity of doctrine and belief and practice is counter-productive to the spread of the gospel. It leads to hypocrisy and has brought dishonor to the gospel, thus leading to many souls falling away. Williams also writes:

> Twelfthly, lastly, true civility and Christianity may both flourish in a state or kingdom, notwithstanding the permission of divers and contrary consciences, either of Jew or Gentile.[311]

True Christianity has always done best when it's allowed to compete with other perspectives. Let all religions and all philosophies have a level playing field, argues Williams. Paul Johnson says of Rhode Island, that not only did it introduce the separation of church and state (in the historical and positive sense of that term), but "it also inaugurated the practice of religious competition."[312]

Tolerance, as properly understood, is a Christian virtue and product of Christianity. Modern secularists today ignore that Williams based his arguments for religious liberty on Scripture, which he held to be the Word of God.

Thomas Jefferson and James Madison agreed with these sentiments of Roger Williams. They did not want state coercion of religious opinions.

James Madison, a key player in the writing of the Constitution, had written an important piece of Virginia legislation in 1785, two years before the convention. I first heard about this legislation from Roy S. Moore (the Ten Commandments judge) whom I met and have interviewed about half a dozen times through the years. The former chief justice of Alabama rightfully noted that Madison's "Memorial and Remonstrance" essentially showed that Christianity gave us our religious freedom. Madison wrote:

> Whilst we assert for ourselves a freedom to embrace, to profess, and to observe the Religion which we believe to be of divine origin, we cannot deny an equal freedom to those whose minds have not yet yielded to the evidence which has convinced us. If this freedom be abused, it is an offence against God, not against man: To God, therefore, not to man, must an account of it be rendered.[313]

In other words, we are convinced Christianity is true. But there are some who are not so convinced. If we try to force them to believe in Christ, we then abuse the freedom that God has given us. We will all give an account before God.

The significance of all this is that Christianity is the source of freedom. People of all religions are free to worship in America. That is a direct outgrowth of Christianity. Madison goes on to point out that Christianity becomes distorted whenever it uses the force of government to try to force itself on any society. He cites centuries of history to make his point.

Even the religiously unorthodox Thomas Jefferson[314] appealed to Jesus Christ ("the holy author of our religion") and His example as to how it is we have religious freedom. In 1786, he wrote:

> Almighty God hath created the mind free...all attempts to influence it by temporal punishments...are a departure from the plan of the holy author of our religion, who being lord both of body and mind, yet chose not to propagate it by coercions on either, as was in his Almighty power to do, but to exalt it by its influence on reason alone....[315]

So, in other words, the state is not to interfere with the conscience. Even God Himself leaves that up to the individual.

This is important because what has happened today is that secularists are imposing state-sanctioned atheism against the Christian conscience of many in our country. The founders wanted healthy, vibrant Christian freedom—in a "disestablished" way (no governmental authority granted to any religious establishment). They never wanted the state to dictate to the terms of anyone's conscience. It was for this very reason that people fled Europe in the first place.

INDIFFERENCE TO RELIGION?

Most people don't realize the Christian make-up of our country in its earliest days. Even as late as 1775—150 years after the Pilgrims landed—the makeup of America was: 98 percent Protestant Christians; 1.8 percent Catholic Christians; .2 of 1 percent Jews.[316]

In the nineteenth century, one of America's greatest theologians ever, Charles Hodge of Princeton Theological Seminary, said, "The proposition that the United States of America is a Christian and Protestant nation, is not so much the assertion of a principle, as the statement of a fact."[317]

HARMFUL TO GOOD GOVERNMENT?

Today, people seem to think that in some way religion in general, and Christianity in particular, is antithetical to good government and that the purpose of the government is to keep religion away from the governors of our land. Perhaps that is why we have found that our Congress seems to chip away at our liberties every time they meet.

This is a very different view from that held by George Washington who said, "True religion offers to government its surest support."[318] In fact, George Washington said that without a humble imitation of Christ we could never hope to be a happy nation.[319]

Nineteenth-century American statesman Robert C. Winthrop, who served as Speaker of the House of Representatives, said: "It may do for other countries and other governments to talk about the state supporting religion. Here, under our own free institutions, it is religion which must support the State."[320]

Samuel Adams, who was called the firebrand of the American Revolution, said: "Let divines and philosophers, statesmen and patriots, unite their endeavors to renovate the age, by impressing the minds of men with the importance of educating their little boys and girls, of inculcating in the minds of youth the fear and love of the Deity."[321]

Commenting on Adams' point, Dr. Kennedy observes:

> The founders of this country believed we should inculcate in the minds of youth the fear and love of the Deity. But because of our stupidity and unbelief, we have now banned God from the classrooms. We have taken away prayer, the Bible, and the Ten Commandments from our schools and have replaced them with police dogs in the halls and police and metal detectors at the doors. Crime is absolutely epidemic, and teachers are retiring early from battle fatigue. This is the folly of modern America.
>
> The secularists and humanists of our time believe that Christianity is the great danger to freedom and good government. They do not even realize they are taking a position totally antithetical to the founders' position; instead these secularists' position is exactly the same as the atheistic founders of the French Revolution. In France, the Church was held by these atheists to be the great evil, which must be banished and restrained. In America, religion was the surest support of good government, and the principles of Christianity were united in an indissoluble bond in the establishment of this country.[322]

NO NATIONAL CHURCH—PERIOD

The phrase "separation of church and state" is an unfortunate choice of words, because it contains a kernel of truth. America's founding fathers did not want a national church, but they did allow states to have their own state-churches. These eventually died out, but they were never declared unconstitutional. It was only at the federal level, that there was to be no national denomination.

Why not? Because the United States was comprised of Anglicans, Congregationalists, Presbyterians, Quakers, Huguenots, a few Baptists, a few Methodists, and so on. Yet the founders were definitely Christian for the most part. At least 90–95 percent of them were practicing, Trinitarian Christians. For example, you can go to Christ Church in Philadelphia today, where George Washington and several others from the Constitutional Convention worshiped that long, hot summer of 1787. John Adams, normally a Congregationalist, also worshiped at the Presbyterian Church that summer.

In fact, years earlier, during the very first day of the Continental Congress, on September 6, 1774, the members held a discussion on whether they should open in prayer. One of the most committed Christians, John Jay, later our first Chief Justice of the Supreme Court, said he didn't think it wise because of the plethora of denominations represented in the assembly.

But Samuel Adams, a Congregationalist from Massachusetts, stood up and persuaded them to hold prayer. Here's what happened that day, according to eyewitness John Adams:

> Mr. Samuel Adams arose and said that he was no bigot, and could hear a Prayer from any gentleman of Piety and virtue, who was at the same time a friend to his Country. He was a stranger in Philadelphia, but had heard that Mr. Duché deserved that character and therefore he moved that Mr. Duché, an Episcopal clergyman, might be desired to read Prayers to Congress tomorrow morning.[323]

So the next day, September 7, 1774, Rev. Jacob Duché led the whole group in prayer in a service that lasted three hours. It was a very moving service, wherein he read Psalm 35, the reading for that particular day in the Anglican "pontificals." It just so happened (by God's providence) to be exactly what the Congressmen needed to hear.

In Psalm 35, David, who is being unjustly persecuted, pours out his heart to God, and he asks to be vindicated: "Plead my cause, Oh, Lord, with them that strive with me, fight against them that fight against me. Take hold of buckler and shield, and rise up for my help."

Even as these words were read, some of the delegates from Massachusetts understood that British troops were attacking their homes and farms. John Adams wrote his wife, Abigail, about the impact of this psalm and prayer meeting:

I never saw a greater effect upon an audience. It seemed as if heaven had ordained that Psalm to be read on that morning. After this, Mr. Duché, unexpectedly to every body, struck out into an extemporary prayer, which filled the bosom of every man present. I must confess, I never heard a better prayer, or one so well pronounced.... It has had an excellent effect upon everybody here. I must beg you to read that Psalm."[324]

At the very beginning of Congress, the representatives opened in prayer. And they have been praying ever since. How does this square with the supposed "separation of church and state" that the liberals try to shove in our face?

The Heritage Foundation, a conservative think-tank in Washington, D.C., has compiled a large commentary on the Constitution. Here is what they write in the opening of their section on the first amendment:

In recent years the Supreme Court has placed the Establishment and the Free Exercise of Religion Clauses in mutual tension, but it was not so for the Framers. None of the Framers believed that a governmental connection to religion was an evil in itself. Rather, many (though not all) opposed an established church because they believed that it was a threat to the free exercise of religion.[325]

TEN MAJOR REASONS

Here are ten major reasons I am concerned to reveal and document that we have Christian roots as a nation and that therefore the atheistic-leaning judges should turn down the ACLU and similar kinds of lawsuits seeking to strip away our Christian heritage. Some of this is by way of review:

1. *Our nation's birth certificate, the Declaration of Independence, mentions God four times—and not in any minor way.* God is the source of our rights, according to this document. The Declaration also argues that the British king is guilty of trying to take away something that God has given us; therefore, King George III ought not to be obeyed. If the ACLU interpretation of strict "separation of church and state" (really, the separation of God and state) were correct, then the Declaration would be unconstitutional (even though the founders said the Constitution is predicated on the Declaration as its foundation). Children would not be allowed to read it in school.

2. *The very same men who gave us the First Amendment also wrote the Northwest Ordinance in 1787 (and in 1789).* This was one of our nation's four most important founding documents—along with the Declaration (which mentions God four times), the Constitution (which was signed "in the Year of our Lord,"[326] i.e., Jesus), and the Articles of Confederation (which mentions God this way: "whereas it has pleased the Great Governor of the World..."[327]). In the Northwest Ordinance, the founders' goal was that they would retain a certain degree of uniformity as new states were being added to the new nation. Article III of the Northwest Ordinance states: "Religion, morality, and knowledge being necessary to good government and the happiness of mankind, schools and the means of education shall be forever encouraged."[328] Religion and morality, according to our founders, were to be driving forces in school; they were not to be systematically censored as they are so often today.

3. *The Treaty of Paris of 1783, negotiated by Ben Franklin, John Adams, and John Jay, acknowledged the Trinity as it made official our separation from Great Britain.* This was the peace treaty that formally ended the Revolutionary War, which had ended unofficially at the Battle of Yorktown two years earlier. How does it begin? "In the name of the most holy and undivided Trinity."[329] I suppose this, too, would be unconstitutional. Does that mean we will have to go back to being British subjects? That is absurd, but so also is the driving out of anything Christian from the public arena from a nation with such thorough Christian roots.

4. *Chaplains have been in the public payroll from the very beginning.* This is true for both the Congress and the military. They would have to go. (In fact, the ACLU has unsuccessfully challenged chaplains.) Before we were even a nation, our government allocated public funding for congressional and military chaplains. The entire chaplain system absolutely violates the current, popular, and totally wrong view of strict "separation of church and state." If the ACLU interpretation were correct, then the founding fathers were grossly violating "church and state" on this matter, as in many others.

5. *The Constitutions of all fifty states mention God in one way or another,* every single one of them, usually in the preamble. We pointed this

out earlier with a few examples; here are a few more instances:

* ⋆ "We, the people of Alaska, grateful to God...."[330]
* ⋆ "The People of Connecticut acknowledging with gratitude, the good providence of God, in having permitted them to enjoy a free government...."[331]
* ⋆ "We, the people of the State of Florida, grateful to Almighty God for our constitutional liberty...."[332]
* ⋆ "We, the people of Missouri, with profound reverence for the Supreme Ruler of the Universe, and grateful for His goodness...."[333]

Each of these constitutions would be unconstitutional according to the ACLU's logic. So would the other forty six.

6. *Every president, from George Washington to President Barack Obama, has been sworn in on the Bible, saying the words, "So help me God."* This too would have to be stopped. This custom is not actually spelled out in the Constitution, but George Washington started the practice, because that had been the common way to take an oath in the Western world for centuries. All presidents have followed suit. Furthermore, prayers have been said at the swearing in of each president. These, too, would have to be stopped. In fact, the atheist who sued to get the phrase *under God* in the Pledge of Allegiance banned also sued former President George W. Bush, unsuccessfully, because he had the audacity to let Rev. Franklin Graham officiate in prayer at his inauguration, something presidents have done from the beginning. They also tried to sue to prevent Rev. Rick Warren from praying at President Barack Obama's inauguration.

George Washington even stooped over and kissed the Bible when he was sworn in as president. Then he led everyone present across the street (in New York City, our capital in 1789) where they participated in a two-hour prayer service at St. Paul's Chapel, which still stands a block away from where the World Trade Center stood. Miraculously, St. Paul's survived 9/11 while some nearby buildings did not (see p. 6).

7. *Virtually every president has mentioned God in their inaugural addresses and also has called for national days of prayer, of fasting, of thanksgiving.* George Washington, Abraham Lincoln, Ronald Reagan.

This, too, is a long-standing practice in the United States—from the very beginning. Before the birth of the nation, the settlers of the colonies called for hundreds of prayer days, fasting days, and days of thanksgiving in their individual colonies. Also, every president has mentioned God in his inaugural address. Several of them have quoted the Bible. Consider a small sampling:

* On March 4, 1841, William Henry Harrison, our ninth president, spoke of unscrupulous men taking advantage of democracies, who then pervert them to dictatorship, "...and, like the false Christs whose coming was foretold by the Savior, seeks to, and were it possible would, impose upon the true and most faithful disciples of liberty."[334]

* On March 4, 1905, Teddy Roosevelt, the twenty-sixth president, said, "My fellow-citizens, no people on earth have more cause to be thankful than ours, and this is said reverently, in no spirit of boastfulness in our own strength, but with gratitude to the Giver of Good who has blessed us with the conditions which have enabled us to achieve so large a measure of well-being and of happiness."[335]

* On January 20, 1977, Jimmy Carter, the thirty-ninth president declared, "Here before me is the Bible used in the inauguration of our first President, in 1789, and I have just taken the oath of office on the Bible my mother gave me a few years ago, opened to a timeless admonition from the ancient prophet Micah: 'He hath showed thee, O man, what is good; and what doth the Lord require of thee, but to do justly, and to love mercy, and to walk humbly with thy God.'" (Micah 6:8, KJV)[336]

Not only did the presidents mention God, but we also see the practice that they have sworn into oath, along the lines of our Judeo-Christian tradition. In fact, in our courtrooms (and even today), oaths have invoked God from the beginning. Up until recently, the belief was that one might lie before men, but would hesitate to lie before God Almighty. The Bible can still be found in some courtrooms, although it is disappearing in others. The ACLU has even filed suit to allow someone in North Carolina to swear on the Koran. But America was not founded on the Koran; it was founded on the Bible. Note that people in lands based on the Koran try to come to America to live, but you do not see many Americans clamoring to live in a Koran-based country.

8. *When they examined all the evidence in 1892, the Supreme Court declared, "this is a Christian nation" in a decision which has never been abrogated.*[337] The *Trinity* decision provides one of the best summaries I have ever read of how Christianity played a pivotal role in the founding of America. I decided to include major portions of that decision as the Appendix of this book. The *Trinity* decision was unanimous in its declaration, and it was decided after ten years of poring through key charters and documents of American history.

9. *God's name is engraved in stone on numerous monuments and buildings of Washington, D.C.,* many of which were constructed in the 1930s. If they had been built earlier, I would guess that there would be even more references to God. Meanwhile, if the ACLU were right, it would be time to take a sand-blaster to the Washington Monument where "Praise be to God" is written in Latin at the top and numerous Bible verses and plaques are quoted on the way up. They would also have to chisel away the three Bible verses listed (without the Scriptural references) at the Lincoln Memorial. Workers would have to blast away the engraved words at the Jefferson Memorial and the Scriptural references at the Library of Congress, and so on.

Furthermore, they would have to renovate the Supreme Court building. Also built in the 1930s, this magnificent structure has carvings of Moses and of the Ten Commandments. Alabama Attorney General Bill Pryor—long-time defender of the "Ten Commandments judge" Alabama Supreme Court Chief Justice Roy S. Moore—says there are more than twenty artistic depictions of Moses or the Ten Commandments throughout the Supreme Court building.[338] Time to reach for the hammer and chisel? No!

Emblazoned over the Speaker of the Senate in the U.S. Capitol are the words, "In God We Trust." This has been our official National Motto for some fifty years and our unofficial motto for more than a hundred years before that. This, too, would have to go. Not to mention that it would have to be removed from our money. Note that

In God We Trust has been placed on American coins since the days of President Abraham Lincoln and on the currency since President Dwight D. Eisenhower.

10. *Early commentaries on the Constitution showed that the founders did not intend a secular government that would silence any Christian presence in public.* So, for example, Supreme Court Justice Joseph Story, who lived through the formation of this government, wrote a massive commentary on the Constitution of the United States in 1828. He said this concerning the First Amendment: "An attempt to level all religions [Christianity and other religions] and to make it a matter of state policy to hold all in utter indifference, would have created universal disapprobation, if not universal indignation...."[339]

Yet that is precisely what has happened. Christianity is increasingly becoming outlawed in modern America, in a nation with unique and incontrovertible Christian roots.

CONCLUSION

It's time to stop the ACLU and their ilk in their tracks with the facts and in the courts. It's time to rediscover the rich Judeo-Christian heritage that made this nation into the greatest, most free country in the history of the world. It's time to say, "Enough" to the forces of godlessness who would send us to the back of the bus. Or would force us off the bus.

One day in the spring of 1999, Michelle Shocks, a pregnant African-American woman, was riding a bus in Seattle, Washington. She struck up a conversation with a fellow passenger, and they began to discuss church. She told him about her church, and he was quite receptive to it. The bus driver overhead the conversation and asked them both to come forward. The driver told them to stop talking about God in this public setting. If they didn't, she would have to kick them off.

Michelle was shocked at this and returned to her seat. The gentleman next to her asked a quick question about what they had been discussing before since they weren't finished with it. The bus driver then declared, "That's it. At the next stop, you two are off my bus."

Even though she was pregnant, even though it was pouring rain, even though the next bus would not come for quite a while, even though religious liberty (not to mention free speech) is protected by the

Constitution, Michelle got kicked off the bus for talking about God with a fellow passenger. She walked home at least a mile in the rain, on the side of the highway. She felt like an abused "drowned rat" when she finally got home.

So it's not "Go to the back of the bus" for Christians in modern America, it's "Get off the bus." Virtually every one of the founding fathers would have been thrown off that bus, because they mentioned God and quoted the Bible in all kinds of public settings.

In closing, consider the words of Calvin Coolidge, our thirtieth president:

> If American democracy is to remain the greatest hope
> of humanity, it must continue abundantly
> in the faith of the Bible. [340]

What a contrast to the liberal legal groups and judicial decisions trying to strip away every vestige of faith in the Bible from America's public life.

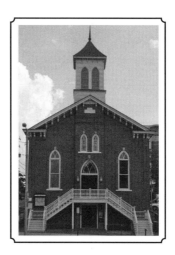

Dexter Avenue Baptist Church, Montgomery, Alabama.

It was in the basement of this church that the civil rights movement was born. In 1955, church member Rosa Parks, after a long hard day at work, was arrested, because she, as a black woman, refused to give up her seat to a white man on the bus. Rev. Martin Luther King Jr. served as pastor of the church and he initiated the bus boycott that launched the civil rights movement, forcing America to live up to its creed—that all men are created equal and receive their rights from the Creator, not the state.

Slavery is a huge sin in the American experience, as is all discrimination on racial grounds. How do we reconcile it and other sins with the Biblical foundation of the U.S.? That's the subject of this chapter.

CHAPTER 9

The Bible and America's Shortcomings

As it is written: "God's name is blasphemed
among the Gentiles because of you."
(Roman 2:24, NIV)

*W*E have seen clearly that America began as a Christian nation. The evidence is overwhelming and irrefutable. But if today you say so, you might have a fight on your hands. Besides, with America's wanton immorality, I am not sure we even want to say America is Christian today. Later generations might well condemn us for allowing widespread abortion, wholesale pornography, ubiquitous drug use, and rampant homosexuality. In this chapter, we want to explore some of the objections to the whole idea that America is or ever was a Christian nation.

One of the key objections is that America has not always lived up to Christian ideals. Shamefully, there have been some serious flaws in our history. The most notable of these in times past was the general mistreatment of the American Indians and the practice of slavery. Even after slavery was abolished, it took about a hundred years to try and overcome our racist past. Some argue that we still have not yet fully overcome it. While the founding fathers did not create a perfect government, they created the means by which such shortcomings could be corrected.

"In Search of Christian America"

In the 1980s, three evangelical professors (i.e., Mark Noll, George Marsden, and Nathan Hatch, all three of them now associated with Notre

Dame) caused quite a stir when they published a book, entitled *In Search of Christian America.* The overall thesis is that there never was a Christian America, that the idea of this country ever having been Christian was a myth, and more important, that it degrades the word "Christian" to say it ever was. A big part of the reason they say this is because of the injustices committed against the Indians and against the slaves. My comment is that those things were bad, but the founders of this country devised means by which the Constitution could be corrected, but not without a great deal of effort. It is not an easy process to amend the Constitution, but it can be done. The mistreatment of the Indians and the institution of slavery are important issues. Let us consider them both in some detail.

SLAVERY

The Bible says that the worker should be paid proper wages for his efforts. It is a sin to withhold due pay: "Behold, the wages of the laborers who mowed your fields, which you kept back by fraud, are crying out against you, and the cries of the harvesters have reached the ears of the Lord of hosts" (James 5:4). Many of our founders knew this.

"I will never concur in upholding domestic slavery. It is the curse of heaven on the States, where it prevails."[341] So said Gouverneur Morris, Constitution signer and the actual author of the preamble to the Constitution (We the people...). Obviously, not everyone agreed with him.

A serious blot on the American experience was its condoning of slavery for so long. Dr. Martin Luther King Jr. liked to point out that a year before the Pilgrim forefathers came over from England, the first group of slaves arrived and were sold here. In 1619, one year before the disembarking of the Pilgrims at Plymouth, a handful of slaves was sold at Jamestown. And thus began "the peculiar institution," which was destined to divide the country some two and half centuries later.

Around the time of the American Revolution, Dr. Samuel Johnson in England asked a penetrating question: "How is it that we hear the loudest YELPS for LIBERTY from the drivers of Negroes?"[342] That is an excellent question. Clearly, this was a major inconsistency with those who clamored for their own freedom, while not allowing for the freedom of their chattel slaves. It is so clear to us today looking back; hindsight is always 20/20. But no doubt we have our own blind spots over which future generations may legitimately skewer us. Also, there were many among the American colonists who opposed slavery, as seen in the Morris quote above and similar founding father quotes to follow. Ironically, some of the stated opposition to slavery came from those who owned slaves.

There are several observations I want to make about America and the problem of slavery. While it had been entrenched here virtually from the beginning of the country, there has also been strong, vocal opposition to it all along.

John Eidsmoe, respected historian, law professor, and author of the classic book, *Christianity and the Constitution*, once told me that there never would have been a United States Constitution if the founding fathers made slavery illegal right away. Some of the southern states, most notably South Carolina, would not have agreed with the document.

Virtually from the introduction of slavery on American soil until its abolition at the end of the Civil War and the fourteenth amendment (1868), there had been strong opposition to slavery—mostly from Christian quarters. For example, in 1652, in Rhode Island, there was a move against slavery, as was true eventually in the other colonies of New England. Providence and Warwick made a law that "no black mankind by covenant, bond, or otherwise," was to be forced to perpetually serve. The master, "at the end of ten years, shall set them free, as the manner is with English servants; and that man that will not let [his slave] go free, or shall send him away, to the end that he may be enslaved to others for a longer time, shall forfeit to the colony forty pounds." Bancroft points out that forty pounds was twice the value of a black slave in those days. Therefore, the colony made slavery illegal and provided financial incentives to not own a slave. Bancroft adds: "The law was not enforced; but the principle did not perish."[343]

Some of the founding fathers fought actively against slavery. For example, one of the key founding fathers was the Rev. John Witherspoon, the president of the College of Princeton, New Jersey, whose ministry was briefly highlighted in the chapter on education. Witherspoon, a Presbyterian minister, signed the Declaration of Independence. William J. Federer, author of *America's God and Country*, said of him: "After his wife died in October of 1789, he re-entered politics, heading up a committee in the New Jersey legislature to abolish slavery."[344]

In 1792, New Hampshire passed its Bill of Rights, which abolished slavery.[345] In 1804, New Jersey's legislature also abolished slavery.[346] This is just a sampling of some of the early opposition to slavery in different northern states.

Furthermore, slavery was not universally accepted in the South. In a 1773 letter, Patrick Henry of Virginia had this to say about the slave trade:

> I take this opportunity to acknowledge the receipt of Anthony Benezet's Book against the slave trade. I thank you for it.... Is it not amazing, that at a time when the rights of humanity are defined and understood with precision in a country above all others fond of liberty, that in such an age and in such a country, we find men professing a religion most humane, mild, meek, gentle and generous, adopting a Principle as repugnant to humanity, as it is inconsistent to the Bible and destructive to liberty?... I will not, I cannot justify it.... I believe a time will come when an opportunity will be offered to abolish this lamentable evil.... It is a debt we owe to the purity of our Religion to show that it is at variance with that law which warrants slavery.[347]

George Mason was one of the Virginia delegates to the Constitutional convention and, while he owned about 200 slaves himself, he became a strong opponent of this great evil. In fact, as noted above, he refused to sign the Constitution because slavery was implicit in its original form. The same year it was written (1787), he wrote: "Every master of slaves is born a petty tyrant. They bring the judgement of heaven upon a country. As nations cannot be rewarded or punished in the next world, they must be in this. By an inevitable chain of causes and effects, Providence punishes national sins, by national calamities."[348]

Even before America declared independence, there was an attempt to end the slave trade. Prior to the first Continental Congress meeting in September 1774, some delegates met in Virginia to discuss various issues, slavery being one of them. Because of illness, Thomas Jefferson was not able to be there, but he sent a paper which declared: "The abolition of domestic slavery is the great object of desire in those Colonies where it was, unhappily, introduced in their infant state. But previous to the enfranchisement of the slaves we have, it is necessary to exclude all further importations from Africa. Yet our repeated attempts to effect this by prohibitions, and by imposing duties which might amount to a prohibition, have hitherto been defeated...." This became the basis for "the Fairfax resolves," which were strong declarations against the slave-trade passed in Virginia that same year. Both George Mason and George Washington played a major part in this proclamation against peddling human flesh: "After the first day of November next we will neither ourselves import nor purchase any slave or slaves imported by any other person, either from Africa, the West Indies, or any other place."[349]

Nonetheless, the British prevented this from taking place. The profits were too high. George Bancroft writes: "The Virginians could plead, and did plead, that 'their assemblies had repeatedly attempted to prevent the horrid traffic in slaves, and had been frustrated by the cruelty and covetousness of English merchants, who prevailed on the king to repeal their merciful acts.'"[350] In other words, key Virginians—while under British rule—tried to abolish slavery, but greedy British merchants who profited from the slave trade prevailed with the king to prevent these merciful acts by the Virginians from being allowed. Again, in 1776, Virginia tried to forbid the importation of more slaves, but England would not let them.[351] This was long before Great Britain abolished the slave trade and freed all slaves in the British Empire, thanks to the five-decade crusade of William Wilberforce and his coterie of fellow evangelicals.

Thus, while there was some strong colonial opposition to slavery, even in the South, there was a British counter-opposition to those measures which would eat into the enormous profits from the slave trade. (Obviously, Virginia and other southern colonies did not follow such a course, even after they became states.)

Furthermore, the Continental Congress of 1776 attempted to prohibit slavery, despite Great Britain's favor of it. George Bancroft notes:

> One kind of traffic which the European maritime powers still encouraged was absolutely forbidden [by the American Congress], not from political reasons merely, but from a conviction of its unrighteousness and cruelty; and, without any limitation as to time or any reservation of a veto to the respective colonies, it was resolved "that no slaves be imported into any of the thirteen united colonies."[352]

The first known American proposal to end all slavery throughout America came from the progressive state of Rhode Island during the founding era. One of the two Rhode Island men who signed the Declaration of Independence was Stephen Hopkins. Notice what Bancroft mentions of his Christian background:

The first who is known to have suggested [to the Continental Congress of 1776] that negroes might be emancipated, and a "provision be made to transport them to Africa, where they might probably live better than in any other country," was Samuel Hopkins of Newport, Rhode Island, a theologian, . . . a firm believer in the coming of the millennium; a theorist who held virtue to require not merely disinterested love, but a love that is willing to make a sacrifice of self.[353]

It is ironic that we think of Rhode Island as progressive. In many ways it was, but, as Bancroft continues on Hopkins, note the source of some of its wealth—the slave trade:

Writing in a town which had grown rich by the slave-trade, Hopkins addressed a memorial to the members of the body representing the United States (i.e., Congress), "entreating them to be the happy instruments of procuring and establishing universal liberty to white and black, to be transmitted down to the latest prosperity."[354]

As we have already seen, the push against slavery in the founding era was not exclusively a Northern phenomenon. Quoting Bancroft further:

Congress had already manifested its own sentiments by the absolute prohibition of the slave-trade; and that prohibition was then respected in every one of the thirteen states, including South Carolina and Georgia. This is the occasion when the slave-trade was first branded as a piracy.[355]

At the Constitutional Convention of 1787, there was considerable debate about slavery. Some wanted to make it completely illegal and state that explicitly in the Constitution. This could not be agreed upon—and some of the pro-slavery states would have walked out, and there would not have been a union, had that happened. However, the Constitution does state that twenty years after the document goes into effect (1789), the slave trade would be abolished (1809). Here's what James Madison wrote in *The Federalist Papers* on that particular stipulation, noting that some of them would have liked the abolition of the slave trade to go into effect immediately. This is from *Federalist #42*:

It were doubtless to be wished, that the power of prohibiting the importation of slaves had not been postponed until the year 1808, or rather that it had been suffered to have immediate operation.... It ought to be considered as a great point gained in favor of humanity, that a period of twenty years may terminate forever, within these States, a traffic which has so long and so loudly upbraided the barbarism of modern policy.... Happy would it be for the unfortunate Africans, if an equal prospect lay before them of being redeemed from the oppressions of their European brethren![356]

We should never forget the fact that within twenty years of the Constitution being written, the founding fathers insisted that the evil slave-trade be abolished once and for all; however, those slaves that were already here continued to repopulate, thus perpetuating the institution. Unfortunately, it would take much longer to free these slaves. Moreover, the invention of the cotton gin would later increase the value of those slaves that were already here. Obviously, these conflicts between pro-slavery and anti-slavery states were not resolved until the Civil War. Then, for a hundred years after that, there were still strong forms of racism that needed to be addressed.

Racism is clearly wrong because the Bible teaches that through one man, God made all the people of the earth (Acts 17:26). It is interesting to note that the West, thanks in large part to Christian influence, has squarely faced the issue of slavery and has abolished it. Yet slavery is still going on in the world, e.g., in the African countries of Sudan and Mauritania, where Muslims capture vulnerable infidels and sell them into slavery. This has been going on for centuries.

In the Western world, opposition to the slave-trade and then slavery itself began in earnest within Christian circles. Again, William Wilberforce, a member of Parliament in the late 1700s and early 1800s, championed the cause against slavery and fought against it decade upon decade, ultimately prevailing. Wilberforce was a committed evangelical, and it was from his relationship with Christ that his crusade against slavery sprang into being. He surrounded himself with like-minded evangelicals and together they successfully fought against this monumental evil. One of those evangelicals, Granville Sharpe, was a scholar of the Greek New Testament. He discovered and articulated an obscure rule of Greek grammar that has never been refuted. It was men who loved and honored the Word of God that abolished slavery.

In America, much of the opposition to slavery came from Christian sources as well. But ultimately it took a war to settle the issue here. Here again, the Scriptures played a role in the freeing of the slaves. Abraham Lincoln, who eventually did so much for abolition, made this remark when he received a copy of the Holy Bible: "In regard to this great book, I have but to say, it is the best gift God has given to men. All the good the Savior gave to the world was communicated through this book. But for it we could not know right from wrong."[357]

While it is true that some professing Christians owned slaves or defended the peculiar institution, it is also true that the death knell against slavery came largely from the influence of the Bible. For example, in his Second Inaugural Address, President Abraham Lincoln said this:

> Fondly do we hope, fervently do we pray, that this mighty scourge of war may speedily pass away. Yet, if God will that it continue until all the wealth piled by the bondsmen's two hundred and fifty years of unrequited toil shall be sunk, and until every drop of blood drawn with the lash shall be paid by another drawn with the sword, as was said three thousand years ago, so still it must be said "the judgments of the Lord are true and righteous altogether."[358]

Furthermore, we know that the Underground Railroad was run by Christians. Also, some owners treated their slaves with kindness.

Has the United States of America been perfect? Not at all. But the founding fathers developed a system of government, based on the Word of God, that allowed for self-correction. The Constitution has now been corrected on the subject of slavery.

As bad as slavery was, and as inexcusable, I wish that school children today would learn that in 1776, the same Congress that declared independence from Great Britain also made the above-cited commitment: Resolved: "that no slaves be imported into any of the thirteen united colonies." I also wish they would learn that the same Congress that declared independence branded slavery "as a crime against humanity."[359] I do not know about you, but I never learned that in school.

THE INDIANS

The way that the Indians were treated by the Europeans and their descendants was partly inexcusable and partly commendable—mostly the former. The history of this nation on that point would have been very different if the native population had been treated as well as the Indians were by the Pilgrims, Roger Williams, or William Penn. All of these tried to go out of their way to work with the Indians, to lead them to Christ, and to be sure that they were treated properly and compensated fairly in all their dealings.

Frankly, though, clashes between the Indians and the Europeans were virtually inevitable. Dr. Peter Lillback, president of Westminster Theological Seminary and author on America's godly heritage, had this to say when I asked him about conflicts between the Jamestown settlers and Indians:

> There were problems on both sides. The Native Indians, if we want to use that term, defended themselves against the intruders. Those that were coming with progress saw themselves as advancing a cause, and they defended themselves as well. So, there is a controversy, but there's also a glory and I think a true celebration affirms both realities. Cultures always clash, change, advance, and humanity goes forward.[360]

What I am about to say does not justify the way the Indians were sometimes mistreated, but it helps to understand the historical context. Sometimes the Indians were very difficult to deal with. For example, even the enlightened historian George Bancroft occasionally calls the Indians "savages." There are innumerable accounts of poor frontiersmen, including women and children, being viciously attacked and brutally murdered by the Indians. Here are just a few snippets that Bancroft mentions in his monumental *History of the United States*. These happen to be dated about the year 1700; they happened to have occurred in the fringes of New England, close to the Canadian border. These are typical of the attacks upon the English settlers by the "savages" and help us to understand three centuries later why they were called savages:

★ "Finding all asleep, they set fire to the homes, and in less than an hour killed two hundred people with most skillfully devised forms of cruelty...."[361] (This includes men, women, and children.)

★ "The Indians burned his home, dashed his new-born child against a tree...."[362]

★ "Benjamin Rolfe, the minister, was beaten to death; one Indian sunk a hatchet deep into the brain of his wife, while another dashed the head of his infant child against a stone."[363]

Bancroft notes that: "Such fruitless cruelties compelled the employment of a large part of the inhabitants as soldiers.... They [these cruelties] fostered a willingness to exterminate the natives."[364]

David Barton tells a horrific story of what the Indians did to men who surrendered in battle. These were soldiers on the British-American side in the French and Indian War, captured by the red man; one of them survived and was able to later provide an eyewitness account of what the Indians did to some of his colleagues. The Indians brought into the fort:

> [A] dozen prisoners, stripped naked, with their hands tied behind their backs.... I stood on the fort walls until I beheld them begin to burn one of these men. They tied him to a stake and kept touching him with fire-brands, red-hot irons, etc., and he screaming in the most doleful manner,—the Indians, in the meantime yelling like infernal spirits. As this scene was too shocking for me to behold, I returned to my lodgings, both sorry and sore.[365]

Catherine Drinker Bowen noted, "Thomas Hobbes had seen the life of the savage as 'solitary, poor, nasty, brutish, and short.' Americans living on Western borders could have wished it even shorter."[366] Bowen also wrote, "the noble savage was a fiction."[367] In addition, she points out, "It is to be doubted if many eighteenth-century colonials looked on the Mohawk or the Cherokee as anything but verminous, thieving, and potentially ferocious nuisances."[368] In 1775, Duncan Cameron wrote, "the Indians could not be restrained from committing the most inhuman barbarities on women and children."[369]

Furthermore, virtually no colonist was exempt from the threat of the Indians. Obviously, those on the frontier were less exempt than those more inland settlers. When the Pilgrims first came, they pursued peace and were able to make a treaty of peace with the Indians that lasted more than five decades. They made this plan with the chief, Massasoit, a very honorable man by all accounts. But later, his son, King Philip, declared war on all the Europeans in that area. Paul Johnson points out that during King Philip's War in 1676, in Massachusetts, and beyond: "Every white family in New England was involved in one way or another."[370]

Certainly, throughout the centuries-long conflict between Indians and the white man, the latter overreacted to Indian cruelties. Bancroft describes inexcusable behavior as seen in an eighteenth-century incident in the south, wherein American colonists violated a recent treaty with the Indians: "The troops of South Carolina, on their return, themselves violated the treaty, enslaving inhabitants of villages which should have been safe under its guarantees; and the massacres on Neuse River were renewed."[371] As we will see in a moment, atrocities toward the Indians reached its zenith in the West in the nineteenth century.

Sometimes Indian cruelty was toward their fellow Indians. George Bancroft writes:

★ "In September 1680, a large war party of the Iroquois made a merciless and infuriated attack upon the Illinois, partly to destroy them as in war, partly to rob them of their store of furs. It was on this occasion that the great village of the Illinois was laid waste."[372]

★ "Of the Illinois village nothing was to be seen but burnt stakes which marked its extent. The heads of the dead remained stuck on poles for the crows to strike at with their talons...."[373]

How Americans mistreated the Indians is not as simple as it is sometimes made out to be today. Some of the colonists who went out of their way to treat the Indians well suffered under their hands.

Attempting to convert the Indians was very difficult and slow-going. Bancroft writes, "Neither John Eliot nor Roger Williams was able to change essentially the mind of and habits of the New England tribes. The Quakers came among the Delawares in the spirit of peace and brotherly love, and with sincerest wishes to benefit them; but the Quakers succeeded no better than the Puritans, not nearly so well as the Jesuits."

Bancroft adds that part of the problem was a restlessness on the part of the Indians. Note what he says about their "hatred of habitual labor":

> In New Hampshire and elsewhere, schools for Indian children were established; but, as they became fledged, they all escaped, refusing to be caged. Harvard college enrolls the name of an Algonkin among its pupils; but the college parchment could not close the gulf between the Indian character of those days and the Anglo-American. No tribe could be trained to habits of regular industry. Their hatred of habitual labor spoiled all. The red men were characterized by a moral inflexibility, a rigidity of attachment to their hereditary customs and manners.[374]

When it was expedient for them to do so, European powers, namely the French and later the British, worsened the relationship of the Indians with the colonists. For example, when France and England were at war in the first part and then the middle of the eighteenth century, the French—who always had better relationships with the Indians than the British—would sometimes use the tribes to wage war on the English settlers in America. The savage examples I quoted above of Indians dashing the brains of babies were from incidents partially incited by the French against the British.

During the ongoing conflict between the British and the Americans in the 1760s and 1770s (that culminated in the American War for Independence), the British sometimes encouraged using Indians to harass the Americans. Guy Johnson was the man chosen for the job to reach the Indians for this cause. He was told by his British masters: "Lose no time...induce them to take up the hatchet against his majesty's rebellious subjects in America."[375] One of the first things Guy Johnson sought to do was to remove the American, Christian *missionaries* from the so-called "Six Nations," a loose confederation of six Indian tribes.[376] In the South Carolina region, writes Bancroft, "a large body of savages stood ready to seize the scalping-knife at the king's behest...."[377]

Even the Declaration of Independence points out this problem in the context of the laundry list of grievances against King George III: "He has excited domestic insurrections amongst us, and has endeavored to bring on the inhabitants of our frontiers, the merciless Indian savages, whose known rule of warfare, is undistinguished destruction of all ages, sexes, and conditions."[378]

Catherine Drinker Bowen, author of *Miracle at Philadelphia: The Story of the Constitutional Convention May to September 1787*, points out that to the Europeans, the red man was a "curiosity." To the Americans, the Indian was a "problem."[379]

In *The Federalist* #24, Alexander Hamilton points out: "The savage tribes on our Western frontier ought to be regarded as our natural enemies...." To which he adds, "Previous to the Revolution, and ever since the peace, there has been a constant necessity for keeping small garrisons on our Western frontier. No person can doubt that these will continue to be indispensable, if it should only be against the ravages and depredations of the Indians."[380]

It is certainly true that the white man supplanted the red man on the American continent. It is true that many injustices were committed against them. It also should be pointed out that one Indian tribe often supplanted another Indian tribe. Indians fought amongst themselves as much as against the white man. The Mohicans were virtually wiped out as a tribe by other Indian groups.

Some of the European settlers paid for their land from the Indians. Others simply seized it. Roger Williams argued how un-Christian the latter posture was. He and others went out of their way to pay a just wage to the Indians.

It should also be pointed out that Indian landownership was not viewed in the same way as European landownership. Most of the Indians were nomads. The majority of them never settled down in any one place permanently. They lived in wide open spaces. They would hunt for game and farm the land, and then they would leave that place when the soil was no longer productive and start the process all over again.

As every school child learned, the Dutch bought Manhattan from the Indians for a mere $24. This may well have been the greatest real estate deal in the history of the world. Many today say that the white man swindled the red man. But Paul Harvey points out a side to this that we never learned in school. Peter Minuit, the shrewd Dutchman who bought Manhattan for the equivalent of $24:

> ...purchased the island from the Canarsie Indians. But the Canarsies did not live there. They were only visiting.
>
> What I'm saying is — the Canarsie Indians sold something they never owned in the first place.
>
> And after they ripped off the world's smartest real estate dealer, they got in their canoes and returned home.
>
> To Brooklyn.
>
> Now you know THE REST OF THE STORY. [emphasis his][381]

How American colonists treated the Indians was commendable in some cases and deplorable in others. Again, I hold up as examples in this realm the Pilgrims, who made a treaty of peace that lasted for more than fifty years, Roger Williams, who chided his fellow Puritans for not always paying equitably for the Indian lands they took, and William Penn, who consistently treated the Indians in a Christian manner. Bancroft points out that justice for all, including the Indians, was important to the Pilgrims of Plymouth. "Murder had ever been severely punished by the Puritans: they had at Plymouth, with the advice of Massachusetts, executed three of their own men for taking the life of one Indian."[382]

Finally, I will say that the greatest travesties against the Indians took place in the nineteenth century. Many of those who most slaughtered the native Americans were Indian haters who had cut their teeth fighting in the Civil War. Some of these veterans may possibly have been professing Christians, but they certainly were not known for their piety—genuine or professed.

Unquestionably, the mistreatment of the Indians on the part of many has been a black-eye on America's history. But we cannot undo the past. Nor should we ignore the atrocities on the part of the Indians that the settlers and founders had to contend with. The truth is that there were cruel and evil people among the whites as well as among the Indians, and one group does not hold all the guilt. Our nation has a Christian heritage, despite some moral failings along the way, including this one.

The Treaty of Tripoli

One of the key objections to the overall thesis that America began as a Christian nation deals with an obscure treaty from the turn of the nineteenth century. This is the Treaty of Tripoli. Groups like People for the American Way (which could well be called "People for Norman Lear's Way," in honor of its founder, the secular humanist Hollywood producer) seek to use the Treaty of Tripoli as a weapon against the religious right. The People for the American Way exist to thwart the religious right's agenda. Period.

During the Washington administration, Muslim pirates from the Barbary coast of Africa (around modern-day Libya) were attacking American ships in unprovoked raids motivated by greed. This sparked the Barbary Powers Conflict, which was waged off and on from Washington's through Madison's administrations. David Barton writes, "The Muslim Barbary Powers (Tunis, Morocco, Algiers, Tripoli, and Turkey) were warring against what they claimed to be the 'Christian' nations (England, France, Spain, Denmark, and the United States). In 1801, Tripoli even declared war against the United States, thus constituting America's first official war as an established independent nation."[383]

Washington's administration initiated peaceful negotiations with the Tripoli government to halt these random attacks. Meanwhile, the United States established the Navy in 1798 to protect American ships because of these pirates. The final result was signed by then-president John Adams in the Treaty of Tripoli in 1797. Here's one version of the wording of Article XI of that treaty:

> As the government of the United States of America is not in any sense founded on the Christian religion as it has in itself no character of enmity against the laws, religion or tranquility of Musselmen [Muslims] and as the said States [United States of America] have never entered into any war or act of hostility against any Mahometan nation, it is declared by the parties that no pretext arising from religious opinions shall ever produce an interruption of the harmony existing between the two countries.

So what does this mean? That the United States never was a Christian nation? Norman Lear and company would have you believe that. What modern secularists like to do is to take the first sentence, but not the rest. They rip this statement out of context: "The government of the United States of America is not in any sense founded on the Christian religion." Plus, many times they falsely attribute this to George Washington. (The treaty was signed after he had retired from the presidency.)

Context or no context, how do we come to terms with this treaty? David Barton weighs in:

> Recall that while the Founders themselves openly described America as a Christian nation...they did include a constitutional prohibition against a *federal* establishment; religion was a matter left solely to the individual States. Therefore, if the article is read as a declaration that the federal government of the United States was not in any sense founded on the Christian religion, such a statement is not a repudiation of the fact that America was considered a Christian nation. [emphasis added]
>
> Reading the clause of the treaty in its entirety also fails to weaken this fact....

Barton then points out that the newly formed American government was telling the Muslims that America was not like the nations of Europe, which had been in conflict with the Muslim nations:

Article XI simply distinguished America from those historical strains of European Christianity which held an inherent hatred of Muslims; it simply assured the Muslims that the United States was not a Christian nation like those of previous centuries (with whose practices the Muslims were very familiar) and thus would not undertake a religious holy war against them.... A clear distinction was drawn between American Christianity and that of Europe in earlier centuries.[384]

Another point, this one made by John Eidsmoe, is that there is even controversy about the original wording of the treaty. There is a question whether Article XI can even be found in the original copy.[385] Article XI as seen above is not necessarily reliable.

Furthermore, Eidsmoe points out that despite the 1797 treaty, the piracy continued, so America went to war with Tripoli and won. This is where the phrase "to the shores of Tripoli" in the *Marine Core Anthem* comes from. After winning the war, we negotiated a new peace treaty, which was accepted April 17, 1806, and it did not contain Article XI or the questionable sentence.[386]

Besides all of that, suppose for a moment that the Treaty of Tripoli (as reproduced above) was legitimate. Suppose they meant by it what Norman Lear and company interpret it to mean. Then it still represents one small sliver of alleged evidence, as opposed to mounds and mounds of real evidence to the contrary. Picture two large tables of evidence in a courtroom. If we put on one all of the documentation for America's Judeo-Christian heritage, the table might buckle under from all the mountains of paperwork that would reach to the ceiling. If we put on the other table the arguments against that thesis, the Treaty of Tripoli could be placed there, all alone, except perhaps for the moral failures and scandals that we have discussed in this chapter. By contrast, this second table would not be very crowded.

Conclusion

To treat American history the way the modern revisionist does is a travesty against the truth. They pick out the presumed negative and overlook the overwhelming positive. They seem to "blame America first," no matter the facts. I hear them rail against America, but then I think about the would-be immigrants who literally risk their lives to try to get here.

Other key objections to the notion of America being a Christian nation can be seen in a misreading of the first amendment. Many secularists today engage in a shell game. They quote someone like James Madison arguing for disestablishment, i.e., no national church. Then they go from there to assume that Madison would approve of the separation of God and state.

Dr. Kennedy once made the following observation when I interviewed him for a portion of our book, *What If Jesus Had Never Been Born?* The immediate context was religious freedom, but what he said could be applied toward all of America's freedoms.

> The perfections of this religious freedom did not spring full blown like Athena from the head of Zeus. But rather it took some time and experimentation and trial and error to work out the flaws and perfect the system which was developing from 1620 for the next 160 years. It went through various stages as it progressed those many decades, and it climaxed with the first amendment to the Constitution with its guarantee of religious freedom.[387]

Again, what he said about religious freedom could apply to all sorts of freedoms. Martin Luther King Jr. used to point out that America was not living up to its creed, that all men were created equal, but that does not mean the creed is wrong. Similarly, the founding fathers did not create a perfect Constitution, (yet very brilliant and Biblically-reasoned), but they built in ways that allowed for it to be corrected, through the amendment process. The American experiment and its founding documents based upon the Bible led to the world's first Christian Constitutional Republic.

Any honest survey of the overall facts of America's roots leads to the same conclusion the Supreme Court came to in 1892: "These, and many other matters which might be noticed, add a volume of unofficial declarations to the mass of organic utterances that this is a Christian nation."[388]

That is where this nation began.

The Liberty Bell is an icon of American freedom. However, many people do not realize that it has a Bible verse on it. "Proclaim liberty throughout all the land unto all the inhabitants thereof" (Leviticus 25:10). Here is the author and his wife, Kirsti, in Philadelphia.

PART FOUR

The Bible and the American Experience

*T*HIS final section will explore some important questions left unanswered. For example, if America truly began as one nation under God, how did we get off track? Secondly, how does the Bible transform a society? Thirdly, how do we, as Christians and other God-fearing Americans today in modern America, attempt in any way to restore America to its Biblical moorings? Should we even try? This final chapter will explore the time-honored question: Where do we go from here?

PHOTO BY CORAL RIDGE MINISTRIES

The Supreme Court in Washington, D.C. It is in this building that so much of the Christian foundation of America has been greatly damaged.

CHAPTER 10

Were Did We Go Wrong?

...take care lest you forget the LORD....
(Deuteronomy 6:12)

HE failed Soviet Union was one of the greatest monstrosities ever
to blight humanity. It was thoroughly atheistic, and it unleashed a
horror that resulted in the murder of tens of millions of their own people.
Aleksandr Solzhenitzyn, the great Russian writer and critic of the USSR,
received the Templeton Prize for Progress in Religion in 1993. When
accepting the prize, he gave a speech wherein he explained how the whole
Soviet enterprise got back to one basic problem: They had forgotten God.
Here is what Solzhenitzyn said:

> More than half a century ago, while I was still a child, I recall
> hearing a number of older people offer the following explanation
> for the great disasters that had befallen Russia: **Men have forgot-
> ten God; that's why all this has happened.**
>
> Since then I have spent well-nigh fifty years working on the
> history of our Revolution; in the process I have read hundreds
> of books, collected hundreds of personal testimonies, and have
> already contributed eight volumes of my own toward the effort
> of clearing away the rubble left by that upheaval. But if I were
> asked today to formulate as concisely as possible the main cause
> of the ruinous [Russian] Revolution that swallowed up some sixty
> million of our people, I could not put it more accurately than to
> repeat: **Men have forgotten God; that's why all this has happened.**
> [emphasis his] [389]

Five years earlier, Solzhenitzyn had spoken at Harvard. In that 1978 speech, he said that America must return to God, at which point he was booed. Dr. Erwin Lutzer says that that response "hurt him more deeply than his suffering in the Russian gulag. He understood more clearly than our self-styled intellectuals that when God is irrelevant anything is permissible."[390] I believe Aleksandr is and was correct and not his rude audience at one of our nation's leading universities.

Why is America seemingly sinking into the abyss? We have forgotten God.

Mass shootings by a deranged gunman seem to be becoming such a common story. These shootings are happening in schools, in malls, and even in churches. The story makes the news for a while, until some other tragedy takes its place. These are all symptoms of the simple truth: We have forgotten God. Just this very day, as of this writing, there was a senseless mass shooting in the peaceful town of Binghamton, New York. These seem to be happening on such a regular basis that we are growing numb to them.

How is it that America began with such great promise and hope and has now come to such a place as this? The answer is we have forgotten God.

Why have we forgotten God?

Pride.

During the calamity that was the Civil War, Abraham Lincoln called for a national day of repentance and prayer. He warned Americans about the sin of pride. He said:

> We have been the recipients of the choicest bounties of Heaven. We have been preserved these many years in peace and prosperity. We have grown in numbers and power as no other nation has ever grown, but we have forgotten God. We have forgotten the gracious hand which preserved us in peace, and multiplied and enriched and strengthened us; and we have vainly imagined, in the deceitfulness of our hearts, that all these blessings were produced by some superior wisdom and virtue of our own. Intoxicated with unbroken success, we have become too self-sufficient to feel the necessity of redeeming and preserving grace, too proud to pray to the God that made us. It behooves us, then, to humble ourselves before the offended Power, to confess our national sins, and to pray for clemency and forgiveness.[391]

The sin of pride is where it all begins. Pride turned Lucifer, the angel of light, into Satan, the demon of darkness (Isaiah 14:12-15). And pride goes before destruction and a fall (Proverbs 16:18). The Bible is very clear that many other sins, which most people take to be far more serious, are peccadilloes compared to the spiritual sin of pride. Pride makes devils.[392]

Think of the Pharisees. What was the sin that blinded them to the reality of the Son of God and caused them to deliver Jesus up to be crucified? Envy fueled by their pride. So pride nailed Christ to the cross.

The warnings in Scripture against pride are numerous. For example:

* "The LORD will destroy the house of the proud, but He will establish the boundary of the widow" (Proverbs 15:25, NKJV).
* "The one who has a haughty look and a proud heart, him I will not endure" (Psalm 101:5, NKJV).
* "Let nothing be done through selfish ambition or conceit, but in lowliness of mind let each esteem others better than himself" (Philippians 2:3, NKJV).
* "God resists the proud, but gives grace to the humble" (James 4:6, NKJV).

The late Dr. D. James Kennedy said:

> We Christians need to humble ourselves, to acknowledge our sins, to acknowledge our unworthiness. We need to pray that God will grant us humility of spirit so we may be able to pray in a way that will be acceptable and pleasing to Him. Until we have first confessed our sins and our unworthiness, our prayers will bounce off Heaven. If we humble ourselves and confess our sins, God will hear from Heaven, answer our prayers, and forgive our sins.[393]

Of course, when we look at American society, we not only see the sin of pride, but all of the seven deadly sins, including envy, greed, anger, lust, gluttony, and sloth.

A CLUELESS GENERATION

I once read that more American children today know who Big Bird is than know who Noah was. Not only is there widespread Biblical illiteracy, but there is widespread illiteracy about our true history.

More people today know the ingredients of a Big Mac than know the Ten Commandments.

More people know contestants on *American Idol* than know basic things about the Bible. What a tragedy.

We have a whole generation of Americans today who have no clue about the godly heritage of this country. Most do not know one-tenth of what we've dealt with in this book. For all they know, America was founded by a group of atheists whose goal was to create an environment where all public places, e.g., schools, courts, government buildings, were to be "religion free zones." For all they know, the founding fathers intended us to experience liberty and licentiousness. For all they know, the founding fathers would be comfortable with the moral filth we now find ourselves wading in. Or they view America as being founded by a group of "dead white guys" who are totally irrelevant today.

The Problem of Prosperity

America became the most successful country in the annals of history. But whenever prosperity comes, there is always the potential for forgetting God, the source of that prosperity. In Deuteronomy 8, Moses even warned the ancient Israelites about this:

> For the LORD your God is bringing you into a good land, a land of brooks of water, of fountains and springs, flowing out in the valleys and hills, a land of wheat and barley, of vines and fig trees and pomegranates, a land of olive trees and honey, a land in which you will eat bread without scarcity, in which you will lack nothing, a land whose stones are iron, and out of whose hills you can dig copper. And you shall eat and be full, and you shall bless the LORD your God for the good land He has given you.
>
> Take care lest you forget the LORD your God by not keeping His commandments and His rules and His statutes, which I command you today, lest, when you have eaten and are full and have built good houses and live in them, and when your herds and flocks multiply and your silver and gold is multiplied and all that you have is multiplied, then your heart be lifted up, and you forget the LORD your God, who brought you out of the land of Egypt, out of the house of slavery, who led you through the great and terrifying wilderness, with its fiery serpents and scorpions and thirsty ground where there was no water, who brought you water out of the flinty rock, who fed you in the wilderness with manna that your fathers did not know, that He might humble

you and test you, to do you good in the end. Beware lest you say in your heart, "My power and the might of my hand have gotten me this wealth." You shall remember the LORD your God, for it is He who gives you power to get wealth, that He may confirm His covenant that He swore to your fathers, as it is this day. And if you forget the LORD your God and go after other gods and serve them and worship them, I solemnly warn you today that you shall surely perish. Like the nations that the LORD makes to perish before you, so shall you perish, because you would not obey the voice of the LORD your God (Deuteronomy 8:7-20).

Tragically, this became Israel's history. God miraculously led them to the Promised Land. They prospered because of Him. Then they forgot Him in their pride and arrogance. Then He judged them. Then they repented, and He helped them. Then they prospered; then they forgot Him. These cycles kept getting worse until He finally had them exiled. He brought back a purified remnant, while paving the way for His Messiah. The overall point is: It is easy to forget God in our prosperity.

The parallels to America (even though there was only one Israel) seem obvious to me. Despite recent economic problems, we are still prosperous overall. If you do not believe me, travel sometime to a Third World country. I remember going on a trip to El Salvador in 2001 with Food for the Poor. When I saw some people living in hovels, living in cardboard boxes, strewn together with chicken coop and corrugated iron (as the kind you would find on a tin roof), I felt so convicted. I remember saying, "Oh God, help me never to complain about anything anymore. Please, forgive me." Unfortunately, I have violated that prayer many times.

Our prosperity often keeps us from God.

Which region is generally more Christian? Western Europe or Eastern Europe. The latter—despite years and years of communist propaganda.

When men prosper, they are often under the delusion that they accomplished everything all by themselves.

In 1702, Cotton Mather once summed up the history of America. If it was true in his time, how much more in our time? He said, "Religion brought forth Prosperity, and the daughter destroyed the mother."[394]

The godliness of the early settlers and founders of this country caused us to prosper as a nation, but that prosperity slowly made many of our fellow Americans feel that they no longer needed God. John Wesley of

Great Britain had some great insights on this whole issue in general, of how religion brings prosperity, and then prosperity eventually undermines religion:

> I fear, wherever riches have increased, the essence of religion has decreased in the same proportion. Therefore I do not see how it is possible, in the nature of things, for any revival of true religion to continue long. For religion must necessarily produce both industry and frugality, and these cannot but produce riches. But as riches increase, so will pride, anger, and love of the world in all its branches.[395]

During the Depression in the 1930s, millions of Americans turned to God. They were comforted spiritually, while their physical needs were great. Church attendance soared during that era. Then, millions of Americans turned to prayer during the 1940s during the Great War. After we won World War II, we experienced unprecedented prosperity in the 1950s and especially 1960s. And then many turned their backs on God.

It is interesting to note that the highest church attendance record in the history of the nation—at any time, including the colonial era—was in 1960 with a whopping 69 percent. By 1970, the number had substantially dropped to 62.4 percent.[396] Today we are down to weekly church attendance of about 40 percent. Yet that is still a huge number of Americans—more than 100 million of us go to church or synagogue each week.

Notwithstanding, prosperity is one of the chief reasons for our nation going secular. If America will again be free and just, Christians must learn to handle wealth for God's glory, rather than yield to the temptation of riches. But then this is exactly what righteousness requires.

THE PROBLEM OF THE MEDIA

Another cause of the secularization of America was (and is) the media. When you consider what the Bible says and then you look at what the mainstream American media says, you will see major conflicts. The media has played a powerful role in de-Christianizing America. They continue to play that role. Note what Abraham Lincoln said on popular views, the kinds of views shaped in our time by the mass media: "Our government rests in public opinion. Whoever can change public opinion can change the government practically just so much."[397]

This is why the age-old argument from Plato is correct: culture precedes politics. To change the politics, you first have to change the culture.

In modern America, we Christians have our work cut our for us, to change the culture. Some Christians may argue that Christ does not call us to change the culture, but just to change lives. That is true in one sense. But it is also true that when Christians authentically live out their faith, it cannot help but impact culture as God intends.

For now, I would think that the media shapes our culture more effectively than the pulpit does.

Historian Paul Johnson points out that there was a major shift in the 1960s and beyond, where the communicators in the media began to have more influence in some ways than the owners or stockholders. TV reporters, anchors, directors, producers, and newspaper editors, writers, and columnists often became more important than owners and managers. Johnson asserts: "Since the latter tended to be overwhelmingly liberal in their views, this was not just a political but a cultural change of considerable importance. Indeed it is likely that nothing did more to cut America loose from its traditional moorings."[398] Here, the great historian is stating that the single most important factor in America jettisoning its heritage was the change of the media.

There have been many studies that show the liberal bias of the secular media. Media Research Center just outside of Washington, D.C., has been tracking and reporting on the liberal bias in the media for years. One of the recent best-sellers, *Bias* by CBS veteran reporter Bernard Goldberg, who is not a Christian, documents in living color the bias he saw firsthand against those with conservative values. Fundamentalist Christians are among the most marginalized by the decision-makers in secular broadcasting. His blockbuster book was an outgrowth of his leaving CBS after seven Emmies and some twenty-eight productive years as a producer/reporter. He ultimately left in 2000 because of the aftershocks of a guest editorial in the *Wall Street Journal* in 1996, for which he became *persona non grata*. What had he said in the editorial so grievous that it cost him his career? He said the media is biased. Goldberg, who says he never voted for a Republican president in his life, wrote in that editorial: "The old argument that the networks and other 'media elites' have a liberal bias is so blatantly true that it's hardly worth discussing anymore."[399] For writing the obvious, he was yanked off the air, shunned, and in effect demoted.

While there are some exceptions here and there, the media have often been very unfair to conservative Christians. This should not surprise us because studies have shown that the key decision-makers usually don't go to church. Consider the research of two social scientists in the famed Lichter-Rothman report. S. Robert Lichter is a research professor in political science at George Washington University. Stanley Rothman is a professor of government at Smith College. Linda Lichter is codirector (along with Robert Lichter) of the Center for Media and Public Affairs in Washington, D.C. They conducted an important survey of 104 of the "most influential television writers, producers, and executives,"[400] which found that these were very liberal people.[401] They learned that 93 percent say they "seldom or never attend religious services." They learned that 97 percent believe that "a woman has the right to decide for herself" whether to have an abortion, and that 80 percent "do not regard homosexual relations as wrong." They even found that only 17 percent "strongly agree that extramarital affairs are wrong."[402] Keep these facts in mind when you watch the evening news. Every story has been carefully filtered by people with a strong bias to the left and a strong bias against the things of God.

In the 2008 election, no matter which candidate you were rooting for (Obama or McCain), anyone with any objectivity would agree that the media was rooting for Obama. Many pundits said that the media has lost any pretense of objectivity. Chris Matthews, host of *Hardball,* said that when Obama spoke, "I felt a thrill going up my leg." Bernard Goldberg wrote a book about that election, titled, *A Slobbering Love Affair: The True (and Pathetic) Story of the Torrid Romance between Barack Obama and the Mainstream Media.*[403] He said that reporters by and large had crossed the *journalistic* line and had become *advocates* for Obama.

So we see that the media has been a major influence in our country's move toward secularism in America. And I have not even mentioned the role of rock music, movies, television, or pornography.

The Problem of the Schools

The public schools have become so secularized that it is shocking.

John Dewey was the father of modern progressive education. He did so much to secularize America's schools. He is viewed as a hero by many. I think he is more of a villain. Thanks to him, millions of school children have not learned about God. They have not learned the truth of how it was Christianity that gave birth to modern science. They have not learned the truth about America's Christian roots. They have not learned the truth about world history in general. (All of these things are documented in the books I wrote with Dr. Kennedy, *What If Jesus Had Never Been Born?* and *What If the Bible Had Never Been Written?*) Instead, education in America, thanks to Dewey and others, has become devoid of God. Yet the Scriptures say that the fear of the Lord is the beginning of wisdom. How can a baseball player make it to home plate, if he never reaches first base?

I am not saying that non-Christian children should have Christian views imposed on them in a compulsory way. What I am saying is that Christian children should not have non-Christian views imposed on them. Yet it happens everyday in America. Thankfully, there are alternatives to government schools, such as homeschooling or Christian schools. There are also pockets here and there (unmolested as yet by ACLU lawsuits) of Christian influence left in some public schools.

Inasmuch as it is possible with us, I do believe parents should try to let their children have a truly Christian education. But I recognize that in today's society that is not always easy or even possible. In that event, then a parent should at least try to supplement the child's education with material and training from a Christian worldview. Regardless of how a parent chooses to teach a child, he or she should recognize that God will hold *parents* accountable.

Dewey was one of the signers of the "The Humanist Manifesto," which was written in the 1930s and rewritten in 1973. It stated:

> We believe, however, that traditional dogmatic or authoritarian religions that place revelation, God, ritual, or creed above human needs and experience do a disservice to the human species.[404]

They add: "No deity will save us; we must save ourselves."[405]

Jacques Barzun, educator and author, said in the *New York Review of Books*: "The once proud and efficient public school system [of the United States] has turned into a wasteland where violence and vice share the time with ignorance and idleness."[406] Now we have millions of illiterates in America that have been turned out by these schools. It is not only unsafe for the children to go there, should they survive the drugs and the other hazards, they may very easily be killed, as recent events have shown. We have also seen how unsafe it is even for teachers.

In our book, *How Would Jesus Vote? A Christian Perspective on the Issues,* D. James Kennedy and I wrote:

> We cannot get rid of religious principle. The founders of this country never intended that religion should not be taught in our schools. The first Congress of the United States passed the Northwest Ordinance in which they said, "Religion, morality, and knowledge being necessary for good government, schools and the means of education shall forever be encouraged." Schools? Yes. For what? Religion, number one. Morality, number two. Knowledge, number three.
>
> We got rid of religion; then we got rid of morality; and now we have gotten rid of education. Oh, we are pretty wise, aren't we? We are so sophisticated and so modern...and so stupid. We are the dumb Americans, but we sure feel good about ourselves.
>
> What we hear from the school unions is that they need more money. Next time you hear that, just remember that we spend more money per student than any other nation in the world...and are producing abysmal results. It is not the money that is the problem; it is the philosophy that has gone wrong. We have brought about a moral educational collapse equivalent to an attack by a hostile foreign power.[407]

Sadly, the secularism of today seems to permeate virtually every level of society, including higher education (even though the phenomenon of the university has Christian roots). This is just where Dewey and his friends started: teach the teachers, journalists, lawyers (future judges), and psychologists.

Walter Kehowski, a community college math professor at Glendale, Arizona, found this out the hard way. He was rebuked for sending an *offensive* e-mail around to his fellow teachers a couple of years ago. Alan Sears, founder of the Alliance Defense Fund, writes:

> But, after receiving e-mails from fellow teachers on everything from the health benefits of bananas to the need for goats in Uganda to quotes for Women's History Month, Kehowski figured the perimeters of "scholarly communication" were being interpreted pretty broadly, somewhere up the line.[408]

So what was the offensive e-mail that caused Kehowski to get in trouble at the school from his fellow teachers, who did not want to be exposed to what he had to share? At Thanksgiving time, he sent out a copy of George Washington's official proclamation of Thanksgiving from 1789. We are in serious trouble today when reminding associates of our true history can get a person in hot water.

THE PROBLEM OF THE COURTS

Another cause of the secularization of America was a whole string of court decisions, which have tried to sever us from our Judeo-Christian roots. Earlier court decisions were favorable to the concept that America is a Christian nation.[409] When did things begin to change on the high court?

The changes began slowly. You may say they devolved, beginning with the acceptance of evolution in the late nineteenth century among many elite leaders. This included Harvard-trained jurists. They changed the rules of court cases. No longer was natural law (based on God's law) the foundation for law.[410] Instead, case law became the norm. It no longer mattered what God said in His law (revealed in nature and in the Scriptures). What mattered is what man said, in previous court decisions. Oliver Wendell Holmes, Jr., a believer in evolution and its implications for law, was a key change agent in this monumental shift from English common law (based on the Bible) to case law (based on man's wisdom).

After World War II, there was a sea change in the interpretation of the Establishment Clause by the United States Supreme Court. The *Everson v. Board of Education* of 1947 was the turning point.

In the *Everson* case, the court upheld a New Jersey statute permitting the state to reimburse parents for the expense of busing their children to and from private (including parochial) schools. However, in doing so, the court ruled for the first time that neither states nor the federal government could "establish a religion." Previously, only the federal government was expressly forbidden from "respecting an establishment of religion." Many of the early colonies in America had state-supported religious institutions. Several of them even had state churches, all of which were eventually abandoned. So these state-supported religious institutions had fallen out of favor over time, but the *Everson* decision constitutionally required that states abandon the practice. Without this application of the establishment clause to individual states as well as to the federal government, there would be no problem with prayer or religious education in taxpayer-supported schools. In other words, the first amendment was being changed from "Congress shall make no law...." to "Congress *and the states* shall make no law...." This eventually would become, "Congress *and the states and local municipalities and any agent of the state, etc.* shall make no law...."[411]

The *Everson* decision found that the transportation legislation did no more than provide a general program to help parents, regardless of their religion. Therefore, the court said, it did not breach the "high and impregnable" wall of separation between church and state. This was the first time the United States Supreme Court imposed Thomas Jefferson's "wall of separation" as a constitutional principle. President Jefferson, who drafted the Declaration of Independence, took no part in drafting the Constitution nor the First Amendment (—again, he was thousands of miles away in France when both of these were written). Jefferson wrote a letter to the Danbury Baptist Convention in 1802. In the letter, he assured this Connecticut church body that it had no need to fear intervention from the federal government because a "wall of separation" had been constitutionally erected between the two. Furthermore, what he meant by that wall of separation was that it protected the church from the state. Now we have this concept that the state must be protected not only from the church, but from any Christian influence or any outward sign of Christianity.

The Court's majority decision in the *Everson* case, written by Justice Hugo Black, stated:

> This Court has said that parents may, in the discharge of their duty under state compulsory education laws, send their children to a religious, rather than a public, school if the school meets the secular educational requirements which the state has the power to impose.... It appears that these parochial schools meet New Jersey's requirements. The State contributes no money to the schools. It does not support them. Its legislation, as applied, does no more than provide a general program to help parents get their children, regardless of their religion, safely and expeditiously to and from accredited schools.
>
> The First Amendment has erected a wall of separation between church and state. That wall must be kept high and impregnable. We could not approve the slightest breach. New Jersey has not breached it here.

This unprecedented conclusion followed a strong statement by the court several pages earlier that specifically spelled out what the "high and impregnable" wall implied:

> Neither a state nor the Federal Government can set up a church. Neither can pass laws which aid one religion, aid all religions, or prefer one religion over another.... No tax in any amount, large or small, can be levied to support any religious activities or institutions, whatever they may be called, or whatever form they may adopt to teach or practice religion.[412]

So the court articulated two theories in 1947: 1) the establishment clause applies to government at all levels, federal, state, and local, and 2) the establishment clause no longer simply means that the United States should not establish a national church, but it means there shall be a strict separation of church and state. These two theories continue to provide the legal basis for the exclusion of prayer from public schools.

BORN OF ANTI-CATHOLIC PREJUDICE

Every judge brings his or her own prejudices to bear in his or her rulings. Hugo Black was no exception. He had a hard time getting accepted on the court in 1937 because he had been active in the Ku Klux Klan as late as the age of thirty-seven in his native Alabama. But the Senate confirmed him, and he did as much as he could to liberalize the high court. Hugo Black was a Unitarian with an anti-Catholic, anti-conservative-Christian bias. Black donated money to Unitarian causes and was interested in "advancing liberal religion."[413]

A few years ago, Black's anti-Catholic prejudice and its significance in the *Everson* decision were brought to light by the *Washington Times*. In an article with the headline "Church, state 'wall,' not idea of Jefferson," Larry Witham writes:

> New research on Thomas Jefferson's "wall of separation" between church and state shows that he [Jefferson] never intended it to be the iron curtain of today, which instead was built on anti-Catholic legal views in the 1940s....
>
> "What we have today is not really Jefferson's wall, but Supreme Court Justice Hugo Black's wall," said American University professor Daniel Dreisbach, whose forthcoming book explores how Jefferson coined the "wall" metaphor....

"You can't understand the period when Justice Black was on the court without understanding the fear American elites had of Catholic influence and power," said Mr. Dreisbach, who is not a Catholic....

In the last two years, Supreme Court Justices Clarence Thomas and Antonin Scalia both have argued that modern anti-Catholicism produced the idea that "sectarian" groups create conflict and must be walled off from public support.

"It was an open secret that 'sectarian' was a code for 'Catholic,'" Justice Thomas wrote in a concurring opinion two years ago. "This doctrine, born of bigotry, should be buried now."[414]

But for now, this doctrine is far from buried.

We have dealt with the *Everson* case at length because it is here where the fountain first began to be polluted. Removing Bible reading, school prayer, and banning even a moment of silence are all outworkings of this 1947 decision. Once the Supreme Court so misinterpreted the establishment clause, the false doctrine of the "separation of church and state" took on a life of its own and destroyed many freedoms and traditions in its path.

Paul Johnson points out that in the twentieth century there was a huge change in how law was to be interpreted. Johnson notes about the practice of law at the time of our founding: "It is vital to grasp that the judicial tradition of the United States, as understood by the Founding fathers, was based upon the English common law and administered statute law."[415] Now, law is decided by prior decisions. One bad decision then leads to another one.

A GREAT CONTRAST TO THE FOUNDERS' VIEW OF LAW

Sir William Blackstone lived in eighteenth-century England and wrote a four-volume definitive treatise on British common law, which was the basis for American law. They were called *Commentaries on the Law*. Blackstone said that the two cornerstones of law both have a divine source: natural law and the "law of revelation," and he said that no human laws should contradict these. He wrote:

Upon these two foundations, the law of nature and law of revelation, depend all human laws; that is to say, no human laws should be suffered to contradict these.[416]

Jumping ahead to the U.S. Supreme Court in the mid-twentieth century, Paul Johnson says that it turned its back on Blackstone, and therefore, on God's law: "...the courts—and especially the Supreme Court—did everything in their power to reduce the hold of religion in the affairs of the state, and particularly in the education of the young."[417]

In the 1980s, former Yale law professor and federal appeals court judge, Robert Bork, was nominated by President Reagan to sit on the Supreme Court. The secularists went all out and smeared the man and his impeccable reputation. He was an advocate for judicial restraint, for judges interpreting law, not making it. He was "borked," and his name has become part of our vocabulary, a verb, which means *to attack systematically.* A few years later, he wrote a book, *The Tempting of America,* on the whole point of how the courts are out of control in this country. Here is what he said about some of their anti-religious decisions:

> The Court has adopted a rigid secularist view of the establishment clause, which would not have disturbed too many people if the clause had not been incorporated to prohibit religious practices that the states had employed for many years. The sense of outrage was particularly intense when the Court prohibited prayer in the public schools, and years later even disapproved some moments of silence. The application of the Bill of Rights to the states in this and other matters has done much to alter the moral tone of communities across the country.[418]

Indeed, numerous court decisions have helped secularize Christian America. The liberals have circumvented the democratic process by getting the courts to do their dirty work for them. This has been the modus operandi of liberal legal groups for years. They have changed the face of America in countless negative ways.

When Robert H. Bork was nominated for the Supreme Court in 1987, he was blindsided in his confirmation hearings in the Senate by liberals who smeared him for his political views, not because of any scandal. He was the first nominee to the high court that was prevented from serving, not because of any moral flaw, but because of his opinions, e.g., that the original intent of the founders was important in constitutional interpretation. He said this, "The abandonment of original understanding in modern times means the transportation into the Constitution of the principles of a liberal culture that cannot achieve those results democratically."[419]

WHERE ARE THE JUSTICE DAVID BREWERS TODAY?

In the chapter that highlighted the early charters of America, we featured some quotes from David Brewer, a former Associate Justice of the Supreme Court. The Appendix of this book includes major portions of the 1892 *Trinity* decision, which provides a terrific summary of the evidence that the Bible made America. In that decision, the high court declared, "This is a Christian nation." [420] David Brewer (1837-1910) was the author of that decision and other materials that documented the pivotal role of the Bible in the founding of America. Brewer, who attended Yale University, served as an associate justice on the United States Supreme Court from 1890 to 1910. *The Oxford Companion to the Supreme Court of the United States* says of him, "David Josiah Brewer was born of Congregational missionary parents in Asia Minor [modern Turkey] and then raised in privilege." [421] Brewer was an idealist, writes *The Oxford Companion*:

> Brewer believed a judge's duty was to remind the people of their highest ideals, to lead rather than to acquiesce. He recognized that there was nothing that a judge could do to stop the inevitable triumph of the masses, but still believed that it was the judge's obligation to try. "It is one thing," Brewer once said, "to fail of reaching your ideal. It is an entirely different thing to deliberately turn your back on it." [422]

His decisions reflected his concern for the original intent of our nation's founders. In *Webster's American Biographies, Van Doren* writes of his decisions: "Conservatively inclined, Brewer generally expressed in his opinions a strict view of the constitutional limitations on federal power...." [423]

This strong Christian judge was also loved and appreciated. Chief Justice Melville W. Fuller said that of the justices that served under him, he found Brewer "one of the most lovable of them all." [424] When he died, the Attorney General of the United States said of David Brewer, the missionary's son: "...the son's life, like the father's, was one of service." [425]

This graduate of Yale was a strict constructionist—meaning he thought it is the job of judges to judge from the bench, not to legislate from the bench. I agree with him—that all judges should decide according to *original intent*, including a "strict view of the constitutional limitations on federal power...." [426]

So here was a born-again Christian serving as a justice of the Supreme Court. Where are all the Christians on the high court today? Or the courts of appeal? Calvin Coolidge, our thirtieth president, once declared, "If good men don't hold office, bad men will."[427]

As I said earlier, I have had the privilege of getting to know Chief Justice Roy Moore, former head of Alabama's judiciary. He is a godly man who loves the Lord and American history. I was there when he unveiled the gigantic Ten Commandments monument that ultimately cost him his job. The monument contained not only the Ten Commandments, but also many excellent quotes from America's founders. Chief Justice Moore pointed out in interview after interview that the founders did not want the government to establish a religion, but that publicly acknowledging God is not the same thing as establishing a religion. Unfortunately, his case proved once again that many in our country today want "freedom from religion," not "freedom of religion." That is a far cry from what our founders wanted. May Roy S. Moore's tribe increase.

There was a time when the Supreme Court justices were all Christians or at least they all held to Judeo-Christian values. Think of some of the famous justices in the early years of our country. John Jay was the first to serve as the Chief Justice of the Supreme Court. Under him and his successors, prayers were a regular part of the opening ceremony of the court activities at every level. Jay said that it's the duty of Christians to vote for Christians:

> Providence has given to our people the choice of their rulers, and it is the duty, as well as the privilege and interest of our Christian nation to select and prefer Christians for their rulers.[428]

You do not get more clear than that.

Perhaps the best known justice in the history of the Supreme Court, the man who brought it to its zenith, would be John Marshall who served in the first part of the nineteenth century. Marshall was an active Episcopalian. He presided over the Supreme Court from 1801 to 1835. Marshall said,

> No person, I believe, questions the importance of religion to the happiness of man even during his existence in this world...the American population is entirely Christian, and with us, Christianity and religion are identified. It would be strange, indeed, if with such a people, our institutions did not presuppose Christianity, and did not often refer to it, and exhibit relations with it.[429]

I think it is safe to say that until the early part of the twentieth century, most of the justices that served on the Supreme Court were Christians. Certainly, they acknowledged the Christian heritage of the country. Again, there was not a change for the worse until the twentieth century and the acceptance of evolution, and specifically, the idea that since everything evolves, then law, too, should evolve and is not based on fixed principles. Oliver Wendell Holmes is an American icon to some. But I would put him in the *hall of shame* for being one of the key change agents in applying evolutionary principles to law.

Earl Warren, serving a few decades later, also deserves a place in the *hall of shame*, for he carried out the logical implications of Holmes' philosophy. That does not mean every decision these men made was bad. There are some worth defending. Anything good they did was because they were piggybacking on the Christian morality of their upbringing. But for the most part, they cut us off from our Judeo-Christian roots and set us adrift in a sea of moral relativism in the realm of law.

In the twentieth century, beginning with Felix Frankfurter and continuing to our own day with Ruth Bader Ginsberg, there have even been ACLU attorneys serving on the high court. While modern Christians have often avoided getting their hands dirty with professions like politics, we have assigned politics to the non-believers—and it's no wonder we are in this current mess.

I believe we have got to lose this notion that the only service you can perform for the Lord is full-time Christian work (not to minimize in any way those engaged in full-time Christian work). We need excellent Christian lawyers. We need superb Christian university professors. The history of the United States shows how God raised up ministers, farmers, lawyers, soldiers, judges, merchants, statesmen, and so on, to help fashion a new nation patterned after His Word. It was not ministers alone. The Calvinist view of "calling"—that each Christian had a specific calling from the Lord—played a role in the founding of America. It would appear that both David Brewer, as a United States Supreme Court Justice, and his father, as an overseas Christian missionary, both fulfilled their callings, different as they may be.

Let me go further on this point. Can you imagine a born-again Christian as a Supreme Court justice? Could you imagine a majority of them on the high court? They could turn this country around—to right side up. So many of the problems in America were ushered in by Supreme Court judges, men and women who did not know our history, or, if they did know it, they intentionally turned their backs on it, to set America on a future course away from our Judeo-Christian roots. One long-standing liberal justice remarked at the time of the classic school prayer case, *Engel v. Vitale*, that they did not have the legal precedent to make this decision, but he thought it was the right thing to do, so he joined with the majority.

Meanwhile, there is a great need for Christian judges to serve on the appeals courts as well. The Supreme Court hears only a small fraction of the cases appealed to them. Therefore, the appeals courts make critical decisions that impact all of us.

For a long time, we as Christians by and large had abandoned politics, the courts, the legal profession, the media, the universities, the law schools. We gave them over to the unbeliever virtually without a fight. We told our young people, if you really want to serve the Lord, then become a minister or a missionary. We neglected other significant ways to serve the Lord. We washed our hands of politics for a time and let the atheists and practical atheists take over. And they did, and we've been playing defensive "catch-up" ever since.

RIDICULOUS LENGTHS

Because of so many liberal judges and so few Christian ones, the courts have sometimes gone to ludicrous lengths to keep any kind of religious—no, I should say Christian—expression out of the public arena. A great example of this can be seen in the case involving the Ten Commandments. In 1980, the high court sided with the secularists in a Kentucky case involving privately-funded copies of the Decalogue of Moses that were displayed in some public schools. Justice William Brennan wrote the decision, striking down public displays of the Ten Commandments with these chilling words:

> If the posted copies of the Ten Commandments are to have any effect at all, it will be to induce the schoolchildren to read, meditate upon, perhaps to venerate and obey, the Commandments. However desirable this might be as a matter of private devotion, it is not a permissible state objective under the Establishment Clause.[430]

Pastor and author George Grant, co-author of the book, *Kids Who Kill,* made this comment on that decision:

> When Justice Brennan feared that children might actually obey the Ten Commandments, what he was really saying was not that we don't want children to have a standard for behavior. He was saying we want an alternative standard for behavior. A secular standard for behavior. Today we're reaping the harvest of that new standard.[431]

Many Supreme Court decisions in the last half a century have made it illegal to do what the founders and their children did, to pray at school, to read the Bible, to venerate the Ten Commandments.

I think one of the worst decisions I have ever heard of in my life came from Judge Samuel Kent in the *Doe v. Santa Fe* decision of 1995. He ruled that in a graduation ceremony, privately sponsored by ministers in a community, that if anyone prayed in the name of any deity, i.e., the name of Jesus, that he would summarily have this minister arrested and thrown in jail for a minimum of six months. He wrote: "Anybody who violates these orders, no kidding, is going to wish that he or she had died as a child when this court gets through with it."[432] This kind of decision is astounding when you consider America's true history. It is astounding from any perspective.

In March 2009, a group of public high schoolers in Kentucky were praying for a classmate whose mother had died in a terrible accident. They were voluntarily praying, in a spontaneous student-led movement, during their lunch break. The Supreme Court has allowed for such speech. But the principal *called the police* to have them arrested.[433] This is how far the animus against Christians has gone in our country. Even President Clinton bemoaned more than a decade ago that our schools should not be "religion-free zones."

And what has been the net effect of our national loss of "religion and morality" (to use George Washington's classic phrase in his Farewell Address)? Not only have we experienced school shootings, but we have seen the brainwashing and the dumbing down of America. A 1998 National Constitution Center Poll found that teenagers are 50 percent more likely to be able to name the Three Stooges than the first three words of the Constitution.

MUCH AT STAKE

In the public schools of America, God has been chased out. But we do not have enough security checkpoints to try and prevent crime. In the 1830s, Dr. Benjamin Rush, one of America's founding fathers, warned us that if the Bible should ever be removed as a textbook, then crimes in school would increase and we'd have to waste lots of money to try and prevent them. One can only wonder what Dr. Rush would say about far too many of today's public schools.

Think of what the settlers and founders went through to establish America. Think of all the sacrifices they undertook for the sake of posterity. As long as we have the opportunity, it is time for Christians in America to become more involved:

* To share our faith with our non-Christian neighbors, coworkers, and friends;

* To vote in a well-informed manner, pleasing to the Lord;

* To make our voice heard in politics, nationally, statewide, and locally. (Let me ask you a question: Why should homosexuals who represent a fraction of the population have greater political capital than evangelicals, of whom there are tens of millions more?)

* To stop supporting and watching the inappropriate movies and television programs Hollywood spews out;

* To pray for genuine repentance, revival, and the healing of our land.

Our heritage is too great to squander.

CONCLUSION

The Bible played a pivotal role in our founding. I believe it could play a pivotal role in saving America. There is a lot at stake. As William Penn once noted, "If we will not be governed by God, we must be governed by tyrants."[434]

Similarly, Robert Charles Winthrop, an American legislator and a descendent of John Winthrop, declared that our choice was between the Scriptures or tyranny. Here is what he said to the Massachusetts Bible Society in Boston on May 28, 1849:

> All societies of men must be governed in some way or other. The
> less they have of stringent State Government, the more they must

have of individual self-government. The less they rely on public law or physical force, the more they must rely on private moral restraint.

Men, in a word, must necessarily be controlled either by a power within them, or a power without them; either by the word of God, or by the strong arm of man; either by the Bible or by the bayonet.[435]

I agree with him totally.

Calvin Coolidge, our thirtieth president, stated:

> If American democracy is to remain
> the greatest hope of humanity,
> it must continue abundantly in the
> faith of the Bible. [436]

Former Alabama Chief Justice Roy Moore and his Ten Commandments monument, for which he was fired, by judicial fiat. More than most judges, Chief Justice Moore recognizes the incredible role the Bible played in the founding of America.

CHAPTER 11

The Bible and Regeneration

Jesus said to him, "I am the way, and the truth, and the life.
No one comes to the Father except through Me."
(John 14:6)

THE purpose of this short chapter is to point out that all change begins in the human heart and proceeds from there. Jesus Christ changes human beings from the inside out and makes them new. He did this for the Pilgrims, the Puritans, the Huguenots, the Quakers, the Presbyterians, and so on.

Our eighteenth president, Rutherford B. Hayes, said, "Now, the best religion the world has ever had is the religion of Christ. A man or a community adopting it, is virtuous, prosperous, and happy."[437]

Virtually all of the early settlers of North America, including the Pilgrims and the Puritans, and our founding fathers believed that Jesus Christ was superior to all others and that only in the Bible is to be found life and liberty and eternal truth. It is because the Bible always shapes the people who read it, that those people were able to shape a nation.

In the light of what our thirtieth president, Calvin Coolidge (who was named after Christian theologian John Calvin), said, "If American democracy is to remain the greatest hope of humanity, it must continue abundantly in the faith of the Bible,"[438] then our land will be free as long as the citizens are free.

What is it that the Bible holds in its pages that changes people and nations and determines the course of history? What is the power, and what is the message?

The message is simple: God created humanity and the world, and it was all very good. But sin entered the world through our ancient parents, Adam and Eve, and so mankind was plunged into decay, entropy, and our will, mind, spirit, bodies, and our very souls became corrupted. In our natural state, we are now under the dominion of the evil one.

Remember how most of the founding fathers learned their ABCs? Through *The New England Primer*. Contained in the first three letters, we have a bare-bones outline of the gospel:

A	B	C
In Adam's Fall,	Thy life to mend,	Christ crucify'd,
We sinned all.	The Bible tend.	For sinners died. [439]

Why was Christ crucified? God in His mercy devised a rescue operation. He sent His Son, Jesus Christ, to conquer evil and to be the sacrifice needed to free us from the corrupting power of sin. Christ freed us and, as liberated people, we become citizens of His kingdom and then live under His dominion for time and eternity.

God saw that evil was so entrenched and so entangled in earthly affairs that no amount of "good works" could make us fit for heaven. People are not good by God's standard of perfection, and left alone we will not follow God's law, nor the law of love. In *Federalist* #51, James Madison once said, "If men were angels, government would not be necessary." [440] But government is necessary, because men are not angels. Madison goes on to point out that because men run government, and because men are not angels, then we also need to be protected from the government. Therefore, because we are not angels, we need a savior.

Man has an eternal desire to be free and independent, and "For freedom Christ has set us free;" (Gal. 5:1a). The virtue of a Christian life, the self-discipline of a converted soul, the moral integrity of the individual Christian have made it possible to found our nation in liberty and establish it in law. Dr. Donald S. Lutz said that virtue was very important to politics in the seventeenth and eighteenth centuries: "In one sense, virtue meant following God's law as found in the Bible. One who did not lie, steal, or fornicate, but who adhered to the golden rule was a virtuous person." Neither freedom, nor virtue for that matter, was viewed as doing whatever one wanted to. Lutz writes, "Throughout the period in question, Americans defined political liberty as the people being subject only to laws based upon their own consent. They were not, however, free to consent to laws that were contrary to their natural liberty, i.e., contrary to the laws of God." Dr. Lutz also points out, "the most fundamental assumption is that *the American people are a virtuous people*," [emphasis his]. He goes on to assert: "Without the belief in a virtuous people, the federal republic would not have been tried." [441]

Thus, virtue was extremely important to the founders of America. As we saw earlier, to George Washington and John Adams and other distinguished founders, religion and morality were keys to our political prosperity. [442] This point—that religion provides the basis for morality—has been grasped throughout our history. For example, our twenty-seventh president, William Howard Taft, declared: "Morality is dependent upon the spread of religious conviction to prevail in the government and civilization of this country." [443]

The power of the Bible is in Christ Jesus and His Spirit. Without the changed heart by the Holy Spirit, man cannot be truly free. This empowers him with Christian self-government (restraint), due to God's sanctification; and without self-government or self-control, freedom will wane.

What Christ Jesus wants is control of our lives. In here lies the paradox of Christianity. It is by giving our life that we gain it. It is by relinquishing the control of our lives that we gain freedom. To gain the freedom Christ has to offer, we must turn from our sin, repent, and receive His forgiveness and by the power of the Holy Spirit live as new subjects in His kingdom and spend the rest of our earthly lives for His glory and the benefit of our fellow man.

We need to understand a few key points:

* We are all sinful.

* God is holy and will judge all our sin. Our sins make us unacceptable to the Lord.

* God sent His Son, Jesus, who lived a perfect life, which no one has ever done or could do.

* Jesus died in our place as a punishment to satisfy divine judgment, paying a price we could never pay.

* If we trust in Him and His finished work on the cross for salvation, He will save us.

If this makes sense to you, please consider saying a prayer along these lines:

Lord Jesus, I can see the enslavement that has taken place in my life, and I come to You now in sorrow and repentance and seek the true freedom only You can give me. Thank You for conquering the evil one on the cross and freeing me from all evil and its power and consequences. Clean and restore my will and my mind, heart, and soul. Let me belong to You for time and eternity. In Your name I pray. Amen.

If you prayed this prayer from your heart, you have been set free and have come home at the same time.

Please, seek a Christ-centered, Bible-believing church to get more information. Please read the Bible for yourself.[446] Let the Bible shape you, for as we yield to the Holy Spirit and let God's Word shape us, we will, in turn, shape our families, our churches, our communities, and our nation.

When I was eighteen, I first fell in love with the Bible. What a great book. I couldn't get enough of it. I still can't. In the last decade, I have even begun to study the Word in the original languages, although I count myself as a neophyte on that point. There are many insights I have gleaned from learning Greek and Hebrew. For example, why is it that so often we see IHS written in churches, e.g., by the altar? What does that mean? It is simply the first three letters of Jesus' name in Greek. The English equivalent would be JES. I learned in Hebrew class that the word Bethlehem means "house of bread." So Jesus, the Bread of Life, was born in the house of bread. God honors His Word. It will not return to Him void.

The Bible was the favorite book during the settling and founding era of America. It is the book that made America. It is the book that can remake America. As the patriotic hymn states:

> *Our Father's God to Thee,*
> *Author of Liberty.*
> *Of Thee we sing:*
> *Long may our land be bright*
> *With freedom's holy light.*
> *Protect us by Thy might,*
> *Great God, our King!* [445]

Chapter 12

"Can an Empire Rise without His Aid?"

Unless the LORD builds the house,
They labor in vain who build it.
(Psalm 127:1, NKJV)

OUR nation's Christian heritage is a precious gift from God. It is being squandered in our time, as the masses lift up the ungodly and perverted as praiseworthy.

If America gets completely cut off from our roots, how can we last—at least as a great nation? The psalmist asks, "If the foundation is destroyed, what can the righteous do?" (Psalm 11:3) But whenever it seems bleakest, then God often intervenes.

Anyone who would deny that we are in a culture war does not seem to be very discerning in my opinion. It is possible that America might not last. No where is it decreed that our nation will last forever. Other nations have arisen and failed. We may just continue to implode and become a shell of what we once were. Consider the history of some past civilizations who neglected God.

We do well to learn from our rich history about where this nation came from. In this last chapter, we want to feature some final considerations, especially concerning the role of prayer at key points in our history.

In 1787, during the Constitutional Convention, the delegates hit an impasse. They had spent nearly two months trying to frame a new governing document and had barely made any progress. The whole exercise appeared fruitless and might even have come to a halt. At that time, the elderly statesman among them, Dr. Benjamin Franklin, reminded them they had forgotten to pray. We will hear more about his amazing speech momentarily.

Unfortunately, we often think of prayer as a last resort, just as our founding fathers did. "Pray—if all else fails." One could well imagine a figurine of praying hands enclosed in a glass frame on a wall (instead of a fire extinguisher) with a bold, red caption: "In case of emergency, break glass!"

I truly believe that if America is ever to experience a rebirth, we need to break that glass. We *are* in an emergency and in great need of making prayer a dominant part of our lives—not just during emergencies.

Only with God's help can America be renewed. He is the One who can truly bring about change. Without His help, we cannot hope for what Abraham Lincoln called "a new birth of freedom."

NATIONAL DAYS OF PRAYER DURING THE REVOLUTION

The founders of this nation certainly thought prayer was important. Do you know how many times Congress called for national days of prayer, humiliation, and fasting during the American War for Independence? Fifteen separate times. In addition, several of the colonies had their own colony-wide days of prayer. In fact, David Barton says, "Between 1633 and 1812, there were over 1700 prayer proclamations issued in the colonies, where the governor would call the state to an annual day of prayer and fasting, or annual day of prayer and thanksgiving."[446]

None of these were like some of today's political prayers, which could just as well be addressed, "To whom it may concern." For example, on July 13, 1775, Governor Jonathan Trumbull of Connecticut wrote to General Washington, telling him of a Congressional call for prayer:

> The Honorable Congress have proclaimed a Fast to be observed by the inhabitants of all the English Colonies on this continent, to stand before the Lord in one day, with public humiliation, fasting, and prayer, to deplore our many sins, to offer up our joint supplications to God, for forgiveness, and for his merciful interposition for us in this day of unnatural darkness and distress.
>
> They have, with one united voice, appointed you to the high station you possess. The Supreme Director of all events hath caused a wonderful union of hearts and counsels to subsist among us. Now therefore, be strong and very courageous.

> May the God of the armies of Israel shower down the blessings of his Divine Providence on you, give you wisdom and fortitude, cover your head in the day of battle and danger, add success, convince our enemies of their mistaken measures, and that all their attempts to deprive these Colonies of their inestimable constitutional rights and liberties are injurious and vain.[447]

Note the Biblical allusions, which Trumbull assumed (correctly) that his hearer would understand. And thankfully, God answered those prayers.

Or how about this example? When John Hancock was the Governor of Massachusetts, he made an official Thanksgiving proclamation on October 5, 1791, in which he prayed for God's prosperity: "that all may bow to the Scepter of our LORD JESUS CHRIST, and the whole Earth be filled with his Glory." [emphasis his] [448] Hancock prayed that the day would come soon that Christ the King would reign on earth.

REVISION OF THE ARTICLES

The delegates to what we now know as the Constitutional Convention originally met to revise the Articles of Confederation (1777), our first governing document as a nation. During the early days of the Convention, they agreed that the Articles were not working; they yielded too much power to the states and too little authority to the national government, which was anemic.

In *Federalist* #30 Alexander Hamilton wrote that the United States was at the precipice of collapse under the Articles. "In America...the government of the Union has gradually dwindled into a state of decay, approaching nearly to annihilation."[449] The entire experiment in self-government might soon find its way onto *the ash heap of history* (to quote Ronald Reagan in a different context).

So here were all these men of Congress meeting initially to discuss how to revise the Articles, and then how to create a more workable document, which we now know as the Constitution. After a grueling May and June, they had made very little headway. The largest impasse dealt with representation of the big states versus the medium states versus the little states. (The ultimate solution was a House of Representatives that reflected the population of each state with a Senate that provided equal representation for each state, regardless of the size of its population. But that was to come later.)

THE ATMOSPHERE AT THE CONVENTION

Men were coming and going at this convention held in Philadelphia, the same place they had framed and adopted the Declaration of Independence. We now call it Independence Hall. Some were leaving because they had to get back to their business concerns—perhaps others because they felt their time was better spent elsewhere.

The days were hot and stifling. So were the nights. This was long before the days of air-conditioning and electric fans. Flies and mosquitoes were a problem.

Tempers flared. Some of the delegates liked to hear themselves speak, even if they had little to say in the conflict. (By some descriptions, Luther Martin, delegate from Maryland who later refused to sign the Constitution, fits this category.) Through it all, George Washington sat silently, stoically, even if his patience was tried on occasion through the whole ordeal.

Finally, on June 28, the elderly Ben Franklin struggled to his feet and made one of the greatest speeches in American history.

I find that it is virtually unknown among secular people. The average high school student knows nothing about Franklin's talk, which is missing from most books about American history or even the Constitution. (I never learned it until I read Gary DeMar's book, *God and Government*, in 1984.) You could interview a hundred Americans, and probably less than two percent have heard of this speech. (Many of them would assume no such thing took place since they assume that the founding fathers intended a completely secular government.) You could attend the tours at Independence Hall and learn nothing about it. You could watch the talking heads on Sunday morning—the political pundits of our age—and not even be aware of it having taken place.

We can be thankful that Franklin's speech can be found in many of the books on America's Christian heritage. Furthermore, it can be found in the original material from the Convention. James Madison, delegate from Virginia, who is sometimes thought of as the Father of the Constitution or its chief architect, took detailed notes at the Convention.

BEN FRANKLIN'S MARVELOUS SPEECH

Ben Franklin was the oldest and perhaps most respected delegate at the Constitutional Convention—the only person who could possibly have been respected more was General Washington, the hero of the late war. Franklin's plea for prayer was essentially a turning point at the Convention. Before his speech, the men were "spinning their wheels" so to speak. After the speech, they began to find traction and were able to accomplish something substantial.

Here's what Dr. Benjamin Franklin said on June 28, 1787 (reproduced, as in the original):

> Mr. President:
>
> The small progress we have made after four or five weeks close attendance [prior to that was sparse attendance, not even enough for a quorum] & continual reasonings with each other—our different sentiments on almost every question, several of the last producing as many noes as ayes, is methinks a melancholy proof of the imperfection of the Human Understanding.
>
> We indeed seem to feel our own want of political wisdom, since we have been running about in search of it. We have gone back to ancient history for models of Government, and examined the different forms of those Republics which, having been formed with the seeds of their own dissolution, now no longer exist. And we have viewed Modern States all round Europe, but find none of their Constitutions suitable to our circumstances.
>
> In this situation of this Assembly, groping as it were in the dark to find political truth, and scarce able to distinguish it when presented to us, how has it happened, Sir, that we have not hitherto once thought of humbly applying to the Father of lights to illuminate our understanding?
>
> In the beginning of the Contest with G[reat] Britain, when we were sensible of danger, we had daily prayer in this room for Divine protection. Our prayers, Sir, were heard, & they were graciously answered. All of us who were engaged in the struggle must have observed frequent instances of a Superintending Providence in our favor.
>
> To that kind Providence we owe this happy opportunity of consulting in peace on the means of establishing our future national felicity. And have we now forgotten that powerful Friend? or do we imagine we no longer need His assistance?
>
> I have lived, Sir, a long time, and the longer I live, the more convincing proofs I see of this truth—that God Governs in the affairs of men. And if a sparrow cannot fall to the ground without

His notice, is it probable that an empire can rise without His aid?

We have been assured, Sir, in the Sacred Writings, that "except the Lord build the House, they labor in vain that build it." I firmly believe this; and I also believe that without His concurring aid we shall succeed in this political building no better than the Builders of Babel: We shall be divided by our partial local interests; our projects will be confounded; and we ourselves shall become a reproach and bye word down to future ages.

And what is worse, mankind may hereafter from this unfortunate instance, despair of establishing Governments by Human wisdom and leave it to chance, war, and conquest.

I therefore beg leave to move—that henceforth prayers imploring the assistance of Heaven, and its blessing on our deliberations, be held in this Assembly every morning before we proceed to business, and that one or more of the clergy of this city be requested to officiate in that service. [quoted exactly as in the original] [450]

Here, Benjamin Franklin, a man considered to be one of the least orthodox of the founding fathers, was asking the delegates to remember God and seek His help.

New Jersey delegate Jonathan Dayton described the impression the old man made on the rest of them:

The Doctor sat down; and never did I behold a countenance at once so dignified and delighted as was that of Washington at the close of the address; nor were the members of the convention generally less affected. The words of the venerable Franklin fell upon our ears with a weight and authority, even greater than we may suppose an oracle to have had in a Roman senate! [451]

That's quite an impression.

Immediately Roger Sherman of Connecticut (one of the few of the founding fathers to sign both the Declaration and the Constitution) seconded the motion. Then the delegates bandied Franklin's suggestion back and forth. They did not officially accept the motion because their treasury was empty—there was no money to hire a chaplain. Nor did they officially vote down his suggestion.

Instead, they agreed on an alternative that accepted the spirit and gist of Franklin's proposal. The alternative was provided by Edmund Jennings Randolph of Virginia, who suggested that:

1) A sermon be preached—at the official request of the Convention —the next week on the Fourth of July to mark the anniversary of Independence, and

2) Prayers be said in the Convention every morning.[452]

What impact did Dr. Franklin's request have on the progress of the Constitutional Convention? New Jersey Delegate Jonathan Dayton tells us what it was like on July 2, just a few days later, when they reconvened for the first time since Franklin's speech: "We assembled again; and...every unfriendly feeling had been expelled, and a spirit of conciliation had been cultivated."[453]

Then on the Fourth of July, the entire Convention attended a special service in the Reformed Calvinistic Lutheran Church, where they heard a sermon by Rev. William Rogers, wherein he prayed:

> We fervently recommend to the fatherly notice...our federal convention.... Favor them, from day to day, with thy inspiring presence; be their wisdom and strength; enable them to devise such measures as may prove happy instruments in healing all divisions and prove the good of the great whole;...that the United States of America may form one example of a free and virtuous government.... May we...continue, under the influence of republican virtue, to partake of all the blessings of cultivated and Christian society.[454]

Think of how "unconstitutional" all this may appear to modern ears. Here all the government officials are attending a *Christian* service in a *Christian* church, where they are being encouraged to act as wise Christians as they choose how the nation's Christian subjects should be governed.

Don't these men know the Constitution? What about "the separation of church and state"? Oh, wait—these are the men who *gave* us the Constitution, and all of this took place as they were writing the document. Looking at Franklin's speech shows us how far we have strayed from our history, our purpose, our mission.

I remember engaging in a series of correspondence by e-mail with an acquaintance who was of the persuasion that the founding fathers were basically secular humanists. When I sent him the details of Ben Franklin's appeal to prayer, he ceased further communication. The facts of history speak for themselves.

ANOTHER PRAYER IN ANOTHER AMERICAN LEGISLATURE

We have gained a small glimpse of the founding fathers' deep abiding respect for prayer and its role in building up the American "empire" for good purposes. To this day, throughout America, our Congress, our Senate, and also the state legislatures open in prayer. During the 1990s, a pastor was invited to say the opening prayer at the statehouse in Kansas. He chose to be anything, but politically correct. Paul Harvey, the noted radio commentator, described the event in this way:

"DOES GOD EVER KNOW!"

> Man, oh, man [does God ever know]! They won't invite Pastor Joe to the Kansas State Legislature again.
>
> They invited Pastor Joe Wright of Wichita's Central Christian Church to deliver the invocation—and he told God on them!
>
> Now, God knows what they've been up to! No sooner had their guest chaplain concluded [reading the] prayer, than three Democrats on the state legislature were on their feet at microphones protesting, "He can't talk like that about us!"
>
> Rep. Delbert Gross considered the invocation gross, calling it "divisive," "sanctimonious," and "overbearing."
>
> Rep. David Haley called it "blasphemous and ignorant."
>
> Rep. Sabrina Standifer echoed the indignation.
>
> What in the world did Pastor Joe say in Topeka that incited the righteous wrath of three Democrats from Hays and Kansas City?
>
> I've secured the entire text of the invocation so you can evaluate it for yourself and decide.

*H*EAVENLY FATHER, we come before You today to ask Your forgiveness and to seek Your direction and guidance.

We know Your Word says, "Woe to those who call evil good," but that is exactly what we have done. We have lost our spiritual equilibrium and inverted our values.

We confess that we have ridiculed the absolute truth of Your Word [and called it] moral pluralism.

We have worshipped other gods and called it multiculturism.

We have endorsed perversion and called it an alternative lifestyle.

We have exploited the poor and called it [the] lottery.

We have neglected the needy and called it self-preservation.

We have rewarded laziness and called it welfare.

We have killed our unborn and called it choice.

We have shot abortionists and called it justifiable.

We have neglected to discipline our children and called it building esteem.

We have abused power and called it political savvy.

We have coveted our neighbors' possessions and called it ambition.

We have polluted the air with profanity and pornography and called it freedom of expression.

We have ridiculed the time-honored values of our forefathers and called it enlightenment.

Search us, O God, and know our hearts today. Try us and see if there be some wicked way in us. Cleanse us from every sin and set us free.

Guide and bless these men and women who have been sent here by the people [of Kansas], and who have been ordained by You to govern this great state.

Grant them Your wisdom to rule, and may their decisions direct us to the center of Your will.

I ask it in the name of Your Son, the living Savior, Jesus Christ. *A*men.[455]

No wonder this gentleman will not be invited back to say an invocation. But his spiritual indictment on contemporary America is an excellent one.

This reminds me of what the late D. James Kennedy once said:

My friends, the hour is late. I think it is important that each one of us carefully consider the Biblical teachings about man, society, the state, and the purpose of life while we still have the freedom to consider them at all.

God has placed us in this free land, yet bit by bit, piece by piece, we have been selling our birthright for a mess of pottage. We have been fearful to stand up and exercise the talents and the abilities God has given us. We have been unwilling to trust Him to provide for our needs, and so we have sold our birthright of freedom for the security of the state, not realizing that we are selling ourselves into bondage.[456]

IF MY PEOPLE

Did you hear about the open prayer sessions in a public high school? Probably not. Several students and even teachers huddled together in a room at this school. Someone asked if there was anyone religious in the room that might be able to lead them in prayer. One of the students volunteered, and they held prayer there at school during normal school hours. What happened next? An ACLU lawsuit?

Not exactly. These students and teachers were fleeing the bloodshed at Columbine High School on April 20, 1999 in Littleton, Colorado, the day of the massacre of twelve students and one teacher, and the double-suicides of the two murderers. Prayer came into a public school in America on that day—only it came too late.

Ours is a nation in need of prayer, in need of a spiritual revival. If America is truly to be renewed, it will not be through the political process, as important as that is. I believe we need a renewed vision, for where there is no vision, the people perish (Proverbs 29:18). God can do the impossible, and so indeed, we can experience a renewal in this land. If there is to be a new birth of freedom in America, then what we need most of all is a genuine revival.

The most appropriate of all Bible verses that spells out the remedy for a nation that has lost its way is 2 Chronicles 7:14: "If My people who are called by My name humble themselves, and pray and seek My face, and turn from their wicked ways, then I will hear from heaven and will forgive their sin and heal their land."

America began, in part, because of the spiritual movement in the mid-eighteenth century known as the Great Awakening. There was a special move of God's Spirit, as He used men of God, in particular, Jonathan Edwards and George Whitefield, to preach the gospel and convert many. The impact on society was profound. John Adams said that the revolution of 1776 was essentially the political outworking of the *spiritual* revolution that had occurred the generation before, i.e., the Great Awakening.

The great British historian, Paul Johnson, author of *A History of the American People,* noted:

> As we have seen, America had been founded primarily for religious purposes, and the Great Awakening had been the original dynamic of the continental movement for independence. The Americas were overwhelmingly church-going, much more so than the English, whose rule they rejected.[457]

George Whitefield was the greatest evangelist of the First Great Awakening. When he first came to Boston in 1740, he saw the outward veneer of religiosity, which was often missing the inner reality. Here is what he wrote on October 12, 1740: "Boston is a large populous place, and very wealthy. It has the form of religion kept up, but has lost much of its power. I have not heard of any remarkable stir for years. Ministers and people are obliged to confess that the love of many is waxed cold. Both seem too conformed to the world...."[458] This was a great example of Cotton Mather's axiom, quoted in an earlier chapter: "Religion brought forth Prosperity, and the daughter destroyed the mother."[459]

Boston prospered because Boston was religious. By 1740, too much of that religion was an outward show. But Whitefield and company helped to change that, by the grace of God, in the First Great Awakening.

My boss for many years, the late Dr. D. James Kennedy, used to say that the only thing that can really change America for the better is true revival. The first Great Awakening, of course, helped lead to the founding of America. The Second Great Awakening helped lead to the end of the evil of slavery. Now, we need a Third Great Awakening.[460] Such a move of God is what this nation desperately needs.

CONCLUSION

The great news is that pastors and laypeople can play an active role in saving our nation's Christian heritage. One potential harbinger of hope in this area is the homeschool movement. Hundreds of thousands of young people have begun to learn about the true history of our nation through homeschooling curriculum. I think of a young man I interviewed for Coral Ridge Ministries-TV. (I've also interviewed him on WAFG radio.) He was the product of a home school, and although he is in his early twenties, he has already written a book, published by a Christian company. The book documents the faith of each of our nation's presidents. His name is Daniel Mount, and the book is titled *The Faith of America's Presidents*.[461]

We have freedom now. But it may be lost one day because of our apathy, not overnight, but over time. May it never be. Our second president, John Adams, once made a solemn warning to us: "Posterity! You will never know how much it cost the present generation to preserve your freedom! I hope you will make good use of it! If you do not, I shall repent in Heaven that I ever took half the pains to preserve it!"[462]

Our twenty-sixth president, Theodore Roosevelt, said, "Fear God; and take your own part!"[463]

We may not succeed, but if God be for us, who can be against us? What kind of an America do we want to leave for our children and grandchildren?

Finally, consider the words of our sixth president, John Quincy Adams, son of John. With his profound axiom, we close:

"Duty is ours; results are God's."[464]

Amen.

Appendix

232

Church of The Holy Trinity
vs.
United States

No. 143.
SUPREME COURT OF THE UNITED STATES
143 U.S. 457, 36 L. Ed. 226, 12 S. Ct. 511
February 29, 1892, Decided

SYLLABUS
t of February 26, 1885, "to prohibit the importation and migra-
foreigners and aliens under contract or agreement to perform
the United States, its Territories, and the District of Columbia,"

PHOTO BY J. NEWCOMBE

The *Trinity* Decision of 1892, the U.S. Supreme Court declared unanimously that this is a Christian nation. That judgment has never been abrogated.

"This Is a Christian Nation"

Blessed is the nation whose God is the LORD....
(Psalm 33:12)

ID you know that the United States Supreme Court declared that America is a Christian nation? They did this in an 1892 decision, the *Trinity* decision, which has never been abrogated.[465] Please note, too, that the section in which they wrote this is not dicta and is therefore not binding either. Nonetheless, every argument they marshal for evidence stands on its own.

The high court did not come to this decision lightly. After having spent ten years reviewing all our founding documents, they finally made this incredible declaration that ours is a Christian land. Furthermore, this was the unanimous conclusion of those seven men (there were not nine justices until F.D.R. packed the court in the 1930s). After reviewing major evidence, the 1892 court concluded: "These and many others which might be noticed, add a volume of unofficial declarations to the mass of organic utterances that this is a Christian nation."[466] It seems amazing that the Supreme Court could make such a ruling. Many decisions made since then have certainly ignored the *Trinity* case or have virtually stood the decision on its head.

The 1892 Supreme Court decision of the *United States v. the Church of the Holy Trinity* sums up the thesis of this book. You may notice the overlap between what is said here and other points made throughout this book. Forgive the repetition, but it is important to see the irrefutable facts of history assembled together in one remarkable document: a Supreme Court decision. To think—the highest court of our land once examined all the evidence and emphatically declared that America is a Christian nation. At least we can say, virtually without controversy, that America was founded as a Christian nation.

I put this section as the Appendix because of the fact that so much of this is repetition from what we have heard earlier and I think it provides a superb summary.

THE BACKGROUND OF THE CASE

The details surrounding the controversy of the *United States v. the Church of the Holy Trinity* are rather complicated. The gist of the dispute was this: Is a church body exempt from some of the laws applied to other kinds of organizations? The court answered that it is, and its rationale comprises the bulk of the *Trinity* decision.

Specifically, the controversy surrounded whether a church in Ohio, an Episcopal one called the Church of the Holy Trinity, violated a law prohibiting the hiring of foreigners. The church hired a minister from overseas and was hauled into court for allegedly violating a law that restricted laborers from abroad to come here, lest they take away American jobs. The case worked its way from lower courts, all the way to the Supreme Court, where the church prevailed.

MAJOR PORTIONS OF THE *TRINITY* DECISION

Here now are major portions of the *Trinity* decision, interrupted by my commentary on the same. I have assigned numbers to the arguments made, just to simplify the points. Again, you will see some of the points made earlier in this book. For example, no one telling America's true history can leave out the Mayflower Compact.

1) OPENING OVERVIEW—WE ARE A CHRISTIAN PEOPLE

The *Trinity* decision begins with all the specifics of the case. Then for page upon page, it explores the deeper question as to why this church in Ohio, or any church in the United States, may possibly be exempt from this particular law—are we or are we not, a Christian nation? The Supreme Court weighs in on the issue:

This is a religious people. This is historically true. From the discovery of this continent to the present hour, there is a single voice making this affirmation. From the discovery of this continent to the present hour, there is a single voice making this affirmation.[467]

When the court wrote in 1892 that we are a "religious people," they are saying we are a "Christian people." Far more than 90 percent of the country at that time were professing Christians. (Even today the number is about 76 percent.[468])

2) The Commission to Christopher Columbus Mentions God

The commission to Christopher Columbus, prior to his sail westward, is from "Ferdinand and Isabella, by the grace of God, King and Queen of Castile," etc., and recites that "it is hoped that by God's assistance some of the continents and islands in the ocean will be discovered," etc.[469]

We see that the Supreme Court takes us back to Columbus, who, was clearly motivated by Christ to undertake his death-defying voyage. Columbus noted: "...it was the Lord who put into my mind (I could feel His hand upon me) to sail to the Indies."[470]

3) The Earliest Charters and Grants All Mention God

Even before Jamestown, even before Plymouth, even before Boston, there was the first charter for Virginia:

> The first colonial grant, that [was] made to Sir Walter Raleigh in 1584, was from "Elizabeth, by the grace of God, of England, France and Ireland, queen, defender of the faith," etc; and the grant authorizing him to enact statutes for the government of the proposed colony provided that "they be not against the true Christian faith now professed in the Church of England." The first charter of Virginia, granted by King James I in 1606, after reciting the application of certain parties for a charter, commenced the grant in these words: "We, greatly commending, and graciously accepting of, their Desires for the Furtherance of so noble a Work, which may, by the Providence of Almighty God, hereafter tend to the Glory of His Divine Majesty, in propagating of Christian Religion to such People as yet live in Darkness and miserable Ignorance of the true Knowledge and Worship

of God, and may in time bring the Infidels and Savages, living in those parts, to human Civility, and to a settled and quiet Government; Do, by these our Letters-Patents, graciously accept and agree to, their humble and well intended Desires." Language of similar import may be found in the subsequent characters of that colony, from the same king, in 1609 and 1611; and the same is true of the various charters granted to the other colonies. In language more or less emphatic is the establishment of the Christian religion declared to be one of the purposes of the grant.[471]

Examine any colonial charter of America. Every one of them mentions a Christian goal as the reason for their coming to these shores.

4) The Mayflower Compact Was Christian. . . .

The celebrated compact made by the Pilgrims onboard the *Mayflower*, 1620, recites: "Having undertaken for the Glory of God, and Advancement of the Christian Faith, and the Honour of our King and Country, a Voyage to plant the first Colony in the northern Parts of Virginia; Do by these Presents, solemnly and mutually, in the Presence of God and one another, covenant and combine ourselves together into a civil Body Politic, for our better Ordering and Preservation, and Furtherance of the Ends aforesaid."[472]

5) . . . As Was One of Our Earliest Constitutions, "The Fundamental Orders of Connecticut"

The Supreme Court now shifts from the Pilgrims to the second full-blown constitution written by American colonists,[473] by the Puritans who established the Connecticut settlement.

The fundamental orders of Connecticut, under which a provisional government was instituted in 1638-39, commenced with this declaration:

> Forasmuch as it hath pleased the Almighty God by the wise disposition of his divine providence so to Order and dispose of things that we the Inhabitants and Residents of Windsor, Hartford and Wethersfield are now cohabiting and dwelling in and upon the River of Conectecotte and the Lands thereunto adjoining; And well knowing where a people are gathered together the word of God requires that to maintain the peace and union of such a people there should be an orderly and

decent Government established according to God, to order and dispose of the affairs of the people at all seasons as occasion shall require; do therefore associate and conjoin our selves to be as one Public State or Commonwealth; and do, for our souls and our Successors and such as shall be adjoined to us at any time hereafter, enter into Combination and Confederation together, to maintain and preserve the liberty and purity of the gospel of our Lord Jesus which we now profess, as also the discipline of the Churches, which according to the truth of the said gospel is now practiced amongst us.[474]

The Puritans were not reticent to mention God or Jesus Christ—the very basis of their colonies—in their political charters, compacts, and constitutions.

6) William Penn's Charter States that God Is the Source of Our Liberty

Next we see the Pennsylvania charter, allowing for religious liberty —under God:

In the charter of privileges granted, in 1701, by William Penn to the province of Pennsylvania and territories thereunto belonging (such territories afterwards constituting the State of Delaware), it is recited: "Because no People can be truly happy, though under the greatest Enjoyment of Civil Liberties, if abridged of the Freedom of their Consciences, as to their Religious Profession and Worship; And Almighty God being the only Lord of Conscience, Father of Lights and Spirits, and the Author as well as Object of all divine Knowledge, Faith and Worship, who only doth enlighten the Minds, and persuade and convince the Understandings of the People, I do hereby grant and declare," etc.[475]

Next, the high court jumps ahead to the time of the American Revolution.

7) The Declaration of Independence Proclaims God As the Source of Our Liberty

Coming nearer to the present time [1892], the Declaration of Independence recognizes the presence of the Divine in human affairs in these words: "We hold these truths to be self-evident, that all men are created equal, that they are endowed by their Creator with certain unalienable Rights, that among these are Life, Liberty, and pursuit of Happiness." "We, therefore, the Representatives of the United States of America, in General Congress, Assembled, appealing to the Supreme Judge of the world for the rectitude of our intentions, do, in the Name and by Authority of the good People of these Colonies, solemnly publish and declare," etc.; "And for the support of this Declaration, with a firm reliance on the Protection of Divine Providence, we mutually pledge to each other our Lives, our Fortunes, and our sacred Honor."[476]

It is such an important point that four times the Declaration of Independence, our nation's birth certificate, mentions God, the source of our liberties. Notice how the court shifted from Penn's charter, which acknowledged their liberties as a gift from Almighty God, to the Declaration, written in Philadelphia, which also declares that our liberties come from God. Man cannot take them away.

8) The State Constitutions Mention God and Often Have Had Specific Religious Requirements, such as for Those Running for Office

As the colonies shifted over to states, these new entities still recognized God:

> If we examine the constitutions of the various States we find in them a constant recognition of religious obligations. Every constitution of every one of the forty-four States contains language which either directly or by clear implication recognizes a profound reverence for religion and an assumption that its influence in all human affairs is essential to the well being of the community. This recognition may be in the preamble, such as is found in the constitution of Illinois, 1870: "We, the people of the State of Illinois, grateful to Almighty God for the civil, political and religious liberty which He hath so long permitted us to enjoy, and looking to Him for a blessing upon our endeavors to secure and transmit the same unimpaired to succeeding generations," etc.[477]

Illinois is obviously just one example. The constitution of every one of the fifty states mentions God somewhere in the document (usually in the Preamble). The Supreme Court continues to look further at state constitutions and the fact that they mention God:

> It may be only in the familiar requisition that all officers shall take an oath closing with the declaration "so help me God." It may be in clauses like that of the constitution of Indiana, 1816 Article XI, section 4: "The manner of administering an oath or affirmation shall be such as is most consistent with the conscience of the deponent, and shall be esteemed the most solemn appeal to God." Or in provisions such as are found in Articles 36 and 37 of the Declaration of Rights of the Constitution of Maryland, 1867: "That as it is the duty of every man to worship God in such manner as he thinks most acceptable to Him, all persons are equally entitled to protection in their religious liberty; wherefore, no person ought, by any law, to be molested in his person or estate on account of his religious persuasion or profession, or for his religious practice, unless, under the color of religion, he shall disturb the good, order, peace or safety of the State, or shall infringe the laws of morality, or injure others in their natural, civil or religious rights; nor ought any person to be compelled to frequent or maintain or contribute, unless on contract, to maintain any place of worship, or any ministry; nor shall any person, otherwise competent, be deemed incompetent as a witness, or juror, on account of his religious belief provide he believes in the existence of God, and that, under His dispensation, such person will be held morally accountable for his acts, and be rewarded or punished therefore, either in this world or the world to come. That no religious test ought ever to be required as a qualification for any office of profit or trust in this State other than a declaration of belief in the existence of God; nor shall the legislature prescribe any other oath of office than the oath prescribed by this constitution."[478]

This Maryland state constitution, quoted at length by the high court, demonstrates the importance of belief in God—and remember, for the vast majority of the lawmakers and the law-abiders, it was the Christian God under consideration. This Maryland constitution of 1867 had been written long after direct Puritan influence in New England had waned.

On the one hand, there was no direct religious test that could be applied for those running for office (e.g., no denominational boundaries).

On the other hand, they had to believe in God. Why would they stipulate that? They tell us why directly: Belief in God implies moral accountability. We shall all stand before the judgment seat of God and give an account before Him. When people believe that, it makes them better citizens. When they don't believe it, they often try to get away with whatever they can. Dostoevsky is quoted to have written, "If God is dead, then all things are permissible."[479] Returning to the *Trinity* decision:

> Or like that in Articles 2 and 3, of Part 1st, of the Constitution of Massachusetts, 1780: "It is the right as well as the duty of all men in society publicly and at stated seasons, to worship the Supreme Being, the great Creator and Preserver of the universe.... As the happiness of a people and the good order and preservation of civil government essentially depend upon piety, religion and morality, and as these cannot be generally diffused through a community but by the institution of the public worship of God and of public instructions in piety, religion and morality: Therefore, to promote their happiness and to secure the good order and preservation of their government, the people of this commonwealth have a right to invest their legislature with power to authorize and require, and the legislature shall, from time to time, authorize and require, the several towns, parishes, precincts and other bodies-politic or religious societies to make suitable provision, at their own expense, for the institution of the public worship of God and for the support and maintenance of public Protestant teachers of piety, religion, and morality in all cases where such provision shall not be made voluntarily."
> Or as in sections 5 and 14 of Article 7, of the constitution of Mississippi, 1832: "No person who denies the being of a God, or a future state of rewards and punishments, shall hold any office in the civil department of this State.... Religion, morality and knowledge being necessary to good government, the preservation of liberty, and the happiness of mankind, schools and the means of education, shall forever be encouraged in this State."
> Or by Article 22 of the constitution of Delaware, 1776, which required all officers, besides an oath of allegiance, to make and subscribe the following declaration, "I, A.B., do profess faith in God the Father, and in Jesus Christ His only Son, and in the Holy Ghost, one God, blessed for evermore; and I do

acknowledge the Holy Scriptures of the Old and New Testament to be given by divine inspiration."[480]

We see here that some of the states, such as Mississippi or Delaware, stipulate a Christian belief system for those running for office. Like the Maryland state constitution, so the Mississippi constitution of 1832 declares that man's accountability to God was an important condition to them for their rulers. They did not want any rogue politicians.

9) The U.S. Constitution Is Indirectly Christian

Now the *Trinity* decision shifts over from some of the state constitutions, which were directly Christian, to the federal one:

> Even the Constitution of the United States, which is supposed to have little touch upon the private life of the individual, contains in the First Amendment, a declaration common to the constitutions of all the States, as follows: "Congress shall make no law respecting an establishment of religion, or prohibiting the free exercise thereof," etc. And also provides in Article 1, section 7, (a provision common to many constitutions,) that the Executive shall have ten days (Sundays excepted) within which to determine whether he will approve or veto a bill.[481]

Note what the court says here about the constitution in general—that it's "supposed to have little touch upon the private life of the individual." This is significant because it shows that in earlier times, the Supreme Court did not view the Constitution as something that regulated what we believe or how we worship.

10) Earlier, Lower Court Decisions Affirm This Is a Christian People

Next the high court reviews some earlier court decisions that affirm the inescapable conclusion that they are building up to:

> There is no dissonance in these declarations. There is a universal language pervading them all, having one meaning; they affirm and reaffirm that this is a religious nation. These are not individual sayings, declarations of private persons; they are organic utterances; they speak the voice of the entire people. While because of a general recognition of this truth the question has

seldom been presented to the courts, yet we find that in *Upde-graph v. The Commonwealth*, 11 S. & R. 394, 400, it was decided that, "Christianity, general Christianity, is, and always had been, a part of the common law of Pennsylvania;...not Christianity with an established church, and tithes, and spiritual courts; but Christianity with liberty of conscience to all men." And in *The People v. Ruggles*, 8 Johns, 290, 294-295, Chancellor Kent, the great commentator on American law, speaking as Chief Justice of the Supreme Court of New York, said: "The people in this State, in common with the people of this country, profess the general doctrines of Christianity, as the rule of their faith and practice; and to scandalize the author of these doctrines is not only, in a religious point of view, extremely impious, but, even in respect to the obligations due to society, is a gross violation of decency and good order.... The free, equal, and undisturbed enjoyment of religious opinion, whatever it may be, and free and decent discussions on any religious subject, is granted and secured; but to revile, with malicious and blasphemous contempt, the religion professed by almost the whole community; is an abuse of that right. Nor are we bound, by any expressions in the Constitution as some have strangely supposed, either not to punish at all, or to punish indiscriminately, the like attacks upon the religion of Mahomet or the Grand Lama; and for this plain reason, that the case assumes that we are a Christian people, and the morality of this country is deeply engrafted upon Christianity, and not upon the doctrines or worship of those imposters." [482]

Do you catch how "politically incorrect" all this is? The Supreme Court of the United States is quoting, with approval, an earlier, lower court decision that dares to call followers of non-Christian religions "imposters."

And in the famous case of *Vidal v. Girard's Executors*, 2 How. 127 (1844), this court, while sustaining the will of Mr. Girard, with its provision for the creation of a college into which no minister should be permitted to enter, observed: "It is also said, and truly, that the Christian religion is part of the common law of Pennsylvania." [483]

Obviously by now, we see that courts in the nineteenth century were much more favorable to Christianity than recent courts have been. Here's the essence of these three court cases they just cited:

* "The people...of this country profess the general doctrines of Christianity...."

* "...we are a Christian people...."

* "...the Christian religion is part of the common law of Pennsylvania."

Now the Court is building up to its climactic conclusion:

11) THE CLIMACTIC CONCLUSION: THIS IS A CHRISTIAN NATION

If we pass beyond these matters to a view of American life as expressed by its laws, its business, its customs and its society, we find everywhere a clear recognition of the same truth. Among other matters note the following: The form of oath universally prevailing, concluding with an appeal to the Almighty; the custom of opening sessions of all deliberative bodies and most conventions with prayer; the prefatory words of all wills, "In the name of God, amen;" the laws respecting the observance of the Sabbath, with the general cessation of all secular business, and the closing of courts, legislatures, and other similar public assemblies on that day; the churches and church organizations which abound in every city, town and hamlet; the multitude of charitable organizations existing every where under Christian auspices; the gigantic missionary associations, with general support, and aiming to establish Christian missions in every quarter of the globe. These and many others which might be noticed, add a volume of unofficial declarations to the mass of organic utterances that this is a Christian nation.[484]

There it is. They may be "fighting words" today. But there it is in black and white. The United States Supreme Court declared that "this is a Christian nation."

THE UNITED STATES: A CHRISTIAN NATION

As marvelous as the *Trinity* decision is, the court marshaled only a fraction of the evidence available. In fact, the Associate Justice who wrote the *Trinity* decision, David Brewer, later wrote a book entitled, *The United States: A Christian Nation*.[485] His book contains many of the observations made in the *Trinity* decision, but it goes beyond that as well. If that material could be viewed as crumbs that fell off the table, they would make a feast. What we want to do for the rest of this chapter is to look at some of that evidence. This is evidence from Justice Brewer that never made it into the final version (or to my knowledge, any version) of the *Trinity* decision.

THE CLASSIFICATION OF NATIONS

In his book, *The United States: A Christian Nation*, Justice David Brewer says something that flies in the face of today's moral sensibilities, with our firm commitment to multiculturalism, the idea that any culture is as good as the next one. (Who are we to look down our noses at cannibals?) Brewer states that there is a link between the Christian faith and civilization:

> It has been often said that Christian nations are the civilized nations, and as often that the most thoroughly Christian are the most highly civilized. Is this a mere coincidence? Study well the history of Christianity in its relation to the nation and it will be found that it is something more than a mere coincidence, that there is between the two the relation of cause and effect, and that the more thoroughly the principles of Christianity reach into and influence the life of the nation the more certainly will that nation advance in civilization.[486]

He also points out that we categorize different countries all the time according to different criteria, including the dominant religion:

> We classify nations in various ways. As, for instance, by their form of government. One is a kingdom, another an empire, and still another a republic. Also by race. Great Britain is an Anglo-Saxon nation, France a Gallic, Germany a Teutonic, Russia a Slav. And still again by religion. One is a Mohammedan nation, others are heathen, and still others are Christian nations. This republic is classified among the Christian nations of the world.[487]

Next, Brewer asks a question still relevant today:

> But in what sense can it be called a Christian nation? Not in the sense that Christianity is the established religion or that the people are in any manner compelled to support it. On the contrary, the Constitution specifically provides that "Congress shall make no law respecting an establishment of religion, or prohibiting the

free exercise thereof." Neither is it Christian in the sense that all its citizens are either in fact or name Christians. On the contrary, all religions have free scope within our borders. Numbers of our people profess other religions, and many reject all. Nor is it Christian in the sense that a profession of Christianity is a condition of holding office or otherwise engaging in the public service, or essential to recognition either politically or socially. In fact, the government as a legal organization is independent of all religions.

Nevertheless, we constantly speak of this republic as a Christian nation—in fact, as the leading Christian nation of the world.

This popular use of the term certainly has significance. It is not a mere creation of the imagination. It is not a term of derision but has a substantial basis—one which justifies its use. Let us analyze a little and see what is the basis.[488]

He then goes on to deal with various charters of the colonies and then various constitutions of the states (post-1776).

Further, Brewer points out what we underscored in an earlier chapter, the Christian nature of the education of the American colonists:

Within less than one hundred years from the landing at Jamestown three colleges were established in the colonies; Harvard in Massachusetts, William and Mary in Virginia, and Yale in Connecticut. The first seal used by Harvard College had as a motto, "In Christi Gloriam," and the charter granted by Massachusetts Bay contained this recital: "Whereas, through the good hand of God many well devoted persons have been and daily are moved and stirred up to give and bestow sundry gifts...that may conduce to the education of the English and Indian youth of this country, in knowledge and godliness." The charter of William and Mary, reciting that the proposal was "to the end that the Church of Virginia may be furnished with a seminary of ministers of the gospel, and that the youth may be piously educated in good letters and manners, and that the Christian faith may be propagated amongst the western Indians, to the glory of Almighty God" made the grant "for propagating the pure gospel of Christ, our only Mediator, to the praise and honor of Almighty God." The charter of Yale declared as its purpose to fit "young men for public employment both in church and civil state," and it provided that the trustees should be Congregational ministers living in the colony.[489]

Going beyond Harvard, William and Mary, and Yale, Brewer talks about the Christian origins of other universities, schools, and academies on our soil:

> It may be added that outside of the institutions with direct State support nearly every academy, college, and university was founded by and is under the control of some one of the several Christian denominations. Indeed, a frequent criticism of many is that they are too much under such control. Certain is it that they would never have come into being but for the denominations back of them. Up to a recent date the rule was that the presidents and an exceedingly large majority of the faculty of all these institutions be ministers. It was a national surprise when first a layman was elected a college president.[490]

He mentions that outside of the state universities, virtually all schools are Christian. The Christian schools came first and paved the way for all others to follow, including the state schools. Brewer continues to marshal his arguments for the Christian origins of our republic:

> I insist that Christianity has been so wrought into the history of this republic, so identified with its growth and prosperity, has been and is so dear to the hearts of this great body of our citizens, that it ought not to be spoken of contemptuously or treated with ridicule.[491]

We can read into his remarks that already by the turn of the twentieth century or so there were some that treated with contempt the Christian roots of America. Already, some were criticizing colleges and universities for being under too much Christian control. Our lament today is precisely the opposite. Alas, in the twenty-first century, unbelief has made incredible inroads to our once-great Christian nation. They seemingly have captured the culture.

But that is at odds with our history.

THE SPIRIT OF 1776

We can see over and over the Spirit of 1776—especially in the state constitutions, many of which were written in 1776 and which served as forerunners to the Declaration of Independence. Also, we can see over and over the unmistakable Christian heritage of America.

THE SHIFT FROM COLONIES TO STATES

When the various colonial settlements shifted over to become states and then when new states were added on, we see again God, the Christian faith, and religious freedom being important to these historic documents.

CONNECTICUT, 1776

Justice Brewer says this of the Connecticut constitution:

> In the preamble of the Constitution of 1776 it is declared, "the free fruition of such liberties and privileges as humanity, civility and Christianity call for, as is due to every man in his place and proportion, without impeachment and infringement, hath ever been, and will be the tranquility and stability of churches and commonwealths; and the denial thereof, the disturbance, if not the ruin of both."[492]

VERMONT, 1777

One of the states born during the revolutionary war was that of Vermont in the New England region:

> The Constitution of Vermont, of 1777, granting the free exercise of religious worship, added, "Nevertheless, every sect or denomination of people ought to observe the Sabbath, or the Lord's day, and keep up and support some sort of religious worship, which to them shall seem most agreeable to the revealed will of God." And this was repeated in the Constitution of 1786.[493]

Brewer could well have cited a Massachusetts court case from 1838, *Commonwealth v. Abner Kneeland*. In this decision the supreme court of that state gave a rundown of various states. Among other things, they stated the following about Vermont:

> In Vermont, with a similar declaration of rights, a statute was passed in 1797, by which it was enacted, that if any person shall publicly deny the being and existence of God or the Supreme Being, or shall contumeliously reproach his providence and

government, he shall be deemed a disturber of the peace and tranquility of the State, and an offender against the good morals and manners of society, and shall be punishable by fine....[494]

In fact, this Massachusetts Supreme Court decision—*Abner v. Kneeland*—made an important observation about religious liberty as perceived by American courts two generations after the Constitution was written. The court declared that the First Amendment "embraces all who believe in the existence of God, as well...as Christians of every denomination.... This provision does not extend to atheists, because they do not believe in God or religion; and therefore...their sentiments and professions, whatever they may be, cannot be called religious sentiments and professions."[495] Thus, much closer to the time the First Amendment was written, it meant freedom *of* religion, not freedom *from* religion.

MAINE

Here's another statement from the same Massachusetts Supreme Court decision, *Commonwealth v. Abner Kneeland*. This is an example of how Maine also began with a godly heritage.

> The State of Maine also, having adopted the same constitutional provision with that of Massachusetts, in her declaration of rights, in respect to religious freedom, immediately after the adoption of the constitution reenacted, the Massachusetts statue against blasphemy....[496]

NEW YORK, 1777

The New York constitution of 1777 was written by an evangelical, John Jay, and it guaranteed religious freedom for all. In Section XXXVIII, the constitution stipulates:

> The free exercise and enjoyment of religious profession and worship, without discrimination or preference, shall forever hereafter be allowed, within this State, to all mankind: Provided, That the liberty of conscience, hereby granted, shall not be so construed as to excuse acts of licentiousness....[497]

Furthermore, this Constitution prohibits ministers from running for office. What? Yes, because they are so vitally needed in the gospel ministry, which is of great value. This is the actual wording of that stipulation:

"...the ministers of the gospel are, by their profession, dedicated to the service of God and the care of souls, and ought not to be diverted from the great duties of their function...."[498] In today's highly secularized milieu, you would not know that ministers were good for anything but public ridicule.

SOUTH CAROLINA, 1778

Returning to Justice Brewer and his book, *The United States: A Christian Nation*, we pick up with what he said about the first state constitution of South Carolina:

> In the Constitution of South Carolina, of 1778, it was declared that "the Christian Protestant religion shall be deemed and is hereby constituted and declared to be the established religion of this State." And further, that no agreement or union of men upon pretense of religion should be entitled to become incorporated and regarded as a church of the established religion of the State, without agreeing and subscribing to a book of five articles, the third and fourth of which were "that the Christian religion is the true religion; that the holy Scriptures of the Old and New Testament are of divine inspiration, and are the rule of faith and practice."[499]

MASSACHUSETTS, 1780

The world's oldest constitution still in force was that of Massachusetts, written mostly by John Adams, who was later to become our second president. This constitution declares:

> We, therefore, the people of Massachusetts, acknowledging, with grateful hearts, the goodness of the great Legislator of the universe, in affording us, in the course of His providence...and devoutly imploring His direction in so interesting a design....[500]
>
> It is the right as well as the duty of all men in society, publicly, and at stated seasons to worship the Supreme Being, the great Creator and Preserver of the universe....[501]
>
> As the public worship of God and instructions in piety, religion and morality, promote the happiness and prosperity of a people and the security of republican government....[502]

SHORT SAMPLES FROM THE CONSTITUTIONS

Earlier we have noted the point that the constitution of every one of the fifty states mentions God somewhere in the document, usually in the preamble. Here are just a few other examples in the order of the dates in which each constitution was adopted:

> * New Hampshire constitution, 1784:
> That morality and piety, rightly grounded on evangelical principles would give the best and greatest security to government, and would lay in the hearts of men the strongest obligation to due subjection; and that the knowledge of these was most likely to be propagated by the institution of the public worship of the Deity and instruction in morality and religion.[503]

> * Maryland, 1776:
> We, the people of the state of Maryland, grateful to Almighty God for our civil and religious liberty....[504]

> * New Jersey, 1844, 1947:
> We, the people of the State of New Jersey, grateful to Almighty God for the civil and religious liberty which He hath so long permitted us to enjoy, and looking to Him for a blessing upon our endeavors to secure and transmit the same unimpaired to succeeding generations, do ordain and establish this Constitution.[505]

> * New York, 1846:
> We, the people of the State of New York, grateful to Almighty God for our freedom, in order to secure its blessings, do establish this Constitution.[506]

> * Indiana, 1851:
> Article I, Section 2. All men shall be secure in their natural right to worship Almighty God.[507]

> * Ohio, 1852:
> We the people of the state of Ohio, grateful to Almighty God for our freedom, to secure its blessings and to promote our common welfare, do establish our Constitution.[508]

> * Iowa, 1857:
> We, the People of the State of Iowa, grateful to the Supreme

Being for the blessings hitherto enjoyed, and feeling our dependence on Him for a continuation of these blessings...establish this Constitution.[509]

* Nebraska, 1867:
We, the people, grateful to Almighty God for our freedom... establish this Constitution.[510]

* North Carolina, 1868:
We the people of the State of North Carolina, grateful to Almighty God, the Sovereign Ruler of Nations, for the preservation of the American Union and the existence of our civil, political, and religious liberties, and acknowledging our dependence upon Him for the continuance of those blessings to us and our posterity, do, for the more certain security thereof and for the better government of this State, ordain and establish this Constitution.[511]

* Idaho, 1889:
We, the people of the State of Idaho, grateful to Almighty God for our freedom, to secure its blessings and promote our common welfare do establish this Constitution.[512]

* Wyoming, 1890:
We, the people of the State of Wyoming, grateful to God for our civil, political, and religious liberties...establish this Constitution.[513]

And on it goes. What more evidence does anyone need that Christianity played a key role in the settling and the founding of this country and even its first hundred years or so after its founding?

There were multiple other examples that the Supreme Court could have cited. The Supreme Court decision of 1892 was very well-researched and well-written. It drew on innumerable primary documents of our nations' founding. But to even quote the *Trinity* decision today is politically incorrect. Yet the facts in the decision still stand, historical revisionism notwithstanding.

The facts are the facts. Something every Christian should know about the founding of America is that the Supreme Court declared, "...this is a Christian nation."

AFTER THE *TRINITY* DECISION....

Although it is so politically incorrect, the idea that America was founded as a "Christian nation" was reaffirmed by an important court as recently as two decades ago. In 1986, U.S. District Judge Frank McGarr, a federal judge in Chicago, said this in a ruling: "The truth is that America's origins are Christian and that our founding fathers intended and achieved full religious freedom for all within the context of a Christian nation in the First Amendment as it was adopted rather than as we have rewritten it."[514]

In the early years of the republic, Associate Justice Joseph Story wrote his famous *Commentaries on the Constitution of the United States*. This member of the Supreme Court, whose *Commentaries* which have been studied by lawyers down through the years, said this: "the real object of the First Amendment was not to countenance much less to advance Mohametanism, or Judaism, or infidelity, by prostrating Christianity, but to exclude all rivalry among Christian sects and to prevent any national ecclesiastical establishment which would give to an hierarchy the exclusive patronage of the national government."[515] So, we see that, far from excluding God, the United States Constitution left the regulation of religion right where it was in the hands of the churches and the states. Remember that when the First Amendment was drafted some of the thirteen states had established religions and they were all some denomination of the Christian religion.

CONCLUSION

French writer and observer of the early American experience, Alexis de Tocqueville reminds us of something we have forgotten. He said, "Moreover, all the sects of the United States are comprised within the great unity of Christianity, and Christian morality is everywhere the same."[516] He reminds us that "Despotism may govern without faith, but liberty cannot."[517] We need to remember that. We cannot have liberty without faith. Tyranny and despotism may be had without faith, but not liberty—because if you dissolve the bonds which faith creates, the government must inevitably move in to create the control which has been lost by the internal self-government upon which the founders of this country based our nation.

Endnotes

INTRODUCTION

1 Woodrow Wilson, remarks at a Denver rally, 1911 in Charles E. Rice, *The Supreme Court and Public Prayer.* (New York: Fordham University Press, 1964), 61-62.

2 George Orwell, quoted in Gary DeMar, *America's Christian History: The Untold Story* (Atlanta: American Vision Publishers, 1993), 22.

3 Francis Schaeffer, quoted by D. James Kennedy, "America: A Christian Nation," pamphlet (Ft. Lauderdale, FL: Coral Ridge Ministries, March 4, 1990).

4 James Madison, Speech in the Virginia Convention, 5 June 1788; Complete Madison, 46, in Caroline Thomas Harnsberger, ed., *Treasury of Presidential Quotations* (Chicago: Follett Publishing Company, 1964), 107.

5 Benjamin Franklin, *Historical Review of Pennsylvania,* 1759, http://www.quotationspage.com/quote/1381.html.

PART ONE: CHAPTER 1

6 Jon Meacham, "The Decline and Fall of Christian America," *Newsweek,* April 13, 2009, 34.

7 E-mail from John Rabe to Jerry Newcombe, April 13, 2009.

8 Steven Mansfield, guest on *Hannity's America,* Fox News Channel, April 10, 2009.

9 Senator John McCain, and Ira N. Forman, as quoted by Don Feder, in "Ibrahim and Ira Meet Christian America" October 23, 2007, http://www.donfeder.com/.

10 Ibid., Don Feder.

11 Transcript of a Coral Ridge Ministries-TV interview with Rabbi Daniel Lapin, May 17, 2001.

12 *The Annals of America,* Twenty volumes (Chicago et al.: *Encyclopaedia Britannica,* 1976). My friend, author and speaker Bill Federer, told me about them, so I purchased my own set, used, on-line. When I told Dr. Kennedy about them, he, too, wanted a set, and I was able to buy them used on-line, for him as well.

13 Cal Thomas points out that we should expect the slander of the world and recognize it as a sign that we're on the right track. He says, "To a very large extent, I welcome 'Christian bashing' if it is for righteousness sake. I think we should look for ways to live even more righteously that the 'bashing' might increase. After all, if they hated Him, they're supposed to hate us too, right?" Source: Letter from Cal Thomas to Jerry Newcombe, April 15, 1995.

14 Transcript of a Coral Ridge Ministries-TV interview with James White, August 2007.

15 Transcript of a Coral Ridge Ministries-TV interview with Robert Spencer, August 2005.

16 Kenneth L. Woodward with David Gates, "How the Bible Made America: Since the Puritans and the pioneers, through wars and social conflicts, a sense of Biblical mission has united us, divided us and shaped our national destiny," *Newsweek,* December 27, 1982, 44.

17 Ezra Bowen, "Looking to Its Roots" *TIME,* May 25, 1987.

18 George Washington, "Farewell Address," September 19, 1796, in *The Annals of America* (Chicago et al.: Encyclopaedia Britannica, 1976), 3:612.

19 Benjamin Hart, "The Wall That Protestantism Built: The Religious Reasons for the Separation of Church and State," *Policy Review,* Fall 1988, 44.

20 Richard Ostling, "In So Many Gods We Trust," *TIME,* January 30, 1995.

21 D. James Kennedy with Jerry Newcombe, *The Gates of Hell Shall Not Prevail* (Nashville, TN: Thomas Nelson Publishers, 1996), 144-145.

22 Transcript from an interview with Ann Coulter, on location in New York City, Coral Ridge Ministries-TV, Ft. Lauderdale, June 2006.

23 Dwight D. Eisenhower, 14 June 1954 quoted in William J. Federer, "Public Papers of Dwight D. Eisenhower 1953-1961," United States Folder in *Library of Classics* (St. Louis: Amerisearch, Inc., 2002), a CD-ROM.

24 Ibid., quoting Dwight D. Eisenhower, recorded for the "Back-to-God" Program of the American Legion, 20 February 1955.

25 Paul Johnson, *A History of the American People* (New York: HarperCollins Publishers, 1997), 204.

26 Ibid., 172.

27 Ibid., 30.

28 John Eidsmoe, *Columbus & Cortez: Conquerors for Christ* (Green Forest, AR: New Leaf Press, 1992), 90.

29 Charter of Virginia, April 10, 1606, William J. Federer, *The Original 13: A Documentary History of Religion in America's first Thirteen States* (St. Louis: Amerisearch, 2007), 33.

30 "Instructions for the Virginia Colony, 1606," in William J. Federer, ed., "United States," *Library of Classics* (St. Louis: Amerisearch, Inc., 2002), a CD-ROM. Note that these instructions were written in 1606, but not read until 1607, after the Jamestown party landed.

31 The Mayflower Compact, 1620, in Bruce Frohnen, ed., *The American Republic: Primary Sources* (Indianapolis: Liberty Fund, 2002), 11.

32 Ibid.

33 "Fundamental Orders of Connecticut," January 14, 1639, *Documents of American History*, ed. Henry Steel Commager, 6th ed. (New York: Appleton Century Crofts, 1958), 26. Quoted in Gary DeMar, *America's Christian History*, 1993 edition, 37.

34 "Charter of Rhode Island and Providence Plantations," July 15, 1663, in William J. Federer, *The Original 13*, 199.

35 Instructions Issued by Queen Christina regarding the New Sweden Colony in 1642, in David Gibbs, Jr., *The Legal Alert* (Seminole, FL: Christian Law Association), October 2001, 3.

36 Charter of Pennsylvania, 1681, granted to William Penn by King Charles II. *A Collection of Charters and Other Public Acts Relating to the Province of Pennsylvania* (Philadelphia: B. Franklin, 1740), 1.

37 Provision 95 of "Charter of Carolina," June 30, 1665, in http://www.yale.edu/lawweb/avalon/states/nc04.htm.

38 Provision 97 of ibid.

39 Peter Sprigg in *Hate Crime Laws: Censoring the Church and Silencing Christians* (Ft. Lauderdale, FL: Coral Ridge Ministries-TV), 2007, a video.

40 Ibid., Ake Green.

41 Ibid., Danny Nahlia.

42 In June 1783, George Washington sent a letter to the governors of all the states. At the end of that "circular," George Washington declared, "I now make it my earnest prayer that God would have you, and the State over which you preside, in His holy protection…that He would most graciously be pleased to dispose us all to do justice, to love mercy, and to demean ourselves with that charity, humility, and pacific temper of mind, which were the characteristics of the Divine Author of our blessed religion, and without an humble imitation of whose example in these things, we can never hope to be a happy nation." Source: George Washington, "Circular to State Governments," June 8, 1783, in John Rhodehamel, ed., *George Washington: Writings* (New York: The Library of America, 1997), 526.

43 William J. Federer in D. James Kennedy, *One Nation Under God* (Ft. Lauderdale, FL: Coral Ridge Ministries-TV, 2005), a video.

CHAPTER 2

44 Catherine Drinker Bowen, *Miracle at Philadelphia: The Story of the Constitutional Convention May to September 1787* (Boston et al.: An Atlantic Monthly Press Book, a division of Little, Brown and Company, 1966/1986), 138.

45 *Life and Works of Abraham Lincoln*, Marion Mills Miller, ed., Centenary Edition, in Nine Volumes, (New York: The Current Literature Publishing Co., 1907), VI:156.

46 Transcript of an interview with Dr. Paul Maier, Coral Ridge Ministries-TV, April 2001.

47 Journalist William Shirer wrote the classic work on Hitler and the Nazis: *The Rise and Fall of the Third Reich*. In the context of Germany's schools, Shirer used that phrase. It applied in Norway and all the places where they took over. William L. Shirer, *The Rise and Fall of the Third Reich* (New York: Simon & Schuster, 1960), 249.

48 Mark Steyn, "Why the world can be thankful for the USA," *The Washington Times: National Weekly Edition*, November 26, 2007, 32.

49 The Liberty Bell was rung from Independence Hall on July 8, 1776, at the first public reading of the Declaration of Independence. This symbol of our freedom has a Bible verse chiseled on it: "Proclaim liberty throughout the land and to all the inhabitants thereof" (Leviticus 25:10).

50 This founding document of America from July 4, 1776, is Part I of our two-part foundation: It tells us why America exists. It declares in no uncertain terms that our rights come from God, and it is the duty of governments to recognize that fact.

51 The Constitution (written 1787 and adopted 1789) is Part II of our two-part foundation. It consists of the "how-to" of government. It is based on the premise laid forth in the Declaration of Independence. As we will see later, it might not have been finished had they not turned to God for help about mid-way. Ironically, one of the least orthodox of the founding fathers, Benjamin Franklin, was the one who reminded them to plead to God for His help.

52 See David Barton, *The Bulletproof George Washington* (Aledo, TX: Wallbuilders, 1990).

53 George Washington letter to Thomas Nelson, 20 August 1778. John C. Fitzpatrick, ed., *The Writings of Washington* (Washington, DC: U.S. Government Printing Office, 1932), XII:343.

54 George Washington, First Inaugural Address, April 30, 1789, in William J. Federer, *America's God and Country Encyclopedia of Quotations* (St. Louis: Amerisearch, Inc., 1994/2000), 652.

CHAPTER 3

55 *Compton's Pictured Encyclopedia and Fact Index* (Chicago: F. E. Compton Co., 1965), 15:192.

56 Author and speaker David Barton knows as much about America's Christian heritage as any human being alive that I am aware of. At his ministry, "Wallbuilders" (named in honor of the wall Nehemiah built) in the Fort Worth area, he has collected tens of thousands of books (originals and reprints), newspapers, proclamations, monographs, and memorabilia from the founding era. I have even had the privilege of videotaping some of these things in his ministry's library.

57 Dr. Peter Lillback is the president of Westminster Theological Seminary and the chief author of *George Washington's Sacred Fire*, a huge book I had the privilege of co-authoring with him.

58 Paul Jehle, D.Ed. is the Executive Director of the Plymouth Rock Foundation, which is dedicated to preserving our nation's Christian roots, and pastor of New Testament Church and school. He leads tours in Plymouth with emphasis on the role the Christian faith played in the lives of the Pilgrims.

59 Author and speaker William J. Federer has written books on the Christian origins of America. His best known has more than half a million copies in print: *America's God and Country Encyclopedia of Quotations* (see note 54).

60 Marshall Foster, D.D., founder of the Mayflower Institute (1975), president of World History Institute, and a speaker on America's Christian heritage for decades, is best known for *The American Covenant: The Untold Story,* coauthored with Mary-Elaine Swanson, first published in 1981, which has sold more than 100,000 copies.

61 Declaration of Independence, 4 July 1776, *The World Almanac and Book of Facts 1998,* 512-513.

62 Arthur Koestler, trans. by Daphne Hardy, *Darkness at Noon* (New York: Bantam Books, 1941/1968), 128.

63 David Barton in Dr. Kennedy, *One Nation Under God* (Ft. Lauderdale, FL: Coral Ridge Ministries-TV, 2005), a video.

64 Remarks of James Hutson, interviewed by Jerry Newcombe, on location at the Library of Congress, Washington, D.C. (Ft. Lauderdale, FL: Coral Ridge Ministries-TV, May 2005).

65 Paul Johnson, *A History of the American People* (New York: HarperCollins Publishers, 1997), 31.

66 "Fundamental Orders of Connecticut," January 14, 1639. Henry Steele Commmager, ed., *Documents of American History,* sixth edition (New York: Appleton-Century-Crofts, 1958), 26.

67 Articles of Confederation, November 15, 1777, proposed by the Continental Congress; signed July 9, 1778; ratified March 1, 1781. Charles W. Eliot, LL.D., ed., *American Historical Documents 1000-1904* (New York: P. F. Collier & Son Company, The Harvard Classics, 1910), 43:168-179.

68 The Constitution, Bruce Frohnen, ed., *The American Republic: Primary Sources* (Indianapolis: Liberty Fund, 2002), 239.

69 Ibid., 227, Northwest Ordinance.

70 Transcript of a Coral Ridge Ministries-TV interview with David Barton, October 10, 2002.

71 Transcript of a Coral Ridge Ministries-TV interview with Donald S. Lutz, April 2005.

72 George Bancroft, *History of the United States of America: From the Discovery of the Continent* (New York: D. Appleton and Company, 1890) IV:196–197.

73 Ibid., 198.

74 Lorraine Boettner, *The Reformed Doctrine of Predestination* (Philadelphia: The Presbyterian and Reformed Publishing Company, 1975), 387.

75 Mecklenburg County, Declaration of Independence of May 20, 1775. *Raleigh* [North Carolina]

Register, April 30, 1819. Charles W. Eliot, LL.D., ed., *American Historical Documents 1000-1904* (New York: P. F. Collier & Son Company, The Harvard Classics, 1910), 43:166.

76 N. S. McFetridge, *Calvinism in History,* 85-88. Quoted in Boettner, *The Reformed Doctrine of Predestination,* 388.

77 Charles E. Rice, *The Supreme Court and Public Prayer,* 167.

78 Ibid., 169.

79 Ibid., 172.

80 The Constitution of Vermont, 1777, in *The Annals of America,* (Chicago: Encyclopaedia Britannica, 2:483.

81 The Constitution of Vermont, 1793, in Rice, *The Supreme Court and Public Prayer,* 175.

82 Andrew Jackson, June 8, 1845, in Henry Halley, *Halley's Bible Handbook* (Grand Rapids, MI: Zondervan, 1927, 1965), 18.

83 Benjamin Franklin, Treaty of Paris, September 3, 1783, in W. Cleon Skousen, *The Making of America* (Washington: The National Center for Constitutional Studies, 1985), 139.

84 Constitutional Convention. September 17, 1787. M. E. Bradford, *A Worthy Company: Brief Lives of the Framers of the United States Constitution* (Marlborough, NH: Plymouth Rock Foundation, 1982), iv-v.

85 John Eidsmoe, *Christianity and the Constitution: The Faith of Our Founding Fathers* (Grand Rapids, MI: Baker Book House, 1987), 41-43.

86 Alexander Hamilton, James Madison, and John Jay, *The Federalist Papers,* with introduction by Clinton Rossiter (New York, et al.: A Mentor Book from New American Library, 1961), vii.

87 Ibid., 301.

88 Bancroft, *History of the United States,* III:77.

89 Samuel Adams, "The Rights of the Colonists" (Boston: Old South Leaflets, 1772), Vol. VII. Selim H. Peabody, ed., *American Patriotism: Speeches, Letters, and Other Papers Which Illustrate the Foundation, the Development, the Preservation of the United States of America* (NY: American Book Exchange, 1880), 34.

90 James Madison, *The Federalist Papers,* #10, 80; and #47, 300-308.

91 John Eidsmoe, *Christianity and the Constitution: The Faith of Our Founding Fathers* (Grand Rapids, MI: Baker Book House, 1987), 101.

92 Catherine Drinker Bowen, *Miracle at Philadelphia: The Story of the Constitutional Convention May to September 1787* (Boston: An Atlantic Monthly Press Book, a div. Little, Brown and Company, 1966/1986), 61.

93 Hamilton, Madison, and Jay, *The Federalist Papers,* 59.

94 Ibid., 110.

95 Ibid., 346.

96 *Life and Works of Abraham Lincoln,* Marion Mills Miller, ed., Centenary Edition. In Nine Volumes: (New York: The Current Literature Publishing Co., 1907), VI:156-157.

97 George Washington, letter to the Synod of the Dutch Reformed Church in North America, October 9, 1789, in John Clement Fitzpatrick, ed., *The Writings of George Washington, from the Original Manuscript Sources 1749-1799,* 39 vols. (Washington, DC: United States Government Printing Office, 1931-1944), XXX:432.

98 http://www.americanvision. org/articlearchive/05-23-05.asp

99 Dwight D. Eisenhower, recorded for the "Back-to-God" Program of the American Legion, 20 February 1955, quoted in ibid. at 1475.

100 George Washington, "First Inaugural Address," April 30, 1789, in John Rhodehamel, ed., *George Washington: Writings* (New York: The Library of America, 1997), 731.

101 Andrew Jackson, September 20, 1838, in a private letter written to an old friend whose brother had suddenly died. Robert V. Remini, *Andrew Jackson and the Course of American Freedom, 1822-1832* (New York: Harper & Row, 1981), 448.

102 John Quincy Adams, September 26, 1810, in a diary entry. Edmund Fuller and David E. Green, *God in the White House: The Faiths of American Presidents* (NY: Crown Publishers, Inc., 1968), 55.

103 Ulysses Simpson Grant, June 6, 1876, letter from Washington during his term as President, to the Editor of the *Sunday School Times* in Philadelphia, in Henry Halley, *Halley's Bible Handbook* (Grand Rapids, MI: Zondervan, 1927, 1965), 18.

104 Theodore Roosevelt in John A. Hash, ed., *The Winning Way* (Murfreesboro, TN: Bible Pathway Ministries, undated), 2.

105 Theodore Roosevelt, October 1917, *Ladies Home Journal,* 12, in Albert Bushnell Hart & Herbert Ronald Ferleger, *Theodore Roosevelt Cyclopedia* (New York: Roosevelt Memorial Association, 1941), 77.

106 Thomas Jefferson to William Canby, Sept. 18, 1813, *Writings*, XIII, 377, in Caroline Thomas Harnsberger, ed., *Treasury of Presidential Quotations* (Chicago: Follett Publishing Company, 1964), 194.

107 Kenneth L. Woodward with David Gates, "How the Bible Made America: since the Puritans and the pioneers, through wars and social conflicts, a sense of Biblical mission has united us, divided us and shaped our national destiny," *Newsweek*, December 27, 1982, 44.

108 (John) Calvin Coolidge, 1923 statement in Charles Fadiman, ed., *The American Treasury* (New York: Harper & Brothers, Publishers, 1955), 127.

109 John Fitzgerald Kennedy, Inaugural Address, January 20, 1961, in *Inaugural Addresses of the Presidents of the United States: From George Washington 1789 to Richard Milhous Nixon 1969* (Washington, DC: United States Government Printing Office; 91st Congress, 1st Session, House Document 91-142, 1969), 267-270.

PART TWO: CHAPTER 4

110 Lew Leadbeater, "Jamestown not worth it," *Virginia Gazette*, July 8, 2006.

111 Transcript of an interview with Doug Phillips, conducted by Jerry Newcombe, shot on location in the Jamestown area (Ft. Lauderdale, FL: Coral Ridge Ministries-TV, 2007).

112 Ibid., Interview with John Eidsmoe.

113 Charter of Virginia, April 10, 1606.

114 http://odur.let.rug.nl/~usa/D/1601-1650/virginia/instru.htm

115 Ibid.

116 Transcript of an interview with Dan Ford, conducted by Jerry Newcombe, shot on location in the Jamestown area (Ft. Lauderdale, FL: Coral Ridge Ministries-TV, 2007).

117 Transcript of an interview with Dr. Peter Lillback, conducted by Jerry Newcombe, shot on location in the Jamestown area (Ft. Lauderdale, FL: Coral Ridge Ministries-TV, 2007).

118 Transcript of an interview with Dr. Paul Jehle, conducted by Jerry Newcombe, shot on location in the Jamestown area (Ft. Lauderdale, FL: Coral Ridge Ministries-TV, 2007).

119 Ibid.

120 Ibid., Interview with John Eidsmoe.

121 Transcript of an interview with Dr. Peter Lillback, conducted by Jerry Newcombe, shot on location in the Jamestown area (Ft. Lauderdale, FL: Coral Ridge Ministries-TV, 2007).

122 John Pory, Speaker, "Proceedings of the First Assembly of Virginia, 1619."

123 Paul Johnson, *A History of the American People* (New York: HarperCollins Publishers, 1997), 27.

124 Captain John Woodlief, December 4, 1619.

125 Transcript of an interview with Dr. Peter Lillback, conducted by Jerry Newcombe, shot on location in the Jamestown area (Ft. Lauderdale, FL: Coral Ridge Ministries-TV, 2007).

126 Transcript of an interview with Dr. Paul Jehle, conducted by Jerry Newcombe, shot on location in the Jamestown area (Ft. Lauderdale, FL: Coral Ridge Ministries-TV, 2007), as reviewed and approved by Dr. Jehle, April 22, 2009.

127 Ibid.

128 Cotton Mather, *The Great Works of Christ in America: Magnalia Christi Americana*, 2 Volumes (Edinburgh: The Banner of Truth Trust, 1702/1853/1979), I:50.

129 Ibid., I:51.

130 John Winthrop, "A Model of Christian Charity," 1630, *The Annals of America* (Chicago et al: Encyclopedia Britannica, Inc., 1976), 1:115.

131 Ronald Reagan quoted in William J. Federer, "American Quotations," Library of Classics (St. Louis: Amerisearch, Inc., 2002), a CD-ROM.

132 John Palfrey, *A History of New England*, 1859, quoted in Verna Hall, *The Christian History of the Constitution of the United States of America: Christian Self-Government* (San Francisco: Foundation for American Christian Education, 1960/1993), 48.

133 Cotton Mather, *The Great Works of Christ in America: Magnalia Christi Americana*, 2 Volumes (Edinburgh: The Banner of Truth Trust, 1702/1853/1979), I:79.

134 Ibid., 80.

135 Ibid., 129.

136 Bancroft, *History of the United States*, 1:240.

137 D. James Kennedy, "The Pilgrim Legacy" (Ft. Lauderdale, FL), 1989

138 Johnson, *A History of the American People*, 46.

139 Ibid., 31.

140 Mather, *The Great Works of Christ in America*, I:119.

141 Johnson, *A History of the American People*, 46.

142 Ibid., 32, 40.

143 Mather, *The Great Works of Christ in America*, 1:93.

144 Ibid., 94.

145 Ibid., 92.

146 Ibid., 103.

147 Ibid., 107.

148 *Church of the Holy Trinity v. the United States.* Please note that the elements quoted here from the 1892 Supreme Court decision were in the "findings" portion of the ruling. While they were presented as evidence in the case, they were not (are not) legally binding. (The Court did not set out to determine: Is America a Christian nation, yes or no? They set out to solve another problem.) Nonetheless, the findings of the Supreme Court in the *Trinity* decision are an excellent summary of America's true history. (See note 337.)

149 David J. Brewer, *The United States: A Christian Nation* (Smyrna, GA: American Vision, 1905/1996), 14-15.

150 Declaration of Independence, July 4, 1776.

151 Brewer, *The United States*, 15.

152 *Church of the Holy Trinity v. the United States.*

153 Brewer, *The United States*, 16.

154 Ibid.

155 The Charter of Maryland, 1632. http://www.yale.edu/lawweb/avalon/states/ma01.htm.

156 Brewer, *The United States*, 16.

157 Ibid.

158 New Jersey, Colony of, 1697, Benjamin Franklin Morris, *The Christian Life and Character of the Civil Institutions of the United States* (Philadelphia: George W. Childs, 1864), 91.

159 William J. Federer, *America's God and Country: Encyclopedia of Quotations* (St. Louis: Amerisearch, Inc., 1994/2000), 259.

160 Francis Newton Thorpe, ed., *The Federal and State Constitutions Colonial Charters, and Other Organic Laws of the States, Territories, and Colonies Now or Heretofore Forming the United States of America* (Washington, DC: Government Printing Office, 1909).

161 Brewer, *The United States*, 18.

162 George Bancroft, *History of the United States of America, From the Discovery of the Continent* (New York: D. Appleton and Company, 1890), II:138.

163 Brewer, *The United States*, 18.

164 For example, see Will Morrisey, "How the Founders Built a Nation on Religion and Philosophy," book review of Michael Novak's *On Two Wings: Humble Faith and Common Sense*, in *The Washington Times*: National Weekly Edition, 23 January 23–February 3, 2002, 28.

165 Lorraine Boettner, *The Reformed Doctrine of Predestination* (Philadelphia: The Presbyterian and Reformed Publishing Company, 1975), 382-383.

166 George Bancroft, *History of the United States of America, From the Discovery of the Continent, Six Volumes* (New York: D. Appleton and Company, 1890), IV:9.

167 Lorraine Boettner, 382-383.

168 Paul Carlson, *Our Presbyterian Heritage* (Elgin, IL: David C. Cook, 1973), 13.

169 Ibid., 384, quoting J. G. Slosser, editor, *They Seek a Country*, 155.

170 Marshall Foster in D. James Kennedy, *One Nation Under God* (Ft. Lauderdale, FL: Coral Ridge Ministries-TV, 2005), a video.

171 Winthrop, "A Model of Christian Charity," *The Annals of America*, 1:115.

CHAPTER 5

172 Michael Weisskopf, *Washington Post* front page story, February 1, 1993 [emphasis mine].

173 D. James Kennedy, *What If Jesus Had Never Been Born?* (Ft. Lauderdale, FL: Coral Ridge Ministries-TV, 2002), a video.

174 James Madison, Second Annual Message to Congress, Dec. 5, 1810, in the *Annals of America*.

175 "Massachusetts School Law," 1647 (originally 1642), *Annals*, 1:84

176 Samuel L. Blumenfeld, *Is Public Education Necessary?* (Boise, ID: The Paradigm Co., 1985), 10.

177 *The New-England Primer* (Boston: Edward Draper's Printing-Office, 1690/1777. Reprinted by David Barton, Aledo, TX: Wallbuilders, 1991), the pages are unnumbered.

178 Cotton Mather, "The Education of Children," http://www.spurgeon.org/~phil/mather/edkids.htm

179 John Eidsmoe, *Christianity and the Constitution: The Faith of our Founding Fathers* (Grand Rapids, MI: Baker Book House, 1987), 51.

180 Ibid., 52.

181 Transcript of an interview with Dr. Donald Lutz, conducted by Jerry Newcombe, on location at the University of Houston (Ft. Lauderdale, FL: Coral Ridge Ministries-TV, 2005).

182 Rosalie J. Slater in her biography, "Noah Webster: Founding Father of American Scholarship and Education," front matter in Noah Webster, *American Dictionary of the English Language* (San Francisco: Foundation for American Christian Education, facsimile 1828 edition, 1995), 11.

183 John A. Garraty and Jerome L. Sternstein, editors, *Encyclopedia of American Biography* (New York: Harper & Row, Publishers, 1974), 1168.

184 Richard Moss, *Noah Webster* (Boston: Twayne Publishers, 1984), 104.

185 Noah Webster, as quoted by Rosalie J. Slater in her biography, "Noah Webster: Founding Father of American Scholarship and Education," front matter in Noah Webster, *American Dictionary of the English Language* (San Francisco: Foundation for American Christian Education, facsimile 1828 edition, 1995), 20.

186 Oscar Handlin, *The History of the United States,* (New York: Holt, Rinehart and Winston, 1967), 1:257.

187 Ibid., 393.

188 Noah Webster, *American Dictionary of the English Language* (San Francisco: Foundation for American Christian Education, 1828, 1995). Note: Webster's 1828 *Dictionary* is without page numbers. The references are to be found by the word entries themselves.

189 Paul Lee Tan, *Encyclopedia of 7,700 Illustrations: Signs of the Times* (Rockville, MD: Assurance Publishers, 1984), 158.

190 "New England's First Fruits," 1642, in *The Annals of America* (Chicago et al.: Encyclopaedia Britannica, 1976), 1:176.

191 Bancroft, *History of the United States of America,* 1:361

192 Elihu Yale, entry in *World Book Encyclopedia* (Chicago: World Book, Inc., 1997), 21:551.

193 "The True Scripture-Doctrine Concerning Some Important Points of the Christian Faith," Boston, 1741 by Rev. Jonathan Dickinson http://personal.pitnet.net/primarysources/ [1741]

194 Stephen K. McDowell and Mark A. Beliles, *America's Providential History* (Charlottesville, VA: Providence Press, 1988), 93.

195 John Eidsmoe, *Christianity and the Constitution: The Faith of our Founding Fathers* (Grand Rapids, MI: Baker Book House, 1987), 81.

196 Transcript of an interview with Dr. Donald Lutz, conducted by Jerry Newcombe, on location at the University of Houston (Ft. Lauderdale, FL: Coral Ridge Ministries-TV, 2005).

197 Transcript of an interview with David Barton, conducted by Jerry Newcombe, on location at Washington, D.C. (Ft. Lauderdale, FL: Coral Ridge Ministries-TV, 2002), as reviewed and approved by Mr. Barton, April 23, 2009.

CHAPTER 6

198 Donald S. Lutz, *The Origins of American Constitutionalism,* (Baton Rouge: Louisiana State University Press, 1988), 153.

199 The Mayflower Compact, in Bruce Frohnen, ed., *The American Republic: Primary Sources* (Indianapolis: Liberty Fund, 2002), 11.

200 Ibid.

201 Transcript of an interview with Marshall Foster, conducted by John Rabe (Ft. Lauderdale, FL: Coral Ridge Ministries-TV, 2003).

202 Bancroft, *History of the United States of America,* 1:207.

203 Paul Johnson, *A History of the American People* (New York: HarperCollins Publishers, 1997), 28.

204 Transcript of an interview with Dr. Paul Jehle, conducted by Jerry Newcombe (Ft. Lauderdale, FL: Coral Ridge Ministries-TV, 2005), reviewed and approved by Dr. Jehle, April 22, 2008.

205 Transcript of an interview with Marshall Foster, conducted by John Rabe (Ft. Lauderdale, FL: Coral Ridge Ministries-TV, 2003), reviewed and approved by Dr. Foster, April 24, 2009.

206 Transcript of an interview with Dr. Paul Jehle, conducted by Jerry Newcombe (Ft. Lauderdale, FL: Coral Ridge Ministries-TV, 2005).

207 John Palfrey, *History of New England*, Vol. II, 1865, in Hall, *Christian History of the Constitution: Christian Self-Government,* 48.

208 Paul Johnson, *A History of the American People* (New York: HarperCollins Publishers, 1997).

209 George Bancroft, *History of the United States of America, From the Discovery of the Continent,* Six Volumes (New York: D. Appleton and Company, 1859/1890), I:227-228.

210 Mather, *The Great Works of Christ in America,* 1:71.

211 John Winthrop, Thomas Dudley, Isaac Johnson, John Wilson, &c, &c, In: Donald Lutz, *A Covenanted People. Religious Tradition and the Origin of American Constitutionalism* (Providence, RI: The John Carter Brown Library, 1987), 12.

212 Dedham Covenant, 1636, http://www.constitution.org/primarysources/covenants.html

213 Covenant of Exeter, New Hampshire, July 5, 1639, http://www.constitution.org/primarysources/covenants.html

214 "Fundamental Orders of Connecticut," January 14, 1639, Documents of American History, ed. Henry Steele Commager, 6th ed. (New York: Appleton Century Crofts, 1958), 26. Quoted in Gary DeMar, America's Christian History, 1993 edition, 37.

215 George Leon Walker, History of the First Church in Hartford (Brown & Gross, 1884), quoted in Verna Hall, The Christian History of the Constitution: Christian Self-Government, 249.

216 Ibid., 252: quoting John Fiske, Beginnings of New England, 1889, [Emphasis mine].

217 German historian von Ranke, quoted in Loraine Boettner, The Reformed Doctrine of Predestination (Philadelphia: The Presbyterian and Reformed Publishing Company, 1975), 389.

218 The New England Confederation, 1643, in The Annals of America (Chicago et al.: Encyclopaedia Britannica, 1976), 1:172.

219 Dr. Donald S. Lutz in D. James Kennedy, One Nation Under God (Ft. Lauderdale, FL: Coral Ridge Ministries-TV, 2005), a video.

220 Donald S. Lutz, The Origins of American Constitutionalism, (Baton Rouge: Louisiana State University Press, 1988), 153, 6-7.

221 Ibid, 25

222 Transcript of an interview with Marshall Foster, conducted by John Rabe (Ft. Lauderdale, FL: Coral Ridge Ministries-TV, 2003), as reviewed and approved by Dr. Foster, April 24, 2009.

223 Donald S. Lutz, The Origins of American Constitutionalism, (Baton Rouge: Louisiana State University Press, 1988), 28.

224 Ibid., 43.

225 The Common Law was itself of Biblical origin under Alfred the Great. The Magna Carta was a reassertion of the Biblically-grounded ancient rights of Englishman.

226 Lutz, 63.

227 Rev. Nathaniel Ward, "Massachusetts Body of Liberties," 1641, Bruce Frohnen, ed., The American Republic: Primary Sources (Indianapolis: Liberty Fund, 2002), 15.

228 Transcript of an interview with Dr. Paul Jehle, conducted by Jerry Newcombe (Ft. Lauderdale, FL: Coral Ridge Ministries-TV, 2005).

229 Transcript of an interview with Dr. Peter Lillback, conducted by Jerry Newcombe on location at Pohick Church, Lorton, Virginia (Ft. Lauderdale, FL: Coral Ridge Ministries-TV, 2005).

230 William Penn, quoted in Verna Hall, The Christian History of the Constitution of the United States of America: Christian Self-Government (San Francisco: Foundation for American Christian Education, 1960/1993), 262a.

231 Donald S. Lutz, The Origins of American Constitutionalism, (Baton Rouge: Louisiana State University Press, 1988), 1.

232 Ibid., 8.

PART THREE: CHAPTER 7

233 Dr. Donald S. Lutz in D. James Kennedy, One Nation Under God (Ft. Lauderdale, FL: Coral Ridge Ministries-TV, 2005), a video.

234 "...the U.S. Constitution is the oldest written constitution in the world. (The Massachusetts Constitution of 1780, although amended and revised many times, is even older)." Michael Kammen, ed., The Origins of the American History: A Documentary History (New York: Penguin Books, 1986), xviii.

235 George Bancroft, History of the United States of America, From the Discovery of the Continent, Six Volumes (New York: D. Appleton and Company, 1890), IV:125.

236 John Adams, Letter to the Officers of the First Brigade of the Third Division of the Militia of Massachusetts, October 11, 1798, in Charles Francis Adams (son of John Quincy Adams and grandson of John Adams), ed., The Works of John Adams: Second President of the United States: with a Life of the Author, Notes, and Illustration (Boston: Little, Brown, and Co., 1854), IX:228-229.

237 John Adams, June 28, 1813, in a letter to Thomas Jefferson. Norman Cousins, In God We Trust: The Religious Beliefs and Ideas of the American Founding Fathers (New York: Harper & Brothers, 1958), 230.

238 George Bancroft, History of the United States of America, From the Discovery of the Continent, Six Volumes (New York: D. Appleton and Company, 1890), IV:425.

239 Ibid., 27.

240 Ibid., III:77.

241 Ibid., IV:132.

242 Ibid., 340.

243 Ibid., V:195.

244 Robert Flood, *The Men Who Shaped America* (Chicago: Moody Press, 1976), 35-36.

245 Samuel Adams, March 20, 1797, as Governor of Massachusetts, in a Proclamation of a Day of Fast. Cushing, ed., *The Writings of Samuel Adams*, II:355-56, in John Eidsmoe, *Christianity and the Constitution: The Faith of Our Founding Fathers* (Grand Rapids, MI: Baker Book House, 1987), 254.

246 *The Annals of America* (Chicago: Encyclopaedia Britannica, 1976), 2:218-219.

247 Samuel Chase in *Runkel v. Winemiller.* William J. Federer, *America's God and Country: Encyclopedia of Quotations* (St. Louis: Amerisearch, 2000), 101.

248 George Bancroft, *History of the United States of America, From the Discovery of the Continent*, Six Volumes (New York: D. Appleton and Company, 1890), IV:241.

249 Ibid., 254.

250 George Washington, July 9, 1776, order issued to the army in response to the reading of the Declaration of Independence by the Continental Congress. Jared Sparks, ed., *The Writings of George Washington*, 12 vols. (Boston: American Stationer's Company, 1837; NY: F. Andrew's, 1834-1847), III:456.

251 George Bancroft, *History of the United States of America, From the Discovery of the Continent*, Six Volumes (New York: D. Appleton and Company, 1890), IV:64-65.

252 Ibid., 94.

253 Ibid., 95, 81.

254 Benjamin Hart, "The Wall That Protestantism Built: The Religious Reasons for the Separation of Church and State," *Policy Review*, Fall 1988, 44.

255 George Bancroft, *History of the United States of America, From the Discovery of the Continent*, Six Volumes (New York: D. Appleton and Company, 1890), IV:98.

256 William J. Federer, *America's God and Country: Encyclopedia of Quotations* (St. Louis: Amerisearch, 2000), 212.

257 Ibid., 213.

258 John Dickinson, in Forrest McDonald, ed., *Empire and Nation* (Englewood Cliffs, NJ: Prentice-Hall, 1962), 15, 17, 20, 28, 83. Tim LaHaye, *Faith of Our Founding Fathers* (Brentwood, TN: Wolgemuth & Hyatt, Publishers, Inc., 1987), 156-157.

259 William J. Federer, *America's God and Country: Encyclopedia of Quotations* (St. Louis: Amerisearch, 2000), 241.

260 George Bancroft, *History of the United States of America, From the Discovery of the Continent*, Six Volumes (New York: D. Appleton and Company, 1890), IV:130.

261 Ibid., 113.

262 Alexander Hamilton, 1787, in Christine F. Hart, *One Nation Under God* (American Tract Society, reprinted by Gospel Tract Society, Inc.), 2. D. P. Diffine, PH.D., *One Nation Under God: How Close a Separation?* (Searcy, AR: Harding University, Belden Center for Private Enterprise Education, 6th ed., 1992), 9.

263 Alexander Hamilton, April 16-21, 1802, in writing to James Bayard. Claude G. Bowers, *Jefferson and Hamilton: The Struggle for Democracy in America* (Boston: Houghton Mifflin Co., 1925, 1937), 40. Broadus Mitchell, Alexander Hamilton: The National Adventure 1788-1804 (New York: MacMillan, 1962), 513-514.

264 John Hancock, April 15, 1775, Massachusetts Provincial Congress declaring a Day of Public Humiliation, Fasting and Prayer. Proclamation of John Hancock from Concord (from an original in the Evans collection, #14220, by the American Antiquarian Society. William Lincoln, ed., *The Journals of Each Provincial Congress of Massachusetts, 1774-1775* (Boston: Dutton and Wentworth, 1838), 114-145 in William J. Federer, *America's God and Country: Encyclopedia of Quotations* (St. Louis: Amerisearch, 2000), 275-276.

265 John Hancock, October 5, 1791 Thanksgiving proclamation, issued while he was Governor of Massachusetts; as printed in the *Columbian Centinel*, October 15, 1791.

266 Patrick Henry, St. John's Church, Richmond, March 1775, Os Guinness, *The Great Experiment* (Colorado Springs, CO: NavPress, 2001), 124.

267 Patrick Henry, Statement to a visitor. William Wirt Henry (grandson of Patrick Henry), editor, *Patrick Henry: Life, Correspondence and Speeches* (New York: Charles Scribner's Sons, 1891), II:519.

268 Ibid., III:606-607.

269 George Bancroft, *History of the United States of America, From the Discovery of the Continent*, Six Volumes (New York: D. Appleton and Company, 1890), IV:31.

270 John Jay, In his Last Will and Testament. William Jay, *The Life of John Jay with Selections from His Correspondence*, 3 vols. (New York: Harper, 1833), I:519-520.

271 John Langdon, October 21, 1785, John Langdon, as President (Governor) of New Hampshire, made an official Proclamation for a General Thanksgiving. Tim LaHaye, *Faith of Our Founding Fathers* (Brentwood, TN: Wolgemuth & Hyatt, Publishers, Inc., 1987), 165-166.

272 Richard Henry Lee, *Journals of Congress*, Volume III, 467-468, in William J. Federer, *America's God and Country: Encyclopedia of Quotations* (St. Louis: Amerisearch, 2000), 362-363.

273 Continental Congress, July 6, 1775, passed the Declaration of the Causes and Necessity for Taking Up Arms, composed by Thomas Jefferson, *Journals of the American Congress - from 1774 to 1788*, Vol. I, Thursday, July 6, 1775. Henry Steele Commager, ed., Documents of American History, 2 vols. (New York: F. S. Crofts & Company, 1934; Appleton-Century-Crofts, Inc., 1948, 6th ed., 1958; Englewood Cliffs, NJ: Prentice Hall, Inc., 9th ed., 1973), I:95.

274 Thomas Jefferson, to Virginia delegates to Congress, August 1774; *Writings, I*, 211, in Caroline Thomas Harnsberger, ed., *Treasury of Presidential Quotations* (Chicago: Follett Publishing Company, 1964), 116.

275 Thomas Jefferson, Notes on Virginia, 1782; *Writings, I*, 227, Harnsberger, ed., *Treasury of Presidential Quotations*, 117.

276 William J. Federer, *America's God and Country: Encyclopedia of Quotations* (St. Louis: Amerisearch, 2000), 369-370.

277 William Livingston, The Independent Reflector—No. 46. *Life and Letters of William Livingston*, reprinted by Theodore Sedgwick, Jr., Stephen Abbott Northrop, D.D., *A Cloud of Witnesses* (Portland, OR: American Heritage Ministries, 1987; Mantle Ministries, 228 Still Ridge, Bulverde, Texas), 288.

278 George Bancroft, *History of the United States of America, From the Discovery of the Continent*, Six Volumes (New York: D. Appleton and Company, 1890), IV:417.

279 Bruce Frohnen, ed., *The American Republic: Primary Sources* (Indianapolis: Liberty Fund, 2002), 327.

280 Luther Martin, in M.E. Bradford, *Religion & The Framers: The Biographical Evidence* (Marlborough, NH: The Plymouth Rock Foundation, 1991), 8.

281 George Bancroft, *History of the United States of America, From the Discovery of the Continent*, 6 vols. (New York: D. Appleton and Company, 1890), IV:121.

282 James McHenry in Bernard Steiner, *One Hundred and Ten Years of Bible Society in Maryland* (Maryland: Maryland Bible Society, 1921), 14.

283 George Bancroft, *History of the United States of America, From the Discovery of the Continent*, Six Volumes (New York: D. Appleton and Company, 1890), IV:155.

284 Ibid., 158, 166.

285 Ibid., 168.

286 The Provincial Congress of Massachusetts gave charge to the Minutemen of the Massachusetts Militia by the Provincial Congress of Massachusetts. Richard Frothingham, *Rise of the Republic of the United States* (Boston: Little, Brown and Co., 1872), 393; quoted in William J. Federer, *America's God and Country*, 427.

287 Gouverneur Morris, circa 1792, in "Notes of the Form for the King of France." John Eidsmoe, *Christianity and The Constitution: The Faith of Our Founding Fathers* (Grand Rapids, MI: Baker Book House, 1987), 188.

288 George Bancroft, *History of the United States of America, From the Discovery of the Continent*, Six Volumes (New York: D. Appleton and Company, 1890), IV:395.

289 Dr. Peter Lillback with Jerry Newcombe, *George Washington's Sacred Fire* (Bryn Mawr, PA: Providence Forum Press, 2006), 30.

290 George Washington, July 4, 1775, in his General Orders from the Headquarters at Cambridge. Jared Sparks, ed., *The Writings of George Washington*, 12 vols. (Boston: American Stationer's Company, 1837, New York: F. Andrew's, 1834-1847), III:491.

291 George Washington, Speech to Delaware Indian Chiefs on May 12, 1779, in John C. Fitzpatrick, ed., *The Writings of George Washington*, (Washington DC: U.S. Government Printing Office, 1932), XV:55.

292 Ibid., III:452: George Washington, "Circular to State Governments," June 8, 1783.

293 George Washington, "Farewell Address," September 19, 1796, in *The Annals of America* (Chicago et al.: Encyclopaedia Britannica, 1976), 3:612.

294 Benjamin Hart, "The Wall That Protestantism Built: The Religious Reasons for the Separation of Church and State," *Policy Review*, Fall 1988, 44.

295 James Wilson, in his *Lectures on Law*, delivered 1789-1791, at the College of Philadelphia. James DeWitt Andrews, *Works of Wilson* (Chicago, 1896), 1:91-93.

296 Witherspoon, John. May 17, 1776, in his sermon entitled, "The Dominion of Providence over the Passions of Men" delivered at The College of New Jersey (Princeton). Varnum Lansing Collins, *President Witherspoon* (New York: Arno Press and The New York Times, 1969), I:197-98.

297 John Witherspoon in Ashbel Green, *The Life of the Rev. John Witherspoon* (Princeton, NJ: Princeton University Press, reprinted 1973, 173.

298 Bruce Frohnen, ed., *The American Republic: Primary Sources* (Indianapolis: Liberty Fund, 2002), 188.

299 George Bancroft, *History of the United States of America, From the Discovery of the Continent*, Six Volumes (New York: D. Appleton and Company, 1890), IV:314.

300 Ibid., 183.

301 John Adams, December 25, 1813, in a letter to Thomas Jefferson in Norman Cousins, *In God We Trust—The Religious Beliefs and Ideas of the American Founding Fathers* (New York: Harper & Brothers, 1958), 255-56.

CHAPTER 8

302 "Lawmakers blast Pledge ruling," June 27, 2002, Posted: 1:11 PM EDT, www.cnn.com/LAW CENTER.

303 Constitution, Article VI, Bruce Frohnen, ed., *The American Republic: Primary Sources* (Indianapolis: Liberty Fund, 2002), 239.

304 Delaware 1776. Article XXII. "Every person who shall be chosen a member of either house, or appointed to any office or place of trust...shall ...make and subscribe the following declaration, to wit: "I, _____, do profess faith in God the Father, and in Jesus Christ His only Son, and in the Holy Ghost, one God, blessed for evermore; and I do acknowledge the holy Scriptures of the Old and New Testament to be given by divine inspiration." George Read, 1776, Constitution of the State of Delaware, Article XXII. *The Constitutions of the Several Independent States of America.* Published by Order of Congress (Boston: Norman & Bowen, 1785), 99-100.

305 John Quincy Adams, quoted by J. Wingate Thornton, Preface to *The Pulpit of the American Revolution*, as found in Verna Hall, *The Christian History of the Constitution of the United States of America: Christian Self-Government* (San Francisco: Foundation for American Christian Education, 1960/1993), 372.

306 Bruce Frohnen, ed., *The American Republic: Primary Sources* (Indianapolis: Liberty Fund, 2002), 88.

307 First amendment, U.S. Constitution, *The World Almanac and Book of Facts 2007* (New York: Work Almanac Books, 2007), 504.

308 Quoted in Verna Hall, *The Christian History of the Constitution of the United States of America: Christian Self-Government* (San Francisco: Foundation for American Christian Education, 1960/1993), IX.

309 George Bancroft, *History of the United States of America, From the Discovery of the Continent*, Six Volumes (New York: D. Appleton and Company, 1859/1890), I:178.

310 Os Guinness, *The Great Experiment* (Colorado Springs, CO: NavPress, 2001), 64.

311 Roger Williams, "A Plea for Religious Liberty," 1644, http://www.constitution.org/bcp/religlib.htm

312 Paul Johnson, *A History of the American People* (New York: HarperCollins Publishers, 1997), 50.

313 Bruce Frohnen, ed., *The American Republic: Primary Sources* (Indianapolis: Liberty Fund, 2002), 328.

314 While Thomas Jefferson may not have been fully orthodox in his beliefs as a professing Christian, he was far from the atheist some modern writers seem to make him. He was not anti-Christian in how he governed as president. Author Mark A. Beliles has assembled an impressive list of some of Jefferson's actions as president:

♢ Promoted legislative and military chaplains,
♢ Established a national seal using a Biblical symbol,
♢ Included the word God in our national motto,
♢ Established official days of fasting and prayer— at least on the state level,
♢ Punished Sabbath breakers,
♢ Punished marriages contrary to Biblical law,

◇ Punished irreverent soldiers,

◇ Protected the property of churches,

◇ Required that oaths be phrased by the words "So Help Me God" and be sworn on the Bible,

◇ Granted land to Christian churches to reach the Indians,

◇ Granted land to Christian schools,

◇ Allowed government property and facilities to be used for worship,

◇ Used the Bible and nondenominational religious instruction in the public schools. He was involved in three different school districts and the plan in each one of these required—required—that the Bible be taught in our public schools.

◇ Allowed clergymen to hold public office and encouraged them to do so,

◇ Funded religious books for public libraries,

◇ Funded salaries for missionaries,

◇ Funded the construction of church buildings for Indians,

◇ Exempted churches from taxation,

◇ Established professional schools of theology. He wanted to bring the entire faculty of Calvin's theological seminary over from Geneva, Switzerland, and establish them at the University of Virginia.

◇ Wrote treaties requiring other nations to guarantee religious freedom, including religious speeches and prayers in official ceremonies.

These are not the actions of a man who was totally godless.

Source: Mark A. Beliles' Introduction to an updated version of Thomas Jefferson's *Abridgement of The Words of Jesus of Nazareth*, 11. For more information, please see Chapter 4, "The Real Thomas Jefferson." in D. James Kennedy and Jerry Newcombe, *What If America Were A Christian Nation Again?* (Nashville, TN: Thomas Nelson, Publishers, 2003).

315 Thomas Jefferson, "Virginia Bill for Establishing Religious Freedom," 1786, Bruce Frohnen, ed., *The American Republic: Primary Sources* (Indianapolis: Liberty Fund, 2002), 330.

316 Benjamin Hart, "The Wall That Protestantism Built: The Religious Reasons for the Separation of Church and State," *Policy Review* (Washington, DC: Heritage Foundation, Fall 1988), 44.

317 Charles Hodge, *Systematic Theology*, 1871 (reprinted Grand Rapids, MI: Wm. B. Eerdmans Publishing Co., 1975), III:343.

318 George Washington to the General Assembly of the Presbyterian Church, 1789, quoted in Os Guinness, *The Great Experiment* (Colorado Springs, CO: NavPress, 2001), 130.

319 George Washington wrote, "I now make it my earnest prayer that God would have you, and the State over which you preside, in His holy protection…that He would most graciously be pleased to dispose us all to do justice, to love mercy, and to demean ourselves with that charity, humility, and pacific temper of mind, which were the characteristics of the Divine Author of our blessed religion, and without an humble imitation of whose example in these things, we can never hope to be a happy nation." Quoted in William J. Federer, *America's God and Country*, 646.

320 Robert C. Winthrop quoted in Gary DeMar, *America's Christian History: The Untold Story* (Atlanta, GA: American Vision Publishers, Inc., 1993), 58.

321 Samuel Adams, letter to his cousin, Vice-President John Adams, 4 October 1790, quoted in Verna M. Hall, *Christian History of the Constitution of the United States of America: Christian Self-Government* (San Francisco: Foundation for American Christian Education, 1960/1993), XIV.

322 D. James Kennedy, "America: A Christian Nation" (Ft. Lauderdale, FL: Coral Ridge Ministries, 1990), a pamphlet.

323 John Adams, letter to wife Abigail, 7 September 1774, quoted in Gary DeMar, *God and Government: A Biblical and Historical Study* (Atlanta, GA: American Vision Press, 1982), I:108.

324 John Adams, letter to wife Abigail, 7 September 1774, from Charles Francis Adams, ed., *Letters of John Adams: Addressed To His Wife* (Boston: Charles C. Little and James Brown, 1841), I:23-24, quoted in William J. Federer, *America's God and Country*, 7.

325 Edwin Meese III, Matthew Spalding, and David Forte, eds., *The Heritage Guide to the Constitution* (Washington, DC: Regnery Publishing, Inc., 2005), 302.

326 Bruce Frohnen, ed., *The American Republic: Primary Sources* (Indianapolis: Liberty Fund, 2002), 239.

327 Articles of Confederation, 1778, in Bruce Frohnen, ed., *The American Republic: Primary Sources* (Indianapolis: Liberty Fund, 2002), 204.

328 Northwest Ordinance, Article III in *The Annals of America*, 3:194-195.

329 Treaty of Paris, 1783, quoted in Gary DeMar, *America's Christian History: The Untold Story* (Atlanta: American Vision, Publishers, 1993), 83.

330 Charles E. Rice, *The Supreme Court and Public Prayer: The Need for Restraint* (New York: Fordham University Press, 1964), 167.

331 Ibid., 168.

332 Ibid.

333 Ibid., 172.

334 J. Michael Sharman, ed., *Faith of the Fathers: Religion and Matters of Faith Contained in the Presidents' Inaugural Addresses from George Washington to Bill Clinton* (Culpeper, VA: Victory Publishing, 1995), 44.

335 Ibid., 82.

336 Ibid., 121.

337 *Church of the Holy Trinity v. the United States*. No. 143. Supreme Court of the United States 143 U.S. 457, 36 L.Ed. 226, 12 S.Ct. 511, 29 February, 1892. Decided.

338 Bill Pryor in D. James Kennedy, *The ACLU v. Judge Roy Moore* (Ft. Lauderdale, FL: Coral Ridge Ministries, 1998), a video.

339 Charles E. Rice, *The Supreme Court and Public Prayer: The Need for Restraint* (New York: Fordham University Press, 1964), 48.

340 Calvin Coolidge, Speech in Washington, D.C., 3 May 1925, quoted in Caroline Thomas Harnsberger, ed., *Treasury of Presidential Quotations* (Chicago: Follett Publishing Company, 1964), 20.

CHAPTER 9

341 Gouveneur Morris, cited in John Eidsmoe, *Christianity and the Constitution*, 180.

342 Paul Johnson, (New York: HarperCollins Publishers, 1997), 72.

343 George Bancroft, *History of the United States of America, From the Discovery of the Continent, Six Volumes* (New York: D. Appleton and Company, 1859/1890), I:294.

344 William J. Federer, *America's God and Country: Encyclopedia of Quotations* (St. Louis: Amerisearch, 2000), 704.

345 Article I, State of New Hampshire, "Bill of Rights," 1792, *The Constitutions of the Sixteen States* (Boston: Manning and Loring, 1797), 50.

346 Joseph Bloomfield, ed., *Laws of the State of New Jersey* (Trenton, NJ: James J. Wilson, 1811), 103–105.

347 Norine Dickson Campbell, *Patrick Henry: Patriot and Statesman* (Old Greenwich, CT: Devin Adair, 1969/1975), 99–100.

348 James Madison, Notes of Debates in the Federal Convention of 1787 (New York: W. W. Norton Co., 1987), 504.

349 George Bancroft, *History of the United States of America, From the Discovery of the Continent*, Six Volumes (New York: D. Appleton and Company, 1890), IV:34.

350 Ibid., 318.

351 Ibid., 338.

352 Ibid., 338.

353 Ibid., 338.

354 Ibid., 338.

355 Ibid., 446.

356 Alexander Hamilton, James Madison, and John Jay, *The Federalist Papers* (New York, et al.: A Mentor Book from New American Library, 1961), 266.

357 Abraham Lincoln, "Remarks upon the Holy Scriptures, in Receiving the Present of a Bible from a Negro Delegation," September 7, 1864, Marion Mills Miller, ed., *Life and Works of Abraham Lincoln: Centenary Edition, In Nine Volumes:* Volume V, (New York: The Current Literature Publishing Company, 1907), 209.

358 Ibid., 225: Abraham Lincoln, Second Inaugural Address, March 4, 1865.

359 George Bancroft, *History of the United States of America, From the Discovery of the Continent, Six Volumes* (New York: D. Appleton and Company, 1890), IV:339.

360 Transcript of an interview of Dr. Peter Lillback by Jerry Newcombe, on location at Jamestown (Ft. Lauderdale, FL: Coral Ridge Ministries-TV, June 2007).

361 George Bancroft, *History of the United States of America*, II:177.

362 Ibid., II:183.

363 Ibid., II:197.

364 Ibid., II:198.

365 Quoted in David Barton, *The Bulletproof George Washington* (Aledo, TX: Wallbuilders, 1990), 42-43.

366 Catherine Drinker Bowen, *Miracle at Philadelphia: The Story of the Constitutional Convention May to September 1787* (Boston et al.: An Atlantic Monthly Press Book, a division of Little, Brown and Company, 1966/1986), 143.

367 Ibid., 145.

368 Ibid., 143.

369 George Bancroft, *History of the United States of America*, IV:257.

370 Paul Johnson, *A History of the American People* (New York: HarperCollins Publishers, 1997), 79.

371 George Bancroft, *History of the United States of America*, II:204-205.

372 Ibid., II:165.

373 Ibid., II:165-166.

374 Ibid., II:127.

375 Ibid., IV:188.

376 Ibid., IV:148.

377 Ibid., IV:256.

378 Bruce Frohnen, ed., *The American Republic: Primary Sources* (Indianapolis: Liberty Fund, 2002), 190.

379 Catherine Drinker Bowen, *Miracle at Philadelphia: The Story of the Constitutional Convention May to September 1787* (Boston et al.: An Atlantic Monthly Press Book, a division of Little, Brown and Company, 1966/1986), 144.

380 Alexander Hamilton, James Madison, and John Jay, *The Federalist Papers*, with introduction by Clinton Rossiter (New York, et al.: A Mentor Book from New American Library, 1961), 161.

381 Paul Aurandt, *Destiny: From Paul Harvey's The Rest of the Story* (Toronto: Bantam Books, 1983), 126.

382 George Bancroft, *History of the United States of America, From the Discovery of the Continent*, Six Volumes (New York: D. Appleton and Company, 1859/1890), I:295.

383 David Barton, *Original Intent* (Aledo, TX: WallBuilder Press, 1996), 126.

384 Ibid., 127.

385 See John Eidsmoe, *Christianity and the Constitution: The Faith of our Founding Fathers* (Grand Rapids, MI: Baker Book House, 1987), 415.

386 Ibid.

387 D. James Kennedy and Jerry Newcombe, *What If Jesus Had Never Been Born?* (Nashville, TN: Thomas Nelson, Publishers, Inc., 1994), 86.

388 *Holy Trinity Church v. United States*, 1892, quoted in Charles E. Rice, *The Supreme Court and Public Prayer: The Need for Restraint* (New York: Fordham University Press, 1964), 58.

PART FOUR: CHAPTER 10

389 Aleksandr Solzhenitsyn, address, "Men Have Forgotten God," A. Klimoff, translator, 1983, http://www.roca.org/OA/36/36h.htm.

390 Erwin W. Lutzer, *Twelve Myths Americans Believe*, (Chicago: Moody Press, 1993), 23.

391 Abraham Lincoln, Marion Mills Miller, ed., *Life and Works of Abraham Lincoln, Centenary Edition*. Nine Vols., (New York: The Current Literature Publishing Co., 1907), IV:156-157.

392 C. S. Lewis, *Mere Christianity* (New York: MacMillan, 1960), 109.

393 D. James Kennedy, "A Shield for America" (Ft. Lauderdale, FL: Coral Ridge Ministries, 2001), a pamphlet.

394 Cotton Mather, *The Great Works of Christ in America: Magnalia Christi Americana* (Edinburgh: The Banner of Truth Trust, 1702/1853/1979), 1:63.

395 Quoted in Max Weber, trans. by Talcott Parsons, *The Protestant Ethic and the Spirit of Capitalism* (New York: Charles Scribner's Sons, 1958), 175.

396 Paul Johnson, *A History of the American People* (New York: HarperCollins Publishers, 1997), 839.

397 Abraham Lincoln, from "Fragment of Speech at a Republican Banquet in Chicago," December 10, 1856, in Lincoln, Abraham, "Writings, Volume II" in William J. Federer, ed., *Library of Classics* (St. Louis: Amerisearch, Inc., 2002), a CD-ROM.

398 Paul Johnson, 847.

399 Bernard Goldberg, *Bias: A CBS Insider Exposes How the Media Distort the News* (Washington, DC: Regnery Publishing, Inc., 2002), 25.

400 S. Robert Lichter, Linda S. Lichter, and Stanley Rothman, with the assistance of Daniel Amundson, *Prime Time: How TV Portrays American Culture* (Washington, DC: Regnery Publishing, Inc., 1994), 422-424.

401 Ibid.

402 Ibid.

403 Bernard Goldberg, *A Slobbering Love Affair: Barack Obama and the Media* (Washington, DC: Regnery 2009).

404 Paul Kurtz, *Humanist Manifestos I and II* (Buffalo, NY: Prometheus Books, 1981), 15.

405 Ibid.

406 Jacques Barzun, 1980, quoted in Joseph Adelson, *Inventing Adolescence* (New Brunswick, NJ: Transaction Books, 1986), 16.

407 D. James Kennedy and Jerry Newcombe, *How Would Jesus Vote? A Christian Perspective on the Issues* (Colorado Springs, CO: WaterBrook Press, 2008), 91.

408 Alan Sears, "Indivisible: No celebration of liberty can ignore America's godly heritage," July 2, 2007, Townhall.com, http://www.thefire.org/index.php/article/8197.html.

409 See, for example, the court decisions listed in the Appendix.

410 An inherent pitfall in the use of the Law of Nature concept, is that those who disregard God can put their own spin on it, just as the Darwinists have done. Truly, without Scripture, men would have a very imperfect view of nature's laws, because sin fatally clouds our judgment.

411 To get a little more technical from a legal perspective: The decision in the case of *Everson v. Board of Education*, made by the United States Supreme Court in 1947, was the first time the Court held that the establishment clause applied to individual states through the due process clause of the fourteenth amendment. Most of the other guarantees of the Bill of Rights had been previously applied to the states as well as to the federal government through the fourteenth amendment. The *Everson* Court expanded this trend to include the religion clauses of the first amendment.

412 *Everson v. Board of Education of Ewing*, 330 US 1 (1947) www.supremecourtus.gov/opinions.

413 Paul A. Fisher, *Behind the Lodge Door* (Rockford, IL: Tan Books and Publishers, 1988/1994), 11.

414 Larry Witham, "Church, state 'wall' not idea of Jefferson," *Washington Times*, August 5, 2002.

415 Paul Johnson, *A History of the American People* (New York: HarperCollins Publishers, 1997), 951.

416 William Blackstone, "Of the Nature of Laws in General," *Blackstone's Commentaries*. Chief Justice Roy S. Moore, Our Legal Heritage (Montgomery, AL: The Administrative Office of Courts, June 2001), 15.

417 Paul Johnson, *A History of the American People* (New York: HarperCollins Publishers, 1997), 967.

418 Robert H. Bork, *The Tempting of America: The Political Seduction of the Law* (New York: A Touchstone Book, Simon & Schuster, 1990), 95.

419 Ibid., 9.

420 *Church of the Holy Trinity v. the United States*. No. 143. Supreme Court of the United States 143 U.S. 457, 36 L.Ed. 226, 12 S.Ct. 511, 29 February, 1892. Decided.

421 Kermit L. Hall, editor in chief, *The Oxford Companion to the Supreme Court of the United States* (New York et al.: Oxford University Press, 1992), 89.

422 Ibid., 90.

423 Charles Van Doren, editor, *Webster's American Biographies* (Springfield, MA: Merriam Webster, Inc., 1984), 135.

424 Kermit L. Hall, editor in chief, *The Oxford Companion to the Supreme Court of the United States* (New York et al.: Oxford University Press, 1992), 89.

425 David J. Brewer, *The United States: A Christian Nation* (Smyrna, GA: American Vision, 1905/1996), 8.

426 Charles Van Doren, editor, *Webster's American Biographies* (Springfield, MA: Merriam-Webster, Inc., 1984), 135.

427 Calvin Coolidge in Caroline Thomas Harnsberger, ed., *Treasury of Presidential Quotations* (Chicago: Follett Publishing Company, 1964), 117

428 Henry P. Johnston, ed., *The Correspondence and Public Papers of John Jay* (New York: Burt Franklin, 1970), IV:393.

429 Quoted in Robert Faulkner, *The Jurisprudence of John Marshall* (Westport, CT: Greenwood Press, 1968), 139.

430 *Stone v. Graham*, 449 U.S. 39 (1980). www.supremecourtus.gov/opinions

431 George Grant in D. James Kennedy, *Violence in the Schoolyard* (Ft. Lauderdale, FL: Coral Ridge Ministries, 1999), a video.

432 Samuel Kent, 1995 ruling, in David Limbaugh, *Persecution: How Liberals Are Waging War Against Christianity* (Washington, DC: Regnery, 2003), 5.

433 http://christianadc.org/news-and-articles/282-police-called-to-stop-students-prayer.

434 William Penn in *The Annals of America* (Chicago: Encyclopaedia Britannica, 1976), 1:189.

435 Robert Charles Winthrop, "Remarks to the Massachusetts Bible Society," Boston, May 28, 1849 in

Addresses and Speeches on Various Occasions (Boston: Little, Brown and Company, 1852), 172.

436 Calvin Coolidge, Speech in Washington, D.C., May 3, 1925; "Foundations," 209, in Caroline Thomas Harnsberger, ed., *Treasury of Presidential Quotations* (Chicago: Follett Publishing Company, 1964), 20.

CHAPTER 11

437 Daniel J. Mount, *The Faith of America's Presidents* (Chattanooga, TN: Living Ink Books, 2007), 209.

438 Calvin Coolidge. Quoted in Caroline Thomas Harnsberger, ed., *Treasury of Presidential Quotations* (Chicago: Follett Publishing Company, 1964), 20.

439 *The New England Primer* (Boston: Edward Draper printing office, 1690/1777. Reprinted by David Barton, Aledo, TX: Wallbuilders, 1991), the pages are unnumbered.

440 James Madison, "Federalist #51" in Alexander Hamilton, James Madison, and John Jay, *The Federalist Papers*, with introduction by Clinton Rossiter (New York, et al.: A Mentor Book from New American Library, 1961), 322.

441 Donald S. Lutz, *The Origins of American Constitutionalism*, (Baton Rouge: Louisiana State University Press, 1988), 28, 74, 85-86.

442 George Washington: "Of all the dispositions and habits which lead to political prosperity, Religion and Morality are indispensable supports."*
John Adams: "Our Constitution was made only for a moral and religious people. It is wholly inadequate to the government of any other."**
(*George Washington, "Farewell Address," September, 19, 1796, in, in *The Annals of America* (Chicago: Encyclopaedia Britannica, 1976), 3:612.)
(**John Adams, October 11, 1798, in a letter to the officers of the First Brigade of the Third Division of the Militia of Massachusetts. Charles Francis Adams (son of John Quincy Adams and grandson of John Adams), ed., *The Works of John Adams: Second President of the United States: with a Life of the Author, Notes, and Illustration* (Boston: Little, Brown, & Co., 1854), IX:228-229.)

443 William Howard Taft. Quoted in Caroline Thomas Harnsberger, ed., *Treasury of Presidential Quotations* (Chicago: Follett Publishing Company, 1964), 195.

444 For more information to help you get grounded in the Christian faith, write to Coral Ridge Ministries, Box 40, Ft. Lauderdale, FL 33308 and ask

for *Beginning Again*. Also I highly recommend a book that has helped me. It is a three-year through-the-Bible study guide, *Search the Scriptures*, edited by Alan Stibbs (Downers Grove, IL: IVP, 1949, 1974). It is now out in paperback.

445 Samuel Smith, "My Country 'Tis of Thee," 1852, 4th verse, in Donald P. Hustad, *Hymns for the Living Church* (Carol Stream, Illinois: Hope Publishing Company, 1984), #525.

CHAPTER 12

446 David Barton, in D. James Kennedy, *One Nation Under God* (Ft. Lauderdale, FL: Coral Ridge Ministries-TV, 2005), a video.

447 Jonathan Trumbull, July 13, 1775, in a letter to General Washington. Quoted in Verna M. Hall, *The Christian History of the American Revolution: Consider and Ponder* (San Francisco: Foundation for American Christian Education, 1976), 511.

448 John Hancock, "Thanksgiving Proclamation, issued while he was Governor of Massachusetts," October 5, 1791, printed in the *Columbian Centinel*, October 15, 1791.

449 Alexander Hamilton, James Madison, and John Jay, *The Federalist Papers*, with introduction by Clinton Rossiter (New York: A Mentor Book from New American Library, 1961), 188-189.

450 Benjamin Franklin, in William J. Federer, *America's God and Country: Encyclopedia of Quotations* (St. Louis, MO: Amerisearch, 2000), 248-249.

451 Ibid, Jonathan Dayton, 249.

452 Edmund Jennings Randolph, in Catherine Drinker Bowen, *Miracle at Philadelphia: The Story of the Constitutional Convention May to September 1787* (Boston: An Atlantic Monthly Press Book, div. Little, Brown and Company, 1966/1986), 38.

453 William J. Federer, *America's God and Country: Encyclopedia of Quotations* (St. Louis, MO: Amerisearch, 2000), 250.

454 Ibid., Rev. William Rogers, 250.

455 Paul Harvey, "God Knows Now!," *Paul Harvey News*, February 10, 1996, Copyright 1996 Paul Harvey Products, Inc., Distributed by Creators Syndicate, Inc., Los Angeles. Prayer text includes additional wording paraphrased from multiple, possibly more original sources for the Prayer later read by Joe Wright as quoted by Paul Harvey, including text from Bob Russell, Pastor, Southeast Christian Church, Louisville, KY, 1995.

456 D. James Kennedy, "The Christian View of Politics" (Ft. Lauderdale, FL: Coral Ridge Ministries, June 1, 1975), a pamphlet. NOTE: this is his prayer at the end of the sermon. I slightly changed the words, from prayer to prose.

457 Paul Johnson, *A History of the American People* (New York: HarperCollins Publishers, 1997), 204.

458 George Whitefield, 12 October 1740. Peter Gomes, "George Whitefield in the Old Colony: 1740," L. D. Geller, ed., *They Knew They Were Pilgrims* (New York: Poseidon Books, Inc., 1971), 93.

459 Cotton Mather, *The Great Works of Christ in America: Magnalia Christi Americana*, 2 Volumes (Edinburgh: The Banner of Truth Trust, 1702/1853/1979), 1:63.

460 D. James Kennedy, *Chapel Remark during the National Day of Prayer*, Coral Ridge Presbyterian Church, Ft. Lauderdale, May 2002.

461 Daniel J. Mount, *The Faith of America's Presidents* (Chattanooga, TN: Living Ink Books, 2007).

462 John Adams to Abigail Adams, 26 April 1777, *Familiar Letters*, 265. Quoted in Caroline Thomas Harnsberger, ed., *Treasury of Presidential Quotations* (Chicago: Follett Publishing Company, 1964), 106.

463 Theodore Roosevelt, 1916; *Works*, XVIII, 199, Caroline Thomas Harnsberger, ed., *Treasury of Presidential Quotations* (Chicago: Follett Publishing Company, 1964), 117.

464 John Quincy Adams, In reply to an inquiry as to his unpopular stance against slavery, in David Barton, *The WallBuilder Report* (Aledo, TX: WallBuilder Press, Summer 1993), 3.

APPENDIX

465 The Trinity case is still good law and is cited frequently, especially for the major proposition of the case, that of statutory construction. The case was cited in the dissent in the case of *Lee v. Weisman*, 112 S. Ct. 2649, as "an aberration" in the long line of Establishment Clause cases holding that there can be no sponsorship of religion. In a 1931 case, the high court reaffirmed this is a "Christian people" in *U.S. v. MacIntosh*, 283 U.S. 605. As late as 1952, in the case of *Zorach v. Clauson*, the Supreme Court noted that, "We are a religious people whose institutions suppose a Supreme Being."

466 *Church of the Holy Trinity v. the United States*. No. 143. Supreme Court of the United States 143 U.S. 457, 36 L.Ed. 226, 12 S.Ct. 511, 29 February, 1892. Decided.

467 Ibid.

468 Jon Meacham, "The Decline and Fall of Christian America," *Newsweek*, April 13, 2009, 34.

469 *Church of the Holy Trinity v. the United States*. No. 143. Supreme Court of the United States 143 U.S. 457, 36 L.Ed. 226, 12 S.Ct. 511, 29 February, 1892. Decided.

470 John Eidsmoe, *Columbus & Cortez, Conquerors for Christ: The Controversy, The Conquest, The Mission, The Vision* (Green Forest, AR: New Leaf Press, 1992), 90.

471 *Church of the Holy Trinity v. the United States*.

472 Ibid.

473 The first full-blown constitution written in America was the Pilgrim Code of Law, written in 1636.

474 *Church of the Holy Trinity v. the United States*.

475 Ibid.

476 Ibid.

477 Ibid.

478 Ibid.

479 Fyodor Dostoevsky's character, Ivan, in *The Brothers Karamazov*, quoted in, Paul Lee Tan, *Encyclopedia of 7700 Illustrations* (Rockville, MD: Assurance Publishers, 1984) 176.

480 *Church of the Holy Trinity v. the United States*.

481 Ibid.

482 Ibid.

483 Ibid.

484 Ibid.

485 David Brewer, *The United States: A Christian Nation* (Originally published by The John C. Winston Company, 1905) (Smyrna, GA: American Vision, 1996).

486 Ibid., 44.

487 Ibid., 13.

488 Ibid., 13-14.

489 Ibid.

490 Ibid., 41.

491 Ibid., 35.

492 Brewer, *The United States*, 15-16.

493 Ibid., 17.

494 *Commonwealth v. Abner Kneeland*, 37 Mass. (20 Pick) 206, 233, 234 (Massachusetts Supreme Court, 1838).

495 Ibid.

496 Ibid.

497 The Constitution of New York, 20 April 1777. Journals of the Provincial Congress, Provincial Convention Committee of Safety and Council of Safety of the State of New York, 1775, 1776 1777, (Albany, NY: Thurlow Weed, 1842), I:892-898.

498 Ibid., Article XXXIX.

499 Brewer, The United States, 17.

500 Preamble to the Constitution of Massachusetts, 1780, quoted in Charles E. Rice, The Supreme Court and Public Prayer: The Need for Restraint (New York: Fordham University Press, 1964), 171.

501 Ibid. (From the Massachusetts Constitution, Declaration of Rights, Article II).

502 Ibid. (From the Massachusetts Constitution, Declaration of Rights, Article III).

503 Constitution of New Hampshire, 1776. Benjamin Franklin Morris, The Christian Life and Character of the Civil Institutions of the United States (Philadelphia: L. Johnson & Co., 1863/George W. Childs, 1864), 235.

504 Constitution of Maryland, 1776. Benjamin Weiss, God in American History: A Documentation of America's Religious Heritage (Grand Rapids, MI: Zondervan, 1966), 155.

505 Tim LaHaye, Faith of Our Founding Fathers (Brentwood, TN: Wolgemuth & Hyatt, Publishers, Inc., 1987), 92.

506 Federer, America's God and Country, 475.

507 Indiana Constitution, 1851, Article I, Section 2. Quoted in Rice, The Supreme Court and Public Prayer, 169.

508 Ibid., 173-174.

509 Iowa Constitution, 1857, Preamble. (See note 169.)

510 Nebraska Constitution, 12 June 1875, Preamble. (See note 172.)

511 LaHaye, Faith of Our Founding Fathers, 92.

512 Idaho Constitution, 1889, Preamble. Rice, The Supreme Court and Public Prayer, 169.

513 "Hearings, Prayers in Public Schools and Other Matters," Committee on the Judiciary, U.S. Senate (87th Cong., 2nd Sess.), 1962, 268 et seq.

514 Marvin E. Frankel, Faith and Freedom: Religious Liberty in America (New York: Macmillan, 1994), 41.

515 Joseph Story, in Charles E. Rice, The Supreme Court and Public Prayer: The Need for Restraint (New York: Fordham University Press, 1964), 47.

516 Alexis deTocqueville, Democracy in America, Vol. I, in Olivier Zunz and Alan S. Kahan, eds., The Tocqueville Reader: A Life in Letters and Politics (New York: Wiley-Blackwell, 2002), 113.

517 Alexis deTocqueville, Democracy in America, Vol. I, translated by Henry Reeve (London: Longmans, Green, and Co., 1875), 312.

Index

A series of meaty, tasty, and easily digestible Theological Studies!

FROM NORDSKOG PUBLISHING

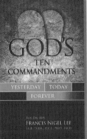

God's Ten Commandments: Yesterday, Today, Forever – Dr. Francis Nigel Lee writes, "God gave man Ten Commandments. Every one of them is vital, in all ages. God Himself is the Root of the Moral Law, and perfectly reflects it. It is the very basis of the United States…and every other Common Law nation in the world." 2007 ISBN: 978-0-9796736-2-7 PB, 5"x8"; 128 PP, $11.95

A Whole New World: The Gospel According to Revelation Greg Uttinger's book is "refreshing for brevity," focusing on the core message . . . that we serve the risen, victorious Lord of time and eternity. His book is "faithful to that 'Revelation of Jesus Christ' (1:1)." – Mark R. Rushdoony, President, Chalcedon Foundation
2007 ISBN: 978-0-9796736-0-3 PB 5"x8"; 100 PP $9.95

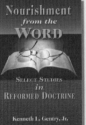

Nourishment from the Word: Select Studies in Reformed Doctrine A collection from Dr. Kenneth L. Gentry, Jr. for serious Christians following the Biblical encouragement to "be a good servant of Jesus Christ, constantly nourished on the words of faith and of sound doctrine" (1 Tim. 4:6). A must for pastors and laypersons alike. Indexed. 2008 ISBN: 978-0-9796736-4-1, PB, 6"x9"; 188 PP $15.95

The Battle of Lexington: A Sermon & Eyewitness Narrative Jonas Clark, 1776 – the pastor at Lexington, tells of . . . principles of personal, civil, and religious liberty, and the right of resistance. Today we need preachers to give their congregations courage to stand and make a difference. Biography of Pastor Clark, facsimile 1776 title page, four poems commemorating Paul Revere's Ride and the "shot heard 'round the world." Illustrated. 2007 ISBN: 978-0-9796736-3-4, PB 5"x8"; 96 PP $9.95

DEC 2008

Died He for Me: A Physician's View of the Crucifixion of Jesus Christ Mark A. Marinella, M.D., F.A.C.P. The death of Jesus for our sins is the heart of the Christian faith. What does a physician have to say about that death? In this important new book, particularly intriguing are the details of the death of Jesus as found in the Old Testament, written hundreds of years before. – Jerry Newcombe, D.MIN. 2008 ISBN: 978-0-9796736-6-5, PB, 6"x9"; 144 PP, $13.95

EXPANDED 2ND ED.

The Fear of God: A Forgotten Doctrine – Dr. Arnold L. Frank gives the reader both a godly rebuke and an impassioned plea to hear the Word of God and the wise counsel of the Puritans speak about the *fear* of God, which precedes the *love* of God. Includes Scripture Index and Study Questions. 2ND EDITION, 2008 PB, 6"x9"; 228 PP, ISBN: 978-0-9796736-5-8, $16.95

FEB 2009

The Death Penalty on Trial: Taking a Life for a Life Taken Dr. Ron Gleason challenges both sides of the death penalty debate with clarity and cogency, citing history, Scripture, the confessionals of the historic Reformed church, and the leading voices of today. He examines the objections from both secularists and liberal Christians, down to the underlying premises. As readers are led to the heart of the matter, they may find themselves drawn persuasively to Gleason's conclusion.

2009 PB, 6"x9"; 152 PP
ISBN: 978-0-9796736-7-2
$14.95

Nordskog Publishing inc.

2716 Sailor Ave.
Ventura, CA 93001
805-642-2070 • 805-276-5129
www.NordskogPublishing.com

Distributed by STL/New Life & Anchor
For bulk sales or an updated list of distributors, contact the publisher.

MEMBER: CSPA

New from
Nordskog Publishing inc.

Sea-bewildered, Blown to a Strange Land

Father Aillil has in his hand a talisman of great power that grants him visions of the future. He knows his duty—be rid of it, cast the evil thing into the farthest sea.

But when his friend Erling Skjalgsson, the Viking chieftain, relinquishes his lands and power rather than do a dishonorable deed, Aillil is tempted to keep it and use it to help Erling.

They sail West Oversea to Greenland, home of Leif Eriksson. Storms and enemies with demonic power lie in wait for them. Their journey will be much longer—and far stranger— than they ever dreamed.

Lars Walker's books are delightful adventures with an undercurrent of commentary on contemporary culture.
REV. PAUL T. McCAIN,
CONCORDIA PUBLISHING HOUSE

Lars Walker understands the unique Norse mindset at the time of the Vikings' conversion to Christianity ... a saga that will keep you on the edge of your chair—and make you think.
JOHN A. EIDSMOE,
AUTHOR OF *Christianity and the Constitution*

ISBN 978-0-9796736-8-9
PB, 5½" X 8½" 296 pp
$12.95

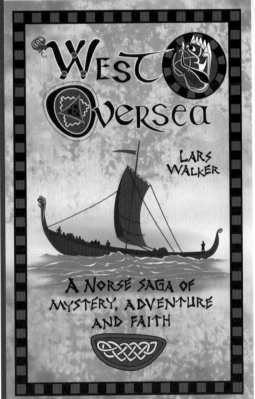

WEST OVERSEA

LARS WALKER

A NORSE SAGA OF MYSTERY, ADVENTURE AND FAITH

Noble Novels

Order from
NORDSKOG PUBLISHING

2716 Sailor Ave, Ventura, CA 93001

✷ www.nordskogpublishing.com ✷

805-642-2070 ✷ 805-276-5129

Also distributed by
STL/New Life & Anchor

MEMBER
Christian
Small
Publishers
Assn.

LARS WALKER is a native of Kenyon, Minnesota, and lives in Minneapolis. He is presently librarian and bookstore manager for the schools of the Association of Free Lutheran Congregations in Plymouth, Minnesota.

He is the author of four previously published novels, and is the editor of the journal of the Georg Sverdrup Society. Walker says, "I never believed that God gave me whatever gifts I have in order to entertain fellow Christians. I want to confront the world with the claims of Jesus Christ."

His Website address is: www.larswalker.com. He blogs at www.brandywinebooks.net.

PHOTO BY RUTH GUNDERSON